African Americans
in U.S. Foreign Policy

African Americans in U.S. Foreign Policy

From the Era of Frederick Douglass to the Age of Obama

Edited by Linda Heywood,
Allison Blakely, Charles Stith,
and Joshua C. Yesnowitz

University of Illinois Press

Urbana, Chicago, and Springfield

Library of Congress Cataloging-in-Publication Data
African Americans in U.S. foreign policy : from the era
of Frederick Douglass to the age of Obama / edited by
Linda Heywood, Allison Blakely, Charles Stith, and
Joshua C. Yesnowitz.
pages cm
Includes bibliographical references and index.
ISBN 978-0-252-03887-7 (hardback) —
ISBN 978-0-252-08041-8 (paperback) —
ISBN 978-0-252-09683-9 (e-book)
1. United States—Foreign relations—20th century—
Citizen participation. 2. United States—Foreign relations—
20th century—Social aspects. 3. African Americans—
Politics and government—20th century. 4. United States—
Race relations—Political aspects. 5. Racism—Political
aspects—United States—History—20th century. 6. African
Americans—Civil rights—History—20th century.
I. Heywood, Linda M. (Linda Marinda), 1945–
II. Blakely, Allison, 1940–
III. Stith, Charles R. IV. Yesnowitz, Joshua C.
E744.A295   2015
323.1196'073—dc23   2014023259

Contents

Acknowledgments

This volume originated in the conference "African Americans and U.S. Foreign Policy" held at Boston University on October 26–28, 2010. The conference included addresses by Johnnie Carson, U.S. assistant secretary of state, and Jendayi Frazer, former U.S. assistant secretary of state, and was attended by more than 350 scholars, former diplomats, State Department officials, students, and members of the general public. We would like to acknowledge the support of the African American Studies Program and the African Presidential Archives and Research Center at Boston University, which co-sponsored the conference. The conference and this collection of essays would not have been possible without the financial support of the Boston University Humanities Foundation, the George and Joyce Wein Fund at Boston University, Blue Cross Blue Shield of Massachusetts, Savings Bank Life Insurance, TD Bank, and USAID.

Preface

Reflections of a
Black Ambassador

WALTER C. CARRINGTON

It was not the lure of liberty but rather its loss that brought enslaved Africans to America's shores. Others, who originally came from Europe
and later from all corners of the earth, could look forward in hope, but those
who came in chains faced nothing but desolation. In the words of the old spiritual, they felt "like a motherless child, a long ways from home." They dreamed
of escaping from this hostile land. Many of them, during their captors' War of
Independence, repaired to the banner of the Union Jack when agents of George
the Third promised them freedom. Although the British lost the war, many
Loyalist blacks claimed that freedom and escaped to Canada and from there
returned to Africa. Those less fortunate were condemned to live in slavery in
the U.S. South or segregation in the North. At times of deepest despair over
their future in America, many blacks followed those who argued, as did Martin
Delany, that Africans in America were a "broken nation" and could be made
whole again only by separating from their white oppressors.

Unwelcome in white churches, blacks formed their own denominations and
often christened them African. Early on, these new black churches saw their
relationship with Africa primarily in terms of helping to Christianize their
"heathen" brethren in Africa; by the late nineteenth century, however, black
churches began to champion the grievances Africans held against their colonial
exploitation. American blacks took the lead in protesting Belgian atrocities in
the Congo and British and French designs on Liberia. Along with blacks in

other parts of the diaspora, they formed the Pan-African movement and saved the German colonies from being swallowed up by the victorious Allied powers at the end of the First World War. America's black colleges educated generations of African leaders, from the founders of the African National Congress to the first heads of state of Ghana, Malawi, and Nigeria. Later blacks moved the American government away from complicity with the apartheid regime in South Africa and toward greater relief to the drought-stricken Sahel and Horn regions. The impetus toward an African identification that had been elite-driven in the nineteenth century had become, by the end of the twentieth, increasingly sparked by the rank and file.

Much of black agitation for a role in the formation of foreign affairs, especially as it affected the Motherland, in the words of Countee Cullen, "from whose loins" he and his ancestors "sprang," coalesced around the doctrine of Pan-Africanism. A West Indian barrister, Henry Sylvester Williams, coined the term "Pan-African" at a 1900 conference on Africa. A thirty-two-year-old William Edward Burghardt Du Bois incorporated it into the conference report and later transformed it into the century's most enduring anthem of a continent's liberation and a race's redemption. Du Bois foresaw in the fall of the kaiser at the end of the First World War a unique advantage to Africa. He persuaded the National Association for the Advancement of Colored People (NAACP) to send him as an observer to the Paris Peace Conference at Versailles. There, with the assistance of Blaise Diagne, the Senegalese member of the French parliament, he called the first Pan-African Conference. Its goal was to influence the Versailles deliberations, and to that end the group submitted eleven resolutions to the Paris Peace Conference.

Most of the demands on behalf of African nationalism fared no better with the victorious Allies than those made in the name of Kurdish or Armenian nationalism. The one exception concerned the fate of the former German colonies. Du Bois and his fellow Pan-Africanists urged that they not be transferred to other colonial powers but instead be placed under international control until their inhabitants could determine their own future. This led to the establishment of the Mandates Commission, under which the League of Nations and later the United Nations Trusteeship Council kept South West Africa (now Namibia) from being formally incorporated into South Africa. While, as chronicled in chapter 1 of this volume, more than sixty African Americans were appointed to diplomatic, consular, or commercial agency positions during the period from the Civil War to the 1920s, their formal participation in foreign policy dates from later in the twentieth century and included great attention to Africa.

Marcus Garvey and the Raising of Mass Consciousness

The Pan-African movement united black intellectuals in the Americas and Africa but left the masses of blacks in the diaspora largely unmoved. While the Pan-Africanists were convening in various European capitals, the condition of the Negro in the United States was deteriorating. Once again, blacks were beginning to despair that they could never hope to live in dignity and security in white America.

It was during this increasingly desperate period that Marcus Garvey arrived from Jamaica to become the greatest mass leader black America had yet known. Garvey went to Harlem in 1916 to talk about his recently established Universal Negro Improvement Association (UNIA). His doctrine of "Africa for the Africans at home and abroad," which he preached with charismatic appeal, caught on quickly. He instilled in the dispirited black masses pride of self and heritage and called for a return to Africa, reigniting the emigration debates of the pre–Civil War years. At the height of his influence in the early 1920s, Garvey had a following of more than a million people. Had the U.S. government not successfully brought controversial mail fraud charges against him in 1923 (and deported him in 1927), there is no telling how much stronger his movement might have grown, especially in the Depression years of the 1930s.

Though Garvey never got to Africa himself nor succeeded in his settlement plans, he had a substantial influence on the continent and upon ordinary black Americans' views toward it. *The Philosophy and Opinions of Marcus Garvey* influenced a broad spectrum of African thinking. Kwame Nkrumah wrote that of all the literature he had studied, none did more to fire his enthusiasm for the liberation of his country than had Garvey's *Philosophy*.[1]

The consciousness about Africa that Garvey had resurrected among the black masses did not disappear with his deportation. The embers of that fire flamed up again in the mid-1930s when Benito Mussolini's Italy invaded Haile Selassie's Ethiopia. Racial pride erupted as never before as the emperor of Abyssinia stood before the League of Nations and warned of a holocaust to come if the nations of the world did not come to his country's aid and stop Fascist Italy in its tracks. The Ethiopian war became the main topic of conversation wherever blacks gathered. A championship boxing match took on mythic proportions as Joe Louis's fists became the instruments of a race's vindication as he delivered a beating to his Italian opponent, Primo Carnera. Volunteers were recruited to go to Ethiopia and fight alongside their African brothers. The country's occupation and the flight of Haile Selassie into exile in London was a deep wound to black pride. Some feared that the conquest of Ethiopia was the beginning of a genocidal plan to annihilate the black race.

Organizing to Influence American Policy

In 1937, a year after the Italian invasion, Max Yergan organized the Council on African Affairs (CAA), the first black-led group dedicated to influencing American policy toward Africa. The council, whose leadership included Paul Robeson, Ralph Bunche, Mordecai Johnson, Adam Clayton Powell, and W.E.B. Du Bois, established close working relationships with African nationalists and labor leaders and lobbied on their behalf with the American government. It paid special attention to South Africa and forged links with the African National Congress. As the end of the war approached in 1945, the council unsuccessfully urged the State Department to convince the British, French, and Belgians to give up their African colonies or at least put them under some sort of international supervision as had previously been done with the German colonies. The council's potential was curtailed in the postwar years by the rise of McCarthyism. It was accused of being a Soviet front and was even denounced as such by its founder, Max Yergan, now a staunch anticommunist, who testified against it before congressional committees.

Anticolonial agitation in Africa in the 1950s caught the attention of more and more American blacks. They supported the Mau Mau rebellion in Kenya and flocked to Kwame Nkrumah's Ghana after independence in 1957. Two important but short-lived groups, the American Society for African Culture (AMSAC) and the American Negro Leadership Conference on Africa (ANLCA), emerged in the 1950s and 1960s. AMSAC was formed by the American delegates to a conference called by the French-language francophone African magazine *Présence Africaine*. The cream of the black intellectual world gathered in Paris in 1956 in the first important celebration of negritude. AMSAC brought important African leaders to the United States; held regular conferences on African issues; published a leading journal, *African Forum*; and helped historically black colleges develop African programs and courses. The ANLCA was founded by the NAACP, Urban League, National Council of Negro Women, sororities, fraternities, and church groups. Through a Washington office it lobbied with the White House, Congress, and the State Department.

Whereas the Council on African Affairs ran afoul of the anticommunist hysteria of the 1950s, AMSAC and the ANLCA were undone by a converse stigma in the 1960s. They were unable to survive revelations that they had accepted funding from the CIA. With the demise of the ANLCA, African issues became less and less a matter of priority for the mainstream civil rights organizations. However, it was not in the mainstream but in countless eddies during the 1960s and 1970s that currents were building that would later cascade down on the leadership and rudely awaken them to the rising tides of black nationalism and Pan-Africanism that had engulfed so many of their erstwhile followers.

When the death of the charismatic young leader of the Congo, Patrice Lumumba, in the final days of the Eisenhower administration was revealed in the early days of the Kennedy presidency, black nationalists, who believed that the United States had conspired in his overthrow and subsequent murder, staged a riot at the United Nations, interrupting a speech by Adlai Stevenson, America's new U.N. ambassador. The tumult was a watershed event. America's mainstream leaders, black and white, were taken aback by the passions that Lumumba's death had unleashed. Those same leaders also were slow to appreciate the mass appeal of a fiery young Muslim minister who called himself Malcolm X. Even as the energies of black Americans were being turned inward and southward during the civil rights movement of the 1960s, the more militant among the young were flirting with nationalist and Pan-African concepts as they sought to link the American struggle with those of people of color around the globe.

Malcolm X had helped them make that connection when, in 1964, he made his pilgrimage to Mecca. While abroad, he made his first visit to Africa and attended the meeting of the Organization of African Unity, where he equated the racist practices of the United States with those of South Africa. Malcolm, who was second only to Martin Luther King in popularity among black Americans, was invited by Stokely Carmichael and others in the Student Nonviolent Coordinating Committee (SNCC) to speak in Selma, Alabama. The militants soon took over the leadership of SNCC as Carmichael was elected to replace John Lewis, the organization's more traditionally integrationist head. Chafing at the strictures that King's ethic of nonviolence placed upon them, SNCC took up Carmichael's cry of "Black Power" in 1966. A delegation from SNCC visited Africa and returned home to step up their nationalist rhetoric.

Meanwhile, Martin Delany's old concept of "the broken nation" was being revived. Robert Williams, a defrocked NAACP leader in North Carolina who argued that blacks had the right to take up arms in self-defense, was named in 1968 as the first president of the Republic of New Afrika while he was in exile in China and Tanzania, from which he returned in late 1969. He claimed the five Southern states with the largest African American populations—Alabama, Georgia, Louisiana, Mississippi, and South Carolina—as the "National Territory of the Black Nation." The attempt to carve a black nation out of the black belt never got much beyond the March 1971 dedication of a parcel of land in Mississippi as "the first African capital of the northern Western Hemisphere." Efforts to relocate American blacks within the borders of the United States were to be no more successful in the twentieth century than the efforts to resettle them beyond its shores had been in the nineteenth.

While the emergence of newly independent African nations opened up new opportunities for American scholars, black pioneers of the field like Rayford

Logan and Leo Hansberry at Howard University found themselves marginalized
by a new white establishment organized into the African Studies Association
(ASA). Black scholars had only a token representation in the top leadership of
the ASA and increasingly resented the perceived influence the association was
wielding with U.S. government policy makers. Just as black missionaries had
been squeezed out of colonial Africa, so black scholars felt they were being
shunted aside in America's relations with independent Africa. It had been blacks
like Horace Mann Bond and Hansberry, for example, who had founded the Institute of African American Relations in 1953 to establish ties with the emerging
leadership of Africa's independence movement. The organizers turned to whites
for financial assistance and soon found the institute under white control, moved
to New York, and renamed the African-American Institute (AAI). The AAI
became the leading private organization promoting ties between African and
American leaders. Its board was overwhelmingly white, and it did not appoint
its first black president until 1989.

The rising tide of black resentment to white hegemony in African affairs
burst through the seawalls at the 1969 annual meeting of the ASA in Montreal.
There, a group of militant black scholars, led by Acklyn Lynch, presented a set
of nonnegotiable demands that were designed to replace "European" control of
the association with "African" control. When the demands were not met, most
of the black delegates walked out and soon after formed the African Heritage
Studies Association under the leadership of one of the patriarchs of Afrocentric
history, John Henrik Clarke. The choice of a historian was symbolic. So much of
the nationalist agitation of the 1960s and '70s had been an attempt to reconcile
black America with its past and from that past to take pride in its blackness and
in its African lineage. The search for the latter had been popularized by Alex
Haley in his book and later phenomenally successful television series *Roots*.

Uniting on South Africa

By the 1970s a major debate had begun in the black community over the best
strategy to eliminate apartheid. It was waged between those who favored sanctions and those who, remembering the positive role business had played in the
civil rights struggle in some parts of the South by moderating white resistance,
opposed the pullout of American companies from South Africa. Pushing for
sanctions and divestment were student groups demonstrating on college campuses, liberation support committees being organized throughout the country,
and, perhaps most important of all, black members of the United States Congress.

Resisting sanctions were Andrew Young, ambassador to the United Nations,
and the leaders of the two major civil rights organizations: the NAACP and the

National Urban League. Roy Wilkins and Vernon Jordan had returned from visits to South Africa to announce that American firms could do more good by staying than by leaving, especially if they adopted the codes of conduct promulgated by the Reverend Leon Sullivan, a black activist of the 1960s who now sat on the board of directors of the General Motors Corporation. Pressure from the membership of the NAACP prompted the organization to send another mission to southern Africa after the death of Wilkins. That delegation returned with a recommendation that the NAACP back sanctions and establish an international affairs bureau in its national office.

The passage of the Voting Rights Act of 1965 had moved the civil rights movement from the streets to the polling booths. A critical mass of blacks was now in the House of Representatives, and under the leadership of Congressman Charles Diggs of Detroit they organized the Congressional Black Caucus. Diggs had risen to the chairmanship of the House Subcommittee on African Affairs and had become the most important spokesperson on African issues in the nation. Through his chairmanship, Diggs provided the continent a place on the legislative agenda it had never enjoyed before. His committee counsel, Goler Teal Butcher, was one of the most respected women on Capitol Hill and until her untimely death in 1993 the intellectual leader on a host of progressive African issues from ending apartheid to fostering economic development.

In 1972 the caucus sponsored a meeting on Africa at Howard University. It turned out to be the largest black American conference on Africa ever held in the United States. At the top of the gathering's priority list was the mobilization of black Americans to press for the elimination of white rule from the Portuguese colonies and southern Africa. Success in this campaign was dependent on blacks being able to mount lobbying efforts as effective as those of white ethnic groups on behalf of their own ancestral homelands.

On the eve of the 1976 presidential election, Congressman Diggs called for a National Black Leadership Conference on southern Africa to be held during the Congressional Black Caucus Weekend in September. The conference issued "The African-American Manifesto on Southern Africa," which called for the urgent formation of a black lobby to which representatives of the organizations assembled pledged their financial support. Under the leadership of Randall Robinson, a veteran organizer of student demonstrations on behalf of sanctions and former staff aide to Diggs, the lobby, TransAfrica, opened its doors for business in 1978. Robinson quickly moved to mobilize the black community to defeat efforts to lift sanctions imposed against Southern Rhodesia. He persuaded the leaders of nearly all the major black organizations to go on record for keeping sanctions and rallied black voters in key congressional districts. Sanctions were maintained, and TransAfrica, in existence less than a year, was credited with engineering the first major victory in the foreign policy field ever attributed to the direct political intervention of the black community. Thirty-five years later TransAfrica is still active, demonstrating a staying power that all of its predecessors lacked.

On the nonpolitical side, Africare, another important African-oriented organization, was founded in the 1970s. The drought and famine in the West African Sahel had aroused as much black American concern as the political problems of southern Africa had. C. Payne Lucas, a former Peace Corps official, working closely with the president of Niger, one of the drought-stricken countries, began a relief effort centered in the black community. He tapped ordinary black Americans in a way they had not been solicited for an Africa-related cause since the days of Garvey. From small black churches and large ones, from tiny Southern rural hamlets and great Northern urban ghettos, envelopes poured into the Africare headquarters in Washington in support of starving cousins in Africa. Over time Africare moved from relief to long-term development work and is now, more than three decades later, still recognized as one of the leading American organizations, black or white, of its kind.

The victory of Jimmy Carter in 1976 brought black Americans into the foreign policy mainstream as never before. Andrew Young, because of his closeness to the president, was able to transform the ambassadorship to the United Nations into a politically powerful post. Like his counterpart in the Ford administration, he enjoyed cabinet status and in the public mind became the embodiment of American policy toward Africa. He and his deputy, Donald McHenry, initiated the strategy that finally led to Namibia's independence, in spite of the attempt, for many years, by the Reagan administration to prevent it.

The 1980s saw a diminution of black influence upon foreign policy formation in the executive branch until, in the last year of his presidency, Ronald Reagan appointed General Colin Powell as national security adviser. In the first year of George H. W. Bush's presidency, Powell moved from the highest civilian foreign policy post ever held by a black man to the highest military one when he was appointed chairman of the Joint Chiefs of Staff. During the 1980s black political influence on Africa policy was exerted primarily through the legislative branch. Under the leadership of TransAfrica, a Free South Africa movement was formed soon after the 1984 elections. It organized protests in front of the South African embassy that went on for a year. During that time the issue of apartheid received unprecedented media coverage as television cameras recorded the carefully scripted daily arrests of celebrity protesters in front of the embassy. The evening news programs carried films of the South African government's increasingly brutal crackdown on black protests at home. The Comprehensive Anti-Apartheid Act of 1986 represented the most important legislative victory blacks had achieved since the civil rights laws of the 1960s. It demonstrated that their considerable political power could now be harnessed in support of international as well as domestic causes.

The question now became how that power would be used. Apartheid was an easy enemy to unite against. It mirrored the racism blacks had fought against for so long in this country. It came as no surprise that it was being propped up by the most antiblack presidency since that of Woodrow Wilson. What was surprising was that Colin Powell as Reagan's national security adviser occupied the highest post ever held in foreign policy formulation by any African American. What was dismaying was that a black man so high up could not or would not exercise any leavening effect on Reagan's retrograde Africa policy.

I had been appointed to my first ambassadorship by Jimmy Carter late in his presidency. I arrived in Senegal in September. Soon after the elections in November, a congressional delegation visited Dakar. I was told by a friend, a staff member traveling with the group, that Anne Holloway, the African American ambassador in next-door neighbor Mali, and I were high on the incoming Reagan administration's hit list. Anne had been a top aide to Andy Young at the United Nations, and I, as executive vice president of the African-American Institute, had been an outspoken supporter of tougher measures against the white minority governments of South Africa and Southern Rhodesia. Chester Crocker, who would be the new assistant secretary of state for Africa, did not want us reading his cables that would, as he put it, remove the "polecat" stigma from those regimes. Two weeks after Reagan had been sworn in, Ambassador Holloway and I each received a cable from the new secretary of state, Alexander Haig, thanking us for our service and giving us only two weeks to pack up and vacate our posts.

Black Ambassadorial Appointments

Under President Carter the number of black ambassadors reached an all-time high. It would take Reagan two terms to make as many appointments as Carter had made in a single term. More important, including the unprecedented naming of Andrew Young and Donald McHenry to the United Nations, more than half of the fifteen appointments had been assigned to posts outside the State Department's historic ghetto of sub-Saharan Africa and the Caribbean.

The election of Bill Clinton in 1992 reversed the era of benign neglect toward Africa practiced by the administration of his predecessor George Bush. I had been running an international program at the Joint Center for Political and Economic Studies, a black think tank. The Berlin Wall had fallen and democracy seemed to be blossoming everywhere. As we worked with African democracy activists, we repeatedly heard the same complaint: the Bush administration had no interest in assisting their efforts. Clinton soon changed that. The promotion of democracy enjoyed the highest priority since the Carter presidency. George Moose became the first black assistant secretary of state for Africa. A record number of thirty-eight blacks received ambassadorial appointments—more than twice the number who served under Reagan during his two terms and Carter during his one. But when one goes inside the numbers a more nuanced picture emerges. Clinton, with a higher number of career foreign service officers to choose from than Carter, had named only three more—eighteen in his first term.

More important, Carter had pierced the nearly impenetrable European curtain of exclusion with three appointments—to Spain, Romania, and East Germany—while Clinton in his two terms sent not a single black ambassador to a European capital. Fewer than half of Carter's appointments were to African or Caribbean countries compared to nearly 80 percent of Clinton's appointments. The only white majority country to which Clinton sent an envoy was New Zealand, twice. First, one of the highest-ranking career officers, Edward Perkins, and later, Carol Moseley-Braun, who had lost her bid for reelection to the U.S. Senate. Reforming the State Department appeared to be a much lower priority for the Clinton administration than turning around the other cabinet agency long regarded as a "plantation"—the Department of Agriculture. Mike Espy, a progressive black congressman from Mississippi, was chosen as secretary of the department and made significant strides in his two years of service.

The George W. Bush administration would put to the test whether a black secretary of state could turn hidebound Foggy Bottom around. The results were not very encouraging. While Bush appointed four more black ambassadors than Clinton, his percentage of those sent as his personal representatives to states outside of Africa and the Caribbean was practically the same (24 percent to 22 percent). Only three, the same as under Carter, were in Europe: Iceland, Albania, and Slovenia, all lower-rated posts.

As this is being written, midway through Barack Obama's second term, the number of his black ambassadorial appointments have not yet caught up with the record set by the man whom Toni Morrison and Congresswoman Eddie Bernice Johnson once suggested might be America's "first black president." However, Obama has far exceeded the percentage assigned to posts outside the Africa-Caribbean bubble, although none have presented their credentials to the head of state of any of our major strategic allies or adversaries. In addition to his important selection of Susan Rice as permanent representative to the United Nations, he also placed blacks in such non-stereotyped positions as ambassador to the European Union; the European Office of the United Nations; the United Nations Agencies for Food and Agriculture; and ambassador-at-large for International Religious Freedom.

One would hope that four centuries later an ambassador is far more than Sir Henry Wotton's famous assessment: "an honest man sent abroad to lie and intrigue for the benefit of his country." Diplomacy is, of course, no longer the special preserve of well-born gentlemen. Men and women of all classes now ply that ancient trade. It is their duty to speak sometimes unpalatable truths not only to people and governments to which they are assigned but also to those back home with the expectation that their insights can have an important impact on the formation of the policies they are expected to carry out. In this regard America's first black envoy, Ebenezer Bassett, set a standard to which all should try to emulate. During his posting in Haiti from 1869 to 1879, he was a fearless champion of human rights, giving diplomatic refuge to opponents of a dictatorial government. He earned the ire of both the Haitian dictator and of his secretary of state back in Washington. When one of the men he had sheltered in the embassy later became president, he appointed Bassett, by then retired from the State Department, as Haiti's consul in New York. Haiti was for Bassett's generation of blacks what South Africa was for ours. There can be no doubt that his actions in Port-au-Prince were inspired by his blackness and his earlier endeavors as a champion of Reconstruction in the United States. It is hard to believe that in that racist age a white envoy would have undertaken the same risks on behalf of the people who had first overthrown slavery in the Western hemisphere.

As the opportunities for blacks to be makers and practitioners of American foreign policy in our own time have expanded, the question must be asked: how much difference has it made to the issues that have historically most concerned African Americans? Under George W. Bush blacks were brought into the inner foreign policy circle as they had never been before. Condoleezza Rice became the most influential shaper of American policy since Henry Kissinger. She had been Bush's tutor during the 2000 campaign and built up a personal rapport and trust with her president that Kissinger never enjoyed with Nixon. Rice's predecessor, Colin Powell, was more in the tradition of previous secretaries of state, whose charge is to be the president's chief foreign affairs adviser and to carry out the president's foreign policies through the State Department. Despite Rice's constant turf battles with Vice President Dick Cheney, as national security adviser she was the person who most often made the final input into Bush's decision making. Rice was skillfully backstopped on African issues by Jendayi Frazer, former ambassador to South Africa, and like the secretary of state a highly regarded academic.

A conventional wisdom has developed that George W. Bush's Africa policy was one of the most successful in American history. How could it be otherwise with three such accomplished blacks in the highest rungs of the Department of State and on the National Security Council? However, it is probably time to temper that nostalgia with a dose of reality. Candidate Bush declared in 2000 that "the U.S. has no vital interests in Africa." By the end of his eight-year presidency, Africa was a significant part of the American national security matrix. It was seen as an important battleground in the "war on terrorism."

On September 10 and 11, 2001, the leading story featuring the United States in African newspapers concerned the walkout of the American delegation, ordered by Secretary Powell, from the World Conference on Racism being held in South Africa. The criticism was scathing. The United States' explanation—that it withdrew because of fear that the conference would call for reparations for slavery and that language in an early draft statement had castigated Israel for its treatment of the Palestinians—was unacceptable. A day later the vitriol was replaced by an outpouring of stories reporting on the horror, grief, and sympathy being expressed by Africans over the attacks on the World Trade Center and the Pentagon. After September 11 the Bush administration followed what seemed to be a two-tier policy toward Africa. Vital interests were perceived mostly as they forwarded the global war on terrorism.

The G8 summit had begun inviting a group of African heads of state to their meetings in order to develop a partnership between the world's richest countries and the world's poorest continent. As America's turn to host the summit approached, President Bush announced that the United States would not invite any Africans. He did not want the meeting distracted from a laser-like focus on the war on terrorism. It was only under considerable pressure from Tony Blair and others that Bush finally relented.

The number one example offered in support of an enlightened Bush policy is his President's Emergency Plan for AIDS Relief (PEPFAR). Under this program more money was authorized for HIV/AIDS prevention than ever before. However, it was hobbled by religion-driven requirements such as promoting abstinence and forbidding funds to be spent on condoms and safe-sex education. Despite the millions spent, a recent report in the *Annals of Medicine* reveals that the rate of new infections in the PEPFAR countries has not been slowed, but is in fact on the rise. Uganda, which had been the signal country for reducing the spread of AIDS, found its progress reversed after adopting the PEPFAR strictures.

Throughout his presidency, Bush viewed Africa mainly through the prism of terrorism. Emphasis was placed more on military engagement than diplomatic engagement with the African continent. Consulates were closed in key areas, and military basing and overflight rights were sought in others on a continent that had more Muslims than all of Arabia. To the consternation of most Africans, Bush set up an Africa Command (or AFRICOM as it has come to be known). It was so unpopular, however, that no country, except Liberia, would agree to host its headquarters. As a result, the organization still operates out of Germany. While many African specialists in the United States greeted with enthusiasm the fact that at least some part of the government was paying more attention to the continent, many others, myself included, argued that Africa would benefit from a posture of benign neglect from the Pentagon.

In most of Africa no institution is more distrusted by its people than their own military, which has so often carried out coups against lawfully constituted governments. AFRICOM particularly boasted of its successes in working with the Malian military to mold it into an effective fighting force against terrorists. The result was a disaster. What many of us feared came to pass. The Malian army, led by General Amadou Sanogo, who had been AFRICOM's poster child, staged a coup against one of Africa's oldest democracies. The situation fell apart and the northern half of the country tried to break away. Mali's AFRICOM-trained army wilted in the face of secessionist and jihadist militias. French troops had to intervene to clean up the mess.

Under Obama, initial fears of AFRICOM dragging Africa into the war on terrorism are being realized. Muslims who have long been comfortable with the concept of the secular state and democracy are apt to become more and more radicalized. There is no sign that Susan Rice, one of AFRICOM's most enthusiastic champions, is likely from her new perch as national security adviser to counsel the president to rein it in or abolish it. Unfortunately, the way of American diplomats, black or white, who wish to spread the values of democracy will be more difficult to navigate in the age of Guantanamo and the Patriot Act, neither of which was an impediment during the four years I served as President Clinton's ambassador to Nigeria. I could confidently occupy the moral high ground when confronting that country's military dictatorship. Without fear of contradiction I could criticize Nigeria's leadership for abuses of human rights that could never take place in the United States—such as torture, indefinite detention, and attempts to suspend habeas corpus and to oust the courts from judicial review of aspects of security decrees.

I hope that the essays in this book will further the understanding of the role African Americans have played in exercising their right and duty to be as concerned about the role their country plays abroad as well as at home. As the war in Iraq and others have shown, their children will disproportionately pay the costs of defending the country in a military that finds it politically more expedient to entice into its ranks the poorer sections of American society than to draft in equal measure members of the middle and upper classes.

Note

1. Patricia Romero, "W.E.B. Dubois, Pan-Africanists, and Africa, 1963–1973," *Journal of Black Studies* 6, no. 4 (1976): 332.

Introduction

For observers both stateside and abroad, the election of Barack Obama evoked the promise of legendary soul singer Sam Cooke's song that "Change Is Gonna Come." Having an African American commander in chief, according to this line of thought, would not only result in demonstrable policy shifts in American foreign policy but would also convey a powerful message to the rest of the world. Because of his cultural heritage, Obama would pursue a global strategy that was sensitive to the needs of the vulnerable and underrepresented, and the willingness of the American public to elect a person of color to the presidency would improve American standing overseas. For African Americans in particular, the new president, a son of Africa and America, would be the catalyst to bring a new luster to "Mother Africa" through a more progressive foreign policy agenda based on shared roots.

At the broadest level these ambitious (and in retrospect naïve) expectations direct our scholarly attention to the relationship between race and the making of foreign policy. What are the policy implications and (the less measurable though often significant) symbolic effects of the "race variable" in American foreign relations? This volume provides a much needed historical perspective that may guide more contemporary discussions. The essays in this edited collection, moreover, contextualize and examine how the role of African American elites in the crafting of American foreign policy has evolved over time from an informal and marginalized presence to one of central policy making on the global stage.

Although African Americans have served as formal and informal representatives of the United States for more than a century, the topic has not received sufficient scholarly attention. Elliott P. Skinner, a former American ambassador

to Upper Volta (now Burkina Faso), explored the ways African Americans influenced early U.S. foreign policy in Africa.[1] While less often referenced today,
earlier works by Jake Miller and George W. Shepherd Jr. also remain seminal
contributions to the still burgeoning field of race and American foreign policy.[2]
More recently the fine volume edited by Michael Clemons provides a rigorous
conceptual framework and includes chapters that examine African American
foreign policy strategies; the leadership styles of Colin Powell and Condoleezza
Rice; and other contemporary "issues, problems, and practices."[3]

    *African Americans in U.S. Foreign Policy: From the Era of Frederick Douglass to
the Age of Obama* can be understood in some respects as a historical companion
to the Clemons text that broadens both the *temporal* and *topical* scopes of analysis. The subtitle of the book is indicative of this wide-ranging approach. Given
the rich history from which this text draws, it is incumbent upon us as editors
to acknowledge that it does not claim to present a comprehensive treatment
of all topics that may be considered within the purview of African Americans
in American foreign policy. Rather, our ambitions are a bit more modest; we
have endeavored to bring together in one volume original work that focuses on
understudied and contemporarily resonant topics—scholarship that illuminates
trends in the study of African American diplomacy, attempts to (re)open lines
of theoretical inquiry, demonstrates creative use of archival materials, and mo-
tivates questions for further research.

    As we describe in this brief introduction, topics range from consideration of
early diplomatic appointees to assessments of those leaders who have served as
policy makers, performers, and cultural ambassadors from the nineteenth century to the present. Chapters are informed by scholarship on African Americans
as formal diplomatic appointees,[4] studies of citizen diplomacy,[5] and research that
seeks to bring a global context to domestic affairs.[6] The volume synthesizes the
extant literature and, in so doing, bridges the scholarly gap between institutional
and extra-institutional (i.e., sociocultural) forms of African American diplomacy
throughout American history and suggests new directions in historiography. In
addition, the book is unique in combining scholarly voices from academia as
well as practitioner insights in their own words, as represented by the thoughts
of former ambassadors Walter C. Carrington and Charles Stith in the preface
and epilogue, respectively.

    Through a close reading of primary source materials (e.g., speeches, letters,
historical archives, diaries, diplomatic cables, and memoirs of policy makers),
contributors provide novel and challenging insights on several animating themes.
First among these themes is *the emergence of African Americans as a political force
and views of political representation.* The first generation of African American
diplomatic appointees, as Allison Blakely describes in chapter 1, were initially

chosen for service in order to "[woo] the newly enfranchised black electorate" in the wake of the Civil War. Employing stronger language, Michael Krenn, in his chapter on Cold War appointments, introduces the notion of "diplomatic tokenism" to understand how African American ambassadors could aid the American cause. Political patronage is a common aspect of the American political system—a sign of political incorporation—but in the African American case it can also be seen as a sign of progress in that it represents the seeking of electoral support from a previously disenfranchised and then neglected constituency group.

As opportunities to participate appear, African American leaders often embrace a specific type of representation. As both Ronald Walters and Robert Smith conclude, increased numbers of African Americans in positions of political influence do not necessarily result in more black interests being represented in the halls of power.[7] To apply Hanna Pitkin's classic formulation, given the formal constraints of the positions that they have held, African Americans have more often engaged in *descriptive* and *symbolic representation* and have been less able to assume the role of *substantive* representative.[8] While prospects have gradually increased—for example, Ambassador Harry K. Thomas Jr., U.S. ambassador to the Philippines (2010–2013), has written about "Breaking the 'Negro Circuit'"[9]— the distinction between placements in African or Caribbean nations and other parts of the world, along with an overwhelming black elite focus on African policy (either by necessity or choice), has been a recurring and complex issue across time. Both Jeffrey Stewart and Lorenzo Morris consider the question of representation(s) within the context of their contributions to this book— the former in an exploration of the position of the black public intellectual in American life through an examination of the career trajectories of Alain Locke and Ralph Bunche, and the latter in a comparative case study of the African American presence at the United Nations.

A related tension revisited throughout the book is *the "paradox of loyalty": contending allegiances to race and nation*.[10] African American representatives have had to balance the often conflicting demands of the positions they hold in government with the interests they wish to advance on behalf of the black community. As Carl Rowan, a State Department spokesperson during the 1950s and 1960s who is profiled in chapter 3, explains, the two roles often have distinct objectives:

> My task is difficult, not merely because of the tenseness of the situation but also because of what I am and what my responsibilities are: on the one hand, I am a Negro with a vital desire, indeed a fierce determination, to see that my children escape the degrading shackles of racism; on the other hand I am a public official

whose job it is to help protect this country's reputation abroad, and an American citizen eager to see his country bind up wounds and wipe out scars of a conflict that should have been forgotten decades ago.

Despite misgivings later in life, Rowan chose to emphasize the progress being made by the United States during his diplomatic career. In embracing a *"from protest to cooperation" strategy,* he called for "responsible militancy" from the African American press, and like Ralph Bunche, chief Africa analyst in the Office of Strategic Services during World War II, who proposed an "insider advocacy of decolonization," Rowan argued that working from within the system was imperfect yet preferable to grievance-based challenges from outside.

At the risk of Establishment co-optation or criticism from African Americans for perceived accommodationism, black leaders have often prioritized the American cause (rather than racial group advancement) to demonstrate fidelity to the nation. Randall Kennedy has written about this "super-patriotism" phenomenon—the overcompensation among some African Americans to prove their loyalty and reassert their citizenship to a nation that because of its past actions does not merit such sentiment.[11] Speaking to these ethno-racial attachments,[12] Brandi Hughes, in her study of the Foreign Mission Board of the National Baptist Convention during the late nineteenth century, and Ibrahim Sundiata, in his exploration of Pan-Africanism in the contemporary era, consider the claims of solidarity and the (historically contingent) feelings of linked fate espoused by African Americans for other peoples of color.

African American elites who aim to influence American foreign policy while maintaining an independence of thought that is unavailable in a formal diplomatic post have often served as cultural envoys. In a chapter building upon his book-length treatment of goodwill sports ambassadors,[13] Damion Thomas investigates the experience of basketball player Bill Russell, among others, in describing how the U.S. government sought to counteract Soviet propaganda by sending popular culture icons abroad during the Cold War era as projections of American prosperity and racial inclusion. While there is more ideological flexibility in these citizen-level approaches to participation—such as religious missions, educational exchanges, or entertainment tours—there are certain *trade-offs of cultural diplomacy.* It will always be difficult to measure the precise impact of American soft power; however, the distinct policy orientations of cultural diplomats are undeniably effective in presenting different aspects of the lived American experience. Cultural emissaries, by definition, have less access to power than formal (institutional) diplomats, but with their singular voice they can make the United States appear less monolithic in its policy decisions to those publics on the receiving end of American foreign policy.

The views of those working outside the restrictions of government may change—Lisa Davenport, for example, in her chapter on jazz diplomacy, describes the evolution of Louis Armstrong's views—as opposed to those within government who must echo the position of the administration in power. As several chapter authors investigate, there are limits to the spectrum of views that are acceptable to the U.S. government. Federally funded projects can be canceled, passports can be revoked, and even non-sponsored cultural diplomats (like sports figures or musicians) acting as private citizens can face repercussions resulting from controversial political speech.

In its entirety this volume speaks to the successes and the setbacks, the promises and the pitfalls of African American contributions to American foreign policy. Examining the influential roles played by—and the constraints imposed upon—African Americans who have represented the nation abroad in various capacities complicates and elucidates our scholarly understanding of individual agency and institutional structures in shaping social, political, and cultural outcomes.

Part I of the text contemplates diplomatic foundations. Each of the three chapters in this section evaluates the impressive achievements of early African American contributors to American foreign policy. Given the limited discursive and political space in which these pioneers were operating, their accomplishments are remarkable and their frustrations about the restrictive bounds of their policy influence are reasonable. In "Blacks in the Diplomatic and Consular Services, 1869–1924," Allison Blakely surveys the experiences of black Americans in the early foreign service. The U.S. Department of State was the first major government department to appoint blacks to positions of prestige. This generation included John L. Waller, Mifflin Wistar Gibbs, and Richard T. Greener, as well as career officer William Henry Hunt. Blakely argues that such progressivism occurred in an atmosphere of pervasive racism and reflected not only the varying interests of the two major political parties but also the growing disenfranchisement of blacks through the Jim Crow laws. Ultimately these early officers faced personal dilemmas born out of contrasting experiences abroad and at home.

In "A New Negro Foreign Policy: The Critical Vision of Alain Locke and Ralph Bunche," Jeffrey C. Stewart structures his study around the provocative claim that African Americans are *natural diplomats* because of the particular circumstances of the black experience in the United States. In order to survive, African Americans have been conditioned to mask their frank judgments about the American "democratic" system. Within this framework, Stewart conceptualizes what he labels the "New Negro foreign policy." As embodied in the work of Locke and Bunche, this perspective is characterized by a critical approach to foreign policy, albeit one that is not too radical or too applicable to the American domestic racial context so as to avoid offending white liberal sensibilities (and therefore jeopardizing patronage opportunities). Representative of sequential stages of development within this foreign policy tradition, Locke and Bunche encountered different levels of political access and policy influence.

In "Carl Rowan and the Dilemma of Civil Rights, Propaganda, and the Cold War," Michael Krenn considers the influence of Cold War politics and policies exerted on journalist and State Department spokesperson Carl Rowan during the 1950s and 1960s. Rowan's contention that "the civil rights issue was being dealt with in an effective and speedy manner" is not, as Krenn argues, an indication of Rowan's naïve optimism about America's racial problem, but rather speaks to his understanding of the need for propaganda in America's struggle against communism. Once the Cold War was well over, as his book *The Coming Race War in America: A Wake-Up Call* attests, Rowan considers America's racial problems in a much less optimistic light.[14]

The next four chapters, which comprise part II of the volume, analyze African American participation in foreign affairs through civil society. Each chapter focuses on groups of African Americans—Baptist missionaries, conscripted soldiers, professional and amateur athletes, and jazz musicians—who engaged in citizen forms of diplomacy during specific temporal periods. While the results of such involvement are often difficult to quantify, the chapters in this section reveal that much can be (politically and personally) accomplished during these cultural exchanges. In addition to serving the interests of the sponsoring organization (e.g., church, government), participation abroad helps to shed light on domestic racial realities while often providing opportunities for racial solidarity and self-awareness.

In "Reconstruction's Revival: The Foreign Mission Board of the National Baptist Convention and the Roots of Black Populist Diplomacy," Brandi Hughes explores how missionary work that began as evangelical outreach developed into a system of shared grievances when African Americans began to see the meaningful parallels and symmetries between their own limited political influence in the Reconstruction South and African communities affected by colonialism. Benefiting from access to the minutes of the annual meeting and publication records of the *Mission Herald,* the National Baptist Convention's monthly newsletter, Hughes traces African American engagement with Africa in the late nineteenth century through the transformation of a historically decentralized religious denomination into a collective space for civic mobilization shaped by diasporic identification and linked social circumstances.

Vera Grant's " White Shame/Black Agency: Race as a Weapon in Post–World War I Diplomacy," represents an arresting parallel to its counterparts in part II on U.S. government employment of sports and music as weapons in cultural diplomacy during the second half of the twentieth century. Grant makes a compelling case that race as a weapon, like sports and music, could be a double-edged sword. On the one hand loyal and talented black U.S. citizens were deliberately used in a callous and cynical fashion to advance their country's interests, but at the same time, those who were manipulated were serendipitously provided an opportunity to enhance their self-esteem and redouble their determination to gain recognition of their full humanity.

In their roles as cultural diplomats, African American athletes and musicians played significant roles in twentieth-century U.S. foreign policy. In "Goodwill Ambassadors: African American Athletes and U.S. Cultural Diplomacy, 1947–1968," Damion Thomas examines the "challenges, contradictions, and political nature" of sports emissaries during the early Cold War era. Recognizing the impact that Soviet declarations of American mistreatment of blacks were having on global public opinion about the United States, government officials planned goodwill trips that would provide opportunities for people around the world to meet successful African Americans whose abilities on the playing field and loyalty to the nation represented a positive counterweight to the claims being posited by adversaries of the United States. Thomas devotes special attention to the response of the program by the athletes themselves, most of whom were initially unaware of the underlying political purpose of their trips. There was an unintended politicizing effect for the athletes, as many used the forum to distance themselves from domestic policies, push for civil rights, and find common cause with subjugated peoples around the world. An increased unwillingness for citizen diplomats to "stay on message" resulted in the programs being scaled back in the late 1960s.

In "The Paradox of Jazz Diplomacy: Race and Culture in the Cold War," Lisa Davenport focuses on the jazz tours that began in July 1954, which were sponsored by the State Department's Bureau of Educational and Cultural Affairs. The jazz tours created a paradox in U.S. Cold War strategy. As Davenport argues, "The cultural expression of one of the nation's most oppressed minorities came to symbolize the cultural superiority of American democracy." Policy makers considered jazz, the "authentic expression of American life," to be an apt instrument in U.S. efforts to contain criticism about America's cultural and racial identity. The tours, suspended in the early 1960s when volatile racial conflicts in urban America and the Vietnam War made them no longer viable, were reinstated in the late 1960s, but with more conservative jazz musicians. In an enlightening expression of Du Boisian double consciousness, Davenport examines the "moral tension" experienced by jazz performers over whether to "affirm their heritage by struggling against racial oppression or seek acceptance into white society."

Part III of the text brings the discussion of African Americans and American foreign policy to the present and considers the impact of African American policy leadership on American foreign relations. In "African American Representatives in the United Nations: From Ralph Bunche to Susan Rice," Lorenzo Morris constructs a typology of "racial pressures" that African Americans must contend with in order to effectively navigate this high-profile position. In explaining possible policy outcomes across similar issue areas, Morris applies this rubric to the service of Ralph Bunche, Andrew Young, Donald McHenry, and Susan Rice and finds distinct pressures and varied levels of effectiveness among the American representatives. In the special case of Susan Rice, Morris reconsiders how the Ellisonian ideal of the "invisible" U.N. ambassador has shifted over time and how being an African American ambassador for the first African American president bears on the assumptions of the racial pressure model.

Has the Obama presidency represented fundamental change or, in many consequential ways, foreign policy continuity? More broadly, what does Obama mean for future African American interest in foreign affairs and the pursuit of diplomatic service? In "Obama, African Americans, and Africans: The Double Vision," Ibrahim Sundiata ponders how the election (and reelection) of President Obama fits into the larger historical narrative that is the focus of earlier chapters. While Obama's ancestral homeland is Africa, Sundiata describes how the process by which one receives broad popular support is incompatible with a Pan-African worldview. The American exceptionalism required for ascension to the highest levels of political power limits the relevance of Pan-Africanism among African American political elites in the twenty-first century.

Providing personal recollections and political analysis, former ambassador Charles Stith reflects on the impact of African Americans on U.S. foreign policy during particular historical periods in the epilogue to the volume. Integrating history and practice, Stith writes about the decisions made and the actions taken by African American diplomats as shapers and makers of American foreign policy.

Notes

1. Elliott P. Skinner, *African Americans and U.S. Policy toward Africa, 1850–1924: In Defense of Black Nationality* (Washington, D.C.: Howard University Press, 1992).

2. Jake C. Miller, *The Black Presence in American Foreign Affairs* (Washington, D.C.: University Press of America, 1978); George W. Shepherd Jr., ed., *Racial Influences on American Foreign Policy* (New York: Basic Books, 1970).

3. Michael Clemons, ed., *African Americans in Global Affairs: Contemporary Perspectives* (Hanover, N.H.: University Press of New England, 2010), xi.

4. Michael L. Krenn, *Black Diplomacy: African Americans and the State Department, 1945–1969* (Armonk, N.Y.: M. E. Sharpe, 1999).

5. Lisa E. Davenport, *Jazz Diplomacy: Promoting America in the Cold War Era* (Jackson: University Press of Mississippi, 2009); Penny Marie Von Eschen, *Satchmo Blows Up the World: Jazz Ambassadors Play the Cold War* (Cambridge, Mass.: Harvard University Press, 2004).

6. Thomas Borstelmann, *The Cold War and the Color Line: American Race Relations in the Global Arena* (Cambridge, Mass.: Harvard University Press, 2003); Mary L. Dudziak, *Cold War Civil Rights: Race and the Image of American Democracy* (Princeton, N.J.: Princeton University Press, 2011); Brenda Gayle Plummer, *Rising Wind: Black Americans and U.S. Foreign Affairs, 1935–1960* (Chapel Hill: University of North Carolina Press, 1996); Brenda Gayle Plummer, ed., *Window on Freedom: Race, Civil Rights, and Foreign Affairs, 1945–1988* (Chapel Hill: University of North Carolina Press, 2003).

7. Robert C. Smith, *We Have No Leaders: African Americans in the Post–Civil Rights Era* (Albany: SUNY Press, 1996); Ronald W. Walters, "Racial Justice in Foreign Affairs," in *African Americans in Global Affairs: Contemporary Perspectives,* ed. Michael Clemons (Hanover, N.H.: University Press of New England, 2010), 1–30.

8. Hanna F. Pitkin, *The Concept of Representation* (Berkeley: University of California Press, 1967).

9. Harry K. Thomas Jr., "Breaking the 'Negro Circuit,'" *State Magazine* (February 2006): 30.

10. The phrase "paradox of loyalty" is appropriated from the title of the book edited by Malveaux and Green that examines African American reactions to the U.S. political climate in the aftermath of the attacks of September 11, 2001. See Julianne Malveaux and Regina A. Green, eds., *The Paradox of Loyalty: An African American Response to the War on Terrorism,* 2nd ed. (Chicago: Third World Press, 2004).

11. Randall Kennedy, *The Persistence of the Color Line: Racial Politics and the Obama Presidency* (New York: Pantheon, 2011).

12. These attitudes are perfectly captured in the title of Alvin Tillery's *Between Homeland and Motherland: Africa, U.S. Foreign Policy, and Black Leadership in America* (Ithaca, N.Y.: Cornell University Press, 2011).

13. Damion L. Thomas, *Globetrotting: African American Athletes and Cold War Politics* (Champaign: University of Illinois Press, 2012).

14. Carl Rowan, *The Coming Race War in America: A Wake-Up Call* (Boston: Little, Brown, 1996).

PART I

Early African American Diplomatic Appointments

Contributions and Constraints

1

Blacks in the U.S. Diplomatic and Consular Services, 1869–1924

ALLISON BLAKELY

The spectacular appointments of two successive black secretaries of state at the turn of the twenty-first century was an almost startling occurrence that for most of the public, both in the United States and abroad, first brought awareness of a significant role of blacks in the diplomatic service. A full century earlier black Americans were playing a very conspicuous part during the formative period of the U.S. Foreign Service, however, and these grand achievements at the dawn of the twenty-first century cannot be fully understood nor appreciated without knowledge of this earlier history. To its credit, the U.S. Department of State was the first major government department to appoint blacks to positions of prestige during the period from the Civil War to the 1920s, when more than sixty African Americans were appointed to diplomatic, consular, or commercial agency positions.[1] In addition to such well-known historical actors as Frederick Douglass, John Mercer Langston, and James Weldon Johnson, those appointed included a host of other, similarly talented figures whose careers have gone unnoticed by later generations, including Richard T. Greener, John L. Waller, and Mifflin W. Gibbs, whose careers I give special attention to in the present chapter. A close look at this fascinating saga (one that still awaits comprehensive scholarly treatment) reveals that this practice, which was undeniably progressive for its time, nevertheless reflected the pervasive racism that was distinctly characteristic of that period of American history. Moreover, the frequency of such appointments showed a direct correlation to the varying interest of the two major political parties, particularly the Republican Party, in wooing the newly enfranchised black electorate. In this regard a telling statistic is that in 1880 there were four black consuls serving, in 1905 the number peaked at seventeen, and in 1920 there were only three.[2] One likely influence on these appointments was the growing disenfranchisement of blacks, the majority of whom still resided in the South, as the Jim Crow system tightened its grip.[3]

A Convergence of State Needs and African American Aspirations

Before the U.S. Foreign Service was formally created and professionalized by the Rogers Act of 1924, which combined the existing diplomatic and consular services and set up a stricter standard examination system, foreign service positions were filled by presidential appointments. This arrangement provided blacks entrée into high-level political appointments that could at times cut through the prevailing strictures of the racial hierarchy still governing American society. It should also be noted, however, that both official and private correspondence related to the subject of assignment of posts makes it abundantly clear that certain regions were designated as "Negro posts." Thus, by far the majority of the assignments for blacks were in Africa, especially Liberia, and in the Caribbean and South America, with roughly a third of the assignments falling in Liberia alone and a fourth in Haiti or Santo Domingo.[4] Although whites were also assigned to these posts at times, both of the political parties in power tended to honor the color designation. For example, when in 1885 the newly elected Democratic administration refused to allow George Washington Williams (1849–1891) to assume the post of minister to Haiti, even after Senate approval and a commission from the State Department, President Grover Cleveland nominated John Edward Thompson, who thereby succeeded John Mercer Langston in that country. From the late 1890s until his death in 1915, Booker T. Washington played a key role in preserving this type of racial preference. Favored by the white establishment as a black leader because of his relatively conservative stance on civil rights, he often had dominant influence in advising both presidents and other powerful political figures on which blacks to reward with government appointments in general. The depth of his involvement in such matters was such that much of the history surrounding the present topic could be written simply by exploiting his voluminous correspondence, which is now available to researchers in the invaluable multivolume related works by the eminent historian Louis Harlan.[5] That such appointments of blacks to consular and diplomatic posts should not be mistaken as clear signs of progress in race relations is evident in the following internal exchange within the State Department regarding the appointment of George Washington Ellis (1875–1919):

Memorandum, July 3, 1907
Mr. Dean:
There is nothing to do but transfer him to the consular service if we want to keep him. Would he be better than some new coon?
R. B. [Robert Bacon]

Memorandum, July 10, 1907
Dear Mr. Carr:
With the possibility of two additional colored brethren coming into the service as a result of the examination do you think it would be desirable to consider transferring Mr. Ellis from the diplomatic to the consular service, and if so where could we send him?
C.R.D. [Dean]

Dear Mr. Dean:
I doubt whether we shall be able to pass more than one colored brethren (adopting your very courteous term), and I think it probable that Ellis could be transferred to the consular service if in making up the list we can find a place for him. Wouldn't he have to be examined?
W.T.C. [Carr]

July 12, 1907 [Alvey A. Adee to Congressman Charles F. Scott]
The Department is in receipt of your letter of June 25, in which you suggest the desirability, if practical, of transferring Mr. George W. Ellis, now Secretary of Legation at Monrovia, Liberia to some other post. I do not know that this can be done, but the matter will have careful consideration. You undoubtedly appreciate that there are difficulties in the way of finding a post where he would be acceptable on account of his race.[6]

A telling commentary on the status of blacks in the service is the fact that Ellis, who was already a respected lawyer and sociologist, never rose beyond his initial rank of secretary of the legation in his eight years of service in Monrovia.[7] Nevertheless, despite the concept of "Negro posts" and a generally low esteem among State Department officials for black officers, other scattered postings spanned the globe, including John Quarles's service in Spain from 1877 to 1880; Richard Greener in Russia at Vladivostok, 1898–1905, and Ivan Smit at Libau in

1908; Mifflin Gibbs and William Henry Hunt in Madagascar, 1897–1901; James G. Carter in Madagascar from 1906 to 1916, in Turkey in 1916, and in France from 1927 to 1940; Hunt in France from 1906 to 1926; Edward B. Cipriani in Wales, England, and Scotland from 1919 to 1921; and Whitney Young in Kobe, Japan, from 1926 to 1929 (and later, beyond the period under review here, in Yokohama in 1932, and in Tientsin, China, in 1938). Regarding these early U.S. consuls and diplomats collectively, it is particularly striking how impressive some of their performance was and how seldom it seemed to be appropriately acknowledged or rewarded. Here it should also be kept in mind that great sacrifice and considerable danger often accompanied the honor these appointments conveyed.

While their white patrons may have considered African Americans more resistant to West Africa's deadly fevers, a number of appointees nevertheless succumbed to them, and others developed chronic illnesses. The very first appointed, Ebenezer Bassett, whom President Ulysses S. Grant appointed minister to Haiti and the Dominican Republic in 1869, died in 1908 but had experienced frequent illnesses associated with malaria or dengue that were first contracted during his initial appointment there. He had also served as consul general for Haiti in New York from 1879 to 1888.[8] Richard Greener was originally appointed to serve in Bombay rather than at the post he finally assumed in Vladivostok, but he had declined to go to India after receiving reports that the bubonic plague was raging there. Health risks continued on into the twentieth century. Ellis suffered from frequent illness throughout his stay in Liberia. His successor there, William D. Crum, served only from 1910 to 1912 and died back home in Charleston, South Carolina, of "African fever," despite his being a physician. An editorial in the *New York Age* even observed that there seemed to be a pattern of such deaths among black diplomats.

Another among the consuls who were also physicians was Henry W. Furniss (1868–1955), who served in Brazil from 1898 to 1905 and in Haiti from 1905 to 1913. In a letter to Congressman James W. Overstreet he reported that the unhealthy conditions there had resulted in his contracting both yellow and black water fever, leaving him with a chronic liver problem. (A daughter-in-law in the United States later reported that late in his life he showed her a cigar box with kidney stones he had passed over the years.) Furniss conveyed this information to the congressman as part of his ongoing plea for a more commensurate salary, pointing out that his pay was several times lower than that of his peers there representing other countries.[9] Despite such risks, foreign service was very attractive to African Americans of talent and ambition, and some were extraordinarily persistent in seeking posts abroad, especially beyond Africa and the Americas, but had very limited success in the latter regard.

An especially poignant illustration of the determination of some to serve is that of George Washington Williams, best known for his pioneering contributions as a historian. His *History of the Negro Race in America from 1619 to 1880*, published by G. P. Putnam's Sons in 1882, was the first scholarly history on this subject by anyone; it was followed in 1887 by Harper's publication of Williams's *History of the Negro Troops in the War of the Rebellion*. His fondest aspiration, however, was to pursue a political career. This nearly came to fruition when President Harrison appointed him minister to Haiti in 1885, but, as noted earlier, he was denied the position by the new Democratic administration. Returning to Boston, where he had been practicing law, he began to pursue his interests in international relations on his own. His attendance at the World Conference on Foreign Missions in London in 1884 and subsequent travels to Europe led him to promote his ideas about the future of Africa. He did so through published articles and a personal tour of four months in the Congo, which he undertook notwithstanding being urged not to go by King Leopold of Belgium, whom he had met during his European travels. In fact in his "Open Letter to His Serene Majesty, Leopold II, King of the Belgians," he directly criticized the king for inhumane treatment of the Congolese people. Other related articles followed, including "Report upon the Congo-State and Country to the President of the Republic of the United States" and "Report on the Proposed Congo Railway." He also visited Portuguese and British possessions in Africa and spent several weeks in Egypt. He had other research and writing in progress when illness led to his untimely death in England in 1891.[10]

Williams thus exhibited the main characteristics common to all the black consuls and diplomats discussed in this chapter: outstanding talent and unbridled ambition. These attributes are sharply reflected in their success in multiple careers. While the main interest here is in their roles in U.S. foreign policy, these were generally highly trained professionals at a time when relatively few of their fellow black Americans were well educated at all. During other phases of their careers they were educators, journalists, lawyers, doctors, politicians, businessmen, and clergymen. One can scarcely conceive of any other grouping of blacks during the half century under discussion that would reveal so many individuals who broke the color barrier by being the "first" in various fields. They were shining exemplars of commitment not only to the "American dream" in terms of their personal aspirations but often as well to the embryonic American imperialism emerging in some aspects of their government's foreign policy. There is more than a little irony in the fact that some of them, though certainly not all, also largely shared the popular perception of Africa and Africans as uncivilized and inferior in culture. Even on the domestic scene some shared the dominant white class and color prejudices regarding the socially constructed "racial" class that they were viewed as being part of. In the era of Booker T. Washington's strongest influence, those successful in gaining his support for appointment were also more likely to ascribe to his conservative political and social views than to the more radical demands for equality being asserted most fiercely by W.E.B. Du Bois.

The Correlation between Qualifications, Performance, and Recognition

The ways in which the lives of these black elites brought them to the U.S. Foreign Service and what they brought of value to the service can best be appreciated by a closer look at a few of them who left extensive informative records. Among the best examples in that respect is Mifflin Wistar Gibbs (1823–1915), whose life included a remarkable number of different careers and lasted into his ninety-third year. Born in 1823 in Philadelphia, his first occupation, at the age of sixteen, was as a carpenter's apprentice, which led to his becoming a journeyman contractor on his own. Meanwhile he gained literacy through a local black men's literary society. Eventually he became active in the Underground Railroad movement with William Still and others, and in 1849 he accompanied Frederick Douglass on a dangerous abolitionist speaking tour in western New York. Upon receiving word the next year of the gold rush in California, he sailed west as a steerage passenger. When racism in San Francisco prevented him from working as a carpenter, he became a partner in a clothing import firm that did so well that his new status allowed him to become a civic leader and a member of state Negro conventions in 1854, 1855, and 1857. He was later prominent at national-level Negro conventions. He was also co-owner and editor of an abolitionist newspaper, *The Mirror of the Times*.[11] In 1858 he moved to British Columbia after gold was discovered there, set up a new store for his firm, and again prospered, well enough to invest in real estate on the side. By 1866 he and his wife, Maria A. Alexander, were settled in Victoria with their five children, and he had been elected to two terms on the city's Common Council, became director of the Queen Charlotte Island Coal Company, and began studying law on the side.

After Gibbs and his wife decided to return to the United States in 1869, he completed formal law training at a business college in Oberlin, Ohio, where his wife had attended Oberlin College, as would three of their children.[12] After touring the South to determine what city seemed to offer the most promising future for Negro residents, Gibbs settled his family in Little Rock, Arkansas. There he again achieved phenomenal success, culminating in his election as municipal judge of Little Rock, the first Negro elected to such office in the United States. In 1876 he was elected a presidential elector for Arkansas on the Republican ticket. In 1877 he received his first federal post when Rutherford B. Hayes appointed him receiver of the U.S. Land Office for the Little Rock District of Arkansas. He was a delegate to all but one of the Republican national conventions from 1868 to 1897, the year he was appointed U.S. consul at Tamatave, Madagascar, serving until ill health forced his resignation in 1901. Thus, Gibbs was a classic example of the foreign service post representing a reward to a Republican stalwart. However, this was by no means the end of his active career. He returned to Little Rock and published his autobiography in 1902, for which Booker T. Washington wrote the introduction. While he was receiver of the Land Office he had encouraged thousands of immigrants and others to homestead virgin Arkansas land and helped them establish schools, emphasizing the trade schools Booker T. Washington would have applauded. In 1903 he became president of the newly organized Capital City Savings Bank in Little Rock, a partner in the Little Rock Electric Light Company, a large shareholder in several other companies, and owner of several pieces of local real estate. For most of the final decade until his death in 1915 he remained active in traveling and giving public lectures.[13]

Although Gibbs's foreign service tour in Madagascar was relatively uneventful, a few years earlier that post had been the center of an episode involving his predecessor once removed, John L. Waller (1850–1907). The incident illustrates some of the pitfalls that confronted prominent blacks who attempted to move beyond the limited realm of activity the establishment deemed acceptable for those of their "race." Waller's career before his consular appointment was almost as varied as Gibbs's and already contained ample evidence that he might try to overstep racial bounds. Though born a slave, he too had become a lawyer, entrepreneur, and journalist and would later serve as a U.S. Army officer as well. His time as consul at Tamatave was far more eventful than that of Gibbs, because it corresponded with the takeover of Madagascar by France, which climaxed with a military invasion in 1894 just after Waller's tenure ended. Then a bizarre twist of affairs began in March 1895 when French authorities arrested Waller because of a private business venture he had remained on the island to pursue. Waller had exploited close ties he had established with the Malagasy government to obtain a large land concession worth millions of dollars in products such as mahogany, teak, and rubber. His intention was to create a colony there through leasing the land and recruiting black settlers from the United States to lease parcels from him. Waller's career showed a lifelong commitment to black colonization projects. Having participated in a wave of black migration to Kansas before his consular post, he would also later float a proposal to have the U.S. Congress appropriate $20 million to sponsor emigration of blacks from the South to Cuba, Puerto Rico, and the Philippines after they had served in Cuba during the Spanish-American War.[14]

There is therefore little reason to doubt Waller's sincerity in the Madagascar land project. Nevertheless, based on flimsy interpretation of a letter of his that the French intercepted, which criticized the French invasion, the French convicted him in a military court on charges of breaking French postal regulations and transmitting military intelligence to the Malagasy. He was sentenced to twenty years of solitary confinement in France. The true French motive appears to have been simply to prevent Waller from restricting their total control of the island and its valuable natural resources. Waller would later publish an account of how during his ocean voyage to France he was chained to the floor of the ship for seven days and without food or water for two days and nights.[15] Reacting to the embarrassment of international reporting on such treatment of a former U.S. consul, and to pressure from Waller's wife, Susan, and the black press, after eleven months of confinement that weakened a health condition that had already been adversely affected by the climate and illness during his service, both houses of Congress passed resolutions directing the State Department to obtain Waller's release. John Mercer Langston was among the attorneys pleading his case. Predictably, the main condition of his release was that no further claims against the French government over the land or his treatment would be considered valid.[16]

The third individual I highlight in this chapter in order to illustrate the gifts these early black consuls brought to their foreign service is Richard T. Greener (1844–1922). His prior career as a lawyer and educator earned him the distinction of being considered the most outstanding black intellectual of his time until W.E.B. Du Bois would surpass him in that regard when he came into his own in the early twentieth century. Son of a sailor, and born in Philadelphia, with the aid of white patrons who early on recognized his potential Greener built upon college preparatory work at Oberlin College and Phillips Academy in Andover, Massachusetts, to become the first black graduate of Harvard College in 1870, winning top prizes for oratory and dissertation writing to boot. His academic career included service as principal at the high schools for black youths in Philadelphia and Washington and as professor of metaphysics and logic at the University of South Carolina during the Reconstruction period. Having meanwhile earned a law degree when the racist backlash ending Reconstruction purged blacks from prestigious academic positions, he returned to Washington, D.C., where he became an instructor and dean at the Howard University Law Department. Greener's most conspicuous role as a lawyer was as part of the legal team in the famous 1881 court-martial of the West Point cadet Johnson C.

Whittaker, who was convicted of the ludicrous charge of self-mutilation after being deliberately attacked by racist fellow cadets. Whittaker also happened to have been one of Greener's students at the University of South Carolina, where radical Republican policies during Reconstruction had imposed the highest percentage of blacks of any white university.

As a reward for campaigning in support of the Republican Party for several years, Greener was appointed secretary of the Grant Monument Association in New York from 1885 to 1892 and as chief examiner of the municipal civil service board for New York City until 1889. It was after struggling throughout the 1890s to find new posts and financial security for his large family that he managed in 1898 to obtain an abortive appointment to Bombay, for which that to Vladivostok was substituted upon his request. Greener left an extraordinarily vivid account of his mission there until 1905 in his consular dispatches back to the State Department and in his personal correspondence.[17] Viewing Siberia as a region of great economic potential and himself as the principal agent for the expansion of American business into Siberia, he strove vigorously to advance both American interests and his own. Serving only at the rank of commercial agent due to the Russian policy of not approving consuls there at that time, Greener nevertheless wrote simultaneously to senators Thomas Platt of New York, Henry Cabot Lodge of Massachusetts, and others offering his candidacy for the rank of consul general should one be established there and to the State Department urging the establishment of one for eastern Siberia.[18]

In his dispatches Greener displayed his exceptional grasp of the historical moment. In the wake of the Spanish-American War, he viewed the United States as now an imperial power competing with the seven other countries that had commercial agents present and as potentially the dominant industrial power in the world, with Germany and Japan as her main rivals. Completion of the Trans-Siberian Railroad during Greener's tenure also underscored Russia's role as a leading world power. The outcome of the Russo-Japanese War of 1904–1905, which concluded with a treaty facilitated by the president of the United States, further vindicated Greener's claim to be in a location of major importance for American national interests. During his first two years he overwhelmed his superiors with so many meticulously written proposals that they responded with complaints about their sheer length and degree of detail: for initiatives such as establishment of a regular American steamship line between the Pacific Coast and Vladivostok, a department store featuring American goods, an American mineral water industry involving a Russian partner, and the introduction of California fruit products into Siberia. He received neither encouragement nor recognition for his efforts. In fact, the only signs of appreciation Greener received for his seven years of service in Russia came from the foreign governments on the scene. He was decorated by the Chinese government for his role in famine relief in North China in the wake of the Boxer Rebellion, and during the Russo-Japanese War he looked after the interests in Vladivostok of both the Japanese and British governments, whose representatives were forced to leave temporarily for diplomatic reasons. To his dismay, his own government dismissed him from his post and from the consular service on the basis of unsubstantiated charges of improper personal conduct and dereliction of duties. When his appeals of this decision failed, Greener retired to Chicago, where he took up his final residence after 1906, still remaining highly respected, especially in the black community.

The few careers considered in some depth so far are all of individuals whose actual periods of service were brief. It may be further instructive, therefore, to also take a closer look at the experience of a career officer with multiple posts of extensive duration. One such person is William Henry Hunt (1869–1951), the launching of whose career might even be said to be the single most significant achievement of Mifflin Gibbs in Madagascar.[19] A Tennessee native, Hunt had met Gibbs by accident after having worked for a decade and a half in the United States and Canada in such jobs as custodian, bellhop, and Pullman porter. A chance acquaintance with the headmaster of Lawrence Academy in Groton, Massachusetts, brought Hunt access to his main formal education. He came to Gibbs's attention through one of his daughters, Ida, who had met Hunt a few years before Gibbs's consular appointment. Gibbs agreed to Hunt's request to be taken along as his informal assistant. Hunt was able to afford this adventure only with the aid of a loan from the Wall Street brokerage firm where he had been employed as a messenger. His formal appointment as vice consul in 1899 began what would become a career of thirty-one years as a consul: in Tamatave as Gibbs's successor, 1901–1906; St. Etienne, France, 1906–1926; Guadeloupe, 1926–1929; the Azores, 1929–1931; and Liberia, 1931–1932. In 1904 he had married Ida Gibbs, who accompanied him at all of his posts. Compared to the experiences of the others treated here thus far, Hunt's life story before, during, and after his foreign service displayed little social activism. It is also interesting to note that the meticulous reports he submitted to the State Department on the economics of the areas where he served, in contrast to the response to Greener's, drew praise from his superiors, and some appeared in government publications as well as a few articles in the *Bulletin of the American Geographical Society of New York*. The St. Etienne post was the high point of Hunt's career and was particularly remarkable because during most of that period he was the only black consul serving in Europe, a region the State Department considered inappropriate for blacks, as shown in the correspondence quoted above regarding G. W. Ellis's assignment. The key factor in Hunt's longevity in the service appears to have been his diplomatic skills and social graces, as he was very popular and active in the local communities. Although Hunt did receive a few promotions within the consular ranks, a strong case could be made for the view expressed by Du Bois in a 1924 *Crisis* article that Hunt's service seemed to merit even higher rank.[20]

Their Legacy

One important consequence, whether intended or not, of the separation of these gifted individuals from the American domestic scene during these crucial decades was a channeling abroad of the energies of some of the strongest potential black leaders at a time when black America was in especially critical need for such leadership at home. While most of them participated to some degree in all of the major social justice initiatives, both local and national, ranging from abolitionism to the twentieth-century advancements of the civil rights movement, the tenor of their critique and activism was restricted during their government service. This contributed to a lack of societal and institutional recognition and preservation of the achievements of these individuals. In fact, apart from the black press, the pervasive racial bias of the time persistently worked to promote a negative legacy. A fairly representative expression of popular opinion of the era appears in an 1896 *New York Times* editorial that, without reference to the actual overall record of performance, declared that "of American Negroes, the better class are not seeking or accepting offices" and that blacks had generally failed as diplomats.[21] Based only on the incomplete data presented here, however, it can be seen that this judgment is patently false. Nevertheless, there was a personal and social dimension of this problem that was quite real, one that centered on the issue of identity. The message of James Weldon Johnson's novel *Autobiography of An Ex-Colored Man,* which he finished during his consular service, is surely an attempt to reconcile some of the contradictory feelings aroused in Johnson by the juxtaposition of his experiences at home and abroad.[22] Johnson was among those who had pleaded in vain for a European post. Greener, whose European post was actually situated in Asia, also struggled with this issue of identity, which in some respects was a counterpart to Du Bois's notion of the double consciousness that arises from the predicament of being black in nominally democratic America.

This dilemma can be seen in a letter Greener wrote from Vladivostok, thus from autocratic Russia, to a friend after having read about race riots occurring in Southern states at home: "As I sit here writing surrounded by my two big flags, while the little one floats over my office, I feel how anomalous our position—I an officer of the Government powerless, or indifferent to my protection at home. Here I am virtual commander of any naval force to protect me or any American interests. At home, in the satrapy of D.C. I could be murdered at will for my political opinions."[23] When abroad they might dine with royalty and socialize freely according to class without regard to the color line, but at home they could not stay in the best hotels regardless of how wealthy they might be. Hunt, who in Madagascar was customarily carried about on a litter shouldered by men, described how he would cushion the shock of reentry into the United States by residing in New York at an exclusive hotel that catered to foreign dignitaries. There he pretended to speak only French, and his light-colored skin completed the disguise.[24]

It is not surprising therefore that some of the light-complexioned chose not to identify as black when given a choice. One example of this was Henry Watson Furniss. Born in Brooklyn, New York, he was well established as a physician and surgeon in Indianapolis when influential Republicans procured his appointment as U.S. consul at Bahia, Brazil, in 1898, where he served until 1905. He then was appointed envoy extraordinary and minister plenipotentiary to Haiti until 1913, when he resigned as is customary with a change to a Democratic administration. In any case, Furniss, who had opposed the U.S. designs for total control of Haiti, could not expect continuation by President Woodrow Wilson, who would soon punctuate the more racist tone of his administration in general by systematically segregating those parts of the federal government that were not already segregated, including even the navy. Back in civilian life and resuming a medical career that would last three decades, the closest Furniss came to taking any kind of political stance was a persistent refusal to use his special knowledge for business ventures in Haiti. The following excerpts from my personal correspondence from 2004 with his granddaughter Diane Furniss Happy provide a rare intimate glimpse into the issue of how Henry Furniss's black identity subsequently played out in her family:

> My grandfather, Henry Watson Furniss, was an early role model for me. While my father was away for almost five years during World War II, I would visit his nearby home in West Hartford almost daily. He inspired my love of botany, of gardening and of nature. It came as quite a surprise, when at age forty (and long after his death), I discovered that my grandfather was African American! This wonderful heritage had never been mentioned in our family and my husband and I were determined to find out more about this fascinating man (and the times he lived in). Since we have retired, we have taken up the search in earnest.
>
> Henry's brother, Sumner Furniss, also a physician, provides an interesting contrast. He returned to Indianapolis, their hometown, where he became a leading activist for African-American causes and often corresponded with Booker T. Washington. On the other hand, Henry, once leaving the diplomatic service, appears to have melded seamlessly into the white enclave of West Hartford. (We discovered that his son, my father, went to prep school, college and medical

school as a "Negro" and then, wanting very much to be a flight surgeon, entered the service in World War II as "white.")[25]

In 1903 Henry Furniss had married Anna Wichmann, a German who would be his companion at his posts and for the rest of his life. A number of the others under discussion were also themselves light-complexioned and married white women. Richard Greener, who could pass for white, had married into a prominent African American family. Apparently, however, after the marriage dissolved into permanent separation in the 1890s, his wife and seven children altered their family name and those who could do so passed for white. The best known of the children, Belle, under the name Belle Da Costa Greene, became closely associated with the financier J. P. Morgan and director of his library. Through her work and travels in that capacity she openly became one of the mistresses of the art critic Bernard Berenson, while just as openly boasting of several other sexual conquests of her own, all amid hushed rumors about her mysterious mixed ancestry.[26] It should be noted, however, that Greener's career as a whole nevertheless left a positive mark, even on the U.S. Foreign Service. Among the consuls counted here was John Stephens Durham (1861–1919), another lawyer, who succeeded Frederick Douglass in Haiti and the Dominican Republic and had been Greener's student when he was principal at the Institute for Colored Youth in Philadelphia. And regarding Greener's seemingly grandiose schemes for Siberia, an interesting recent parallel to Greener's efforts in Vladivostok was the tenure of Pamela Spratlin, an African American, as consul general at Vladivostok at the turn of the twenty-first century.[27]

In considering the degree of direct involvement in public affairs and the social justice movement back home in weighing the legacy of these foreign service officers, it is also important to recognize that some of them were very much involved indirectly. William Henry Hunt is a good example of reticence in overt activism while having obvious extensive ties with important activists. His wife, Ida Gibbs Hunt, was especially committed to the world peace movement, and their location in France facilitated her serving as assistant secretary of the first Pan-African Congress, in Paris in 1919. She subsequently attended the Paris session of the second Pan-African Congress in 1921 as well, and she and W.E.B. Du Bois cochaired the executive committee that planned the third Pan-African Congress, held in London in 1923, where she also presented a paper titled "The Coloured Races and the League of Nations." Among W. H. Hunt's papers are materials from the Niagara movement, the NAACP, Pan-African activities, and the Association for the Study of Negro Life and History.[28]

Ida's sister, Harriet Gibbs Marshall (1868–1941), also carried on the family tradition of activism, both at home and abroad in the foreign service, though not at consular rank. Born while the Gibbs family lived in British Columbia, Harriet was educated at Oberlin and became the first black to finish the full course at its music conservatory. She then went on to found two conservatories for blacks, the most important being the Washington Conservatory of Music, which survived from 1903 to 1960. Her career took an unexpected turn, however, when she married Napoleon Bonaparte Marshall, a Harvard graduate who had practiced law in Massachusetts and New York and had helped her in establishing her conservatory. It was his subsequent career that carried them abroad. Having served with distinction in World War I as a rare black at the rank of captain, and with his father-in-law's contacts, he managed to obtain appointment as a clerk in the legation in Haiti, with a promise of elevation to that of a special attaché that never came. Instead, the couple spent six years working diligently to improve living conditions for Haitians, and their lack of official title allowed them to openly support the unsuccessful efforts to remove the U.S. Marine occupation force.[29]

Arguably the clearest example of a powerful positive legacy from the earliest black foreign service officers is the career of Clifton R. Wharton, who in addition to serving in Monrovia from 1927 to 1939 was simultaneously responsible for the Canary Islands from 1930 to 1939 and would later serve in Romania from 1958 to 1961, and in Norway from 1961 to 1964. Wharton holds the distinctions of being the first black American diplomat to be appointed on the basis of the then new diplomatic examination and, subsequently, the first to become an ambassador by advancing through the professional ranks, as well as the first black foreign service officer to become chief of a diplomatic mission. Before launching his diplomatic career he had received two law degrees from Boston University, in 1920 and 1923. Even more to the point regarding the question of legacy, he was also the father of his even more famous son, Clifton R. Wharton Jr., who would achieve an even more dazzling array of "firsts": the first black PhD in economics, from the University of Chicago, after having graduated from the Boston Latin School and Harvard College; a number of top positions in the corporate and foundations world; and the first black president of a major university in the United States, with his appointment at Michigan State University in 1970. One final example of an indirect legacy of the rich cultural exchange in which the early black foreign service officers participated may be seen in the son of John Waller's daughter Jennie and a Malagasy nobleman. His given name was Paul Andreamentania Rezafkerifo; the one he assumed was Andy Razaf, under which he became one of the leading composers of American popular music in the early twentieth century, best known for "Ain't Misbehavin'" and "Honeysuckle Rose."

The first generation of black foreign service officers thus left a rich legacy in terms of both professional performance and personal achievements. Their history provided a firm foundation and tradition for later officers and speaks volumes in support of persistent demands by black officers a century later to receive just treatment. Particularly striking evidence of its continuity with the present is the lawsuit that was filed in 1986 on behalf of 259 black officers asking that foreign service personnel policies be declared in violation of the Civil Rights Acts of the 1960s. The late twentieth-century configuration of world affairs and the further evolution of democracy in America toward realization of the true spirit of its ideals finally provided a more favorable climate for racial justice. The 1996 settlement of that class action suit provided, among other things, for a $3.8 million payment to black foreign service officers for back pay and raises, promotions for seventeen individuals, and a diversity training program.[30]

Notes

1. My list is compiled primarily from the general records of the Department of State, Record Group (RG) 59. However, I find its list to have omitted a few people about whom I found documentation elsewhere; and some of the information compiled by archives staff is inaccurate due to not detecting a few instances where appointments were made but not actually consummated.

2. Name Index to the Appointment of United States Diplomatic and Consular Officers, 1776–1993. Records of U.S. Department of State, National Archives, Washington, D.C.

3. The frequency of black appointments declined due to the fact that it had been mainly driven by the desire of the Republican Party to maximize its share of the black vote, which became less important as their right to vote was blocked by racist laws and practices established in the Southern states during this period.

4. An informative study focusing on those serving in Africa during this period is Elliott P. Skinner, *African Americans and U.S. Policy toward Africa, 1850–1924: In Defense of Black Nationality* (Washington, D.C.: Howard University Press, 1992).

5. Louis R. Harlan, ed., *The Booker T. Washington Papers* (Urbana: University of Illinois Press, 1972).

6. George Washington Ellis Papers, Bureau of Appointments, RG 59, Box 2.

7. See John E. Fleming and Rayford Logan, "Ellis, George Washington," in Rayford W. Logan and Michael R. Winston, eds., *Dictionary of American Negro Biography* (New York: W. W. Norton, 1982), 211–12.

8. Nancy Gordon Heinl, "Bassett, Ebenezer Don Carlos," in Logan and Winston, *Dictionary of American Negro Biography*, 32.

9. *New York Age*, December 19, 1912, 4. See also Furniss's obituary in the *New York Times*, December 8, 1912, 17. An informative complete biographical sketch is Rayford W. Logan, "Crum, William D[emos]," in Logan and Winston, *Dictionary of American Negro Biography*, 144.

10. John Hope Franklin, "Williams, George Washington," in Logan and Winston, *Dictionary of American Negro Biography,* 657.

11. I. Garland Penn, *The Afro-American Press and Its Editors* (Springfield, Mass.: Willey and Co., 1891), 76.

12. Mifflin Wistar Gibbs, *Shadow and Light: An Autobiography with Reminiscences of the Last and Present Century* (Washington, D.C., 1902 [Lincoln, NE: Bison Books, 1995]), chapter 6.

13. For this sketch of Gibbs's life I have drawn heavily from my offering on him in Logan and Winston, *Dictionary of American Negro Biography,* "Gibbs, Mifflin W[istar]," 258–59.

14. *[Indianapolis] Recorder,* July 8, 1899, 1.

15. *American Citizen,* June 26, 1896, 1.

16. A large collection of documents concerning Waller's ordeal can be found in Foreign Relations of the United States 1895 (Pt. 1, 251–396) and in House Document No. 225 (Ser. No. 3425; 94th Cong., 1st sess., 1895–1896). See also Randall Bennett Woods, *A Black Odyssey: John Lewis Waller and the Promise of American Life, 1878–1900* (Lawrence: Regents Press of Kansas, 1981); and Allison Blakely, "Waller, John L[ouis] 1850–1907," in Logan and Winston, *Dictionary of American Negro Biography,* 627–28.

17. Much of what is presented here on Greener's career is excerpted from three earlier publications of mine: Allison Blakely, "Richard T. Greener and the 'Talented Tenth's' Dilemma," *Journal of Negro History,* vol. 54, no. 4 (1974): 305–21; *Russia and the Negro: Blacks in Russian History and Thought* (Washington, D.C.: Howard University Press, 1986), 44–48; and "Greener, Richard T[heodore]," in Logan and Winston, *Dictionary of American Negro Biography,* 268–69.

18. See Greener to Whitefield McKinlay, February 18, 1902, W. McKinlay Papers, Carter G. Woodson Collection, Manuscript Division, Library of Congress, Washington, D.C.

19. Much of what follows concerning Hunt is excerpted from my *Dictionary of American Negro Biography* entry on him, "Hunt, William H[enry], 336–37.

20. W.E.B. Du Bois, *The Crisis: A Record of the Darker Races* 27, no. 6 (1924): 247–51.

21. *New York Times,* February 22, 1896, 4.

22. I have excerpted this statement from Allison Blakely, "Black U.S. Consuls and Diplomats and Black Leadership, 1880–1920, *Umoja* 1, no. 1 (1997): 9. The broader life and career of Johnson has of course been treated extensively by many scholars, but a helpful, substantial sketch is Rayford W. Logan, "Johnson, James Weldon," in Logan and Winston, *Dictionary of American Negro Biography,* 353–57.

23. Greener letter (only a fragment available), probably to Isaiah Wears, no date indicated, in Jacob C. White Collection, Moorland-Spingarn Research Center, Howard University, Washington, D.C.

24. W. H. Hunt to Ida Gibbs Hunt, February 8, 1904, W. H. Hunt Papers, Moorland-Spingarn Research Center. For an identical account of these experiences of Hunt, see my article "Black U.S. Consuls and Diplomats and Black Leadership, 1880–1920," 9.

25. Letter from Diane Furniss Happy to Allison Blakely, May 17, 2004.

26. See Jean Strouse, *Morgan: American Financier* (New York: Harper Collins, 1999), 509–20.

27. Spratlin later served as chief operating officer and deputy ambassador in Astana, Kazakhstan, then subsequently as ambassador in Bishek, Kyrgyzstan.

28. See Allison Blakely, "Hunt, Ida Alexander Gibbs," and "Hunt, William H[enry], in Logan and Winston, *Dictionary of American Negro Biography*, 336–37.

29. Allison Blakely, "Marshall, Harriet [Hattie] Gibbs," in Logan and Winston, *Dictionary of American Negro Biography*, 426.

30. Appeals of seven who opted out of the settlement went all the way to the Supreme Court, where the final judgment was to let the earlier ruling stand. Norman Kempster, "Blacks Call State Dept. Jobs Policy Racist," *Los Angeles Times*, October 24, 1986 (available at http://articles.latimes.com/1986-10-24/news/mn-7193_1_black-foreign-service -officers); and Richard Carelli, "Court Rejects Appeals of Black Foreign Service Officers," *AP Online*, November 30, 1998 (available at http://www.highbeam.com/doc/1P1-19421517 .html).

2

A New Negro Foreign Policy

The Critical Vision of Alain Locke and Ralph Bunche

JEFFREY C. STEWART

For an America that prides itself on never having been an empire, it is remarkable how sensitive Americans are when African Americans dare to tell us what our approach should be when it comes to Africa. A kinship between the African and the black American that is routinely denied, or if admitted is labeled as the basest essentialism, becomes threatening once the African American subject challenges America about its foreign policy toward Africa. That's because the black American embodies discourses of race and colonialism whenever she or he steps into the foreign policy debates of the United States and Europe. Whether aware of it or not, the African American who takes up the international affairs of the West enters those discussions as a black body inscribed with the crimes of Western imperialism even if he or she has never set foot in Africa. Participation in the world of foreign affairs is thus problematic for African Americans, especially if they want to be *players*—those whose insights, innovations, and vision will actually shape the future of the world—for the suspicion always lingers that the black American can't be trusted.

Such distrust arises because for much of the nation's history America has demanded fawning agreement from the African American, and as a consequence the African American has utilized a series of masks to shield the world, and herself, from the consequences of having lived as a virtual pariah in a "democratic" society. This masking, hiding in plain view the ability to say things that can be taken more than one way, has created a distinct American persona—allowing the "Negro" to survive, but also creating suspicion—that the black commentator is not telling the whole truth. Perhaps the first "New Negro" poet, Paul Laurence Dunbar, articulated this phenomenon of turn-of-the-twentieth-century New Negro consciousness when he broke with his traditional dialect idiom, itself a mask, and in 1896 wrote the poem "We Wear the Mask," which announced in its first two stanzas,

> We wear the mask that grins and lies,
> It hides our cheeks and shades our eyes—
> This debt we pay to human guile
> With torn and bleeding hearts we smile
> And mouth with myriad subtleties.
>
> Why should the world be over-wise,
> In counting all our tears and sighs?
> Nay, let them only see us while
> We wear the mask.[1]

By 1925, when Alain Locke published *The New Negro: An Interpretation*, the idea of the New Negro was of a young, forthright black subject who rejected the "old Negro" persona of always "wearing the mask" and telling white people what they wanted to hear, and instead spoke plainly about the injustice and inhumanity of racism in America.[2] Whatever else the Harlem Renaissance did, it educated sophisticated white people that there was a "double consciousness," as W.E.B. Du Bois famously defined it, of looking at the world as an American and as a Negro and that a tension existed between the two visions of America's interests. While the New Negro concept advertised a break with past strategies of psychological survival and accommodation, "wearing the mask" did not disappear in the Harlem Renaissance. Rather, it moved to a higher level in which a kind of sophisticated New Negro subject emerged, who had attended elite historically white universities and colleges; who had traveled internationally and possessed broad interests and knowledge on a range of scholarly subjects; but who was nevertheless dependent on elite white allies to advance personally and, if lucky, shape the future of the nation through the arts, literature, drama, and public affairs.[3] But the problem facing such potential contributors to a new notion of American foreign policy was how could they garner the access and power to affect the future of American policies globally, and especially in relation to Africa? To what extent would they have to "mask" their criticality toward Western policy on Africa in the very act of trying to change it?

Key to my argument here is that a New Negro foreign policy consciousness did emerge during the first decades of the twentieth century, among African American elites and the rank and file, who, as Alvin B. Tillery argues in *Between Homeland and Motherland,* linked the mentality of American racism to the mentality behind European colonialism and embraced Africans from the entire continent, not just Liberia, as part of a broad-based philosophy of black liberation.[4] This was a significant break with nineteenth-century Negro attitudes that viewed much of sub-Saharan Africa as barbaric.[5] Divisions in opinion among early twentieth-century Negro Americans as to whether European colonialism was a civilizing and Christianizing benefit gave way to an emerging consensus that regardless of those possible benefits, imperialism was a racial institution. Where Tillery sees this "New Negro" attitude about Africa crystallizing with W.E.B. Du Bois's Pan-African Congress in 1919, I suggest that this way of viewing Africa and imperialism had been articulated systematically four years earlier in a series of public lectures, *Race Contacts and Interracial Relations,* given by Alain Locke at Howard University in Washington, D.C. These lectures defined imperialism as the "practice of race" and racism in America as domestic imperialism.[6] Yet, also definitive of the New Negro approach to foreign policy was that Locke and some others tended to hide all the consequences of looking at imperialism as naked racial violence, especially when such intellectuals were interacting with powerful stakeholders in the white foreign policy intelligentsia. They "wore the mask" even as New Negroes.

As Brenda Gayle Plummer suggests in *Rising Wind: Black Americans and U.S. Foreign Policy, 1935–1960,* it has seldom occurred to mainstream policy makers, foreign policy experts, even historians and social scientists, that this New Negro consciousness would have any tangible effects on major foreign policy debates; and when the notion has occurred to white policy thinkers that African Americans might have significant opinions on subjects such as the future of Africa, these have largely been dismissed as grounded in "black commitments [that] have always been utopian and rooted in eccentric modes of thought arising from poverty and oppression."[7] In other words, the African American was not—and arguably is still not—taken seriously as having a distinctive and relevant contribution to make to American foreign policy, of having learned something unique and important about, for example, the interrelationship of peace and justice, globally speaking, from having lived "behind the veil," as Du Bois put it, for centuries in America. But what policy makers may have overlooked is that racial discrimination and the strategies of coping with it by a minority besieged by a hostile majority may make the African American a natural diplomat, for diplomacy is often the masking or veiling of a nation's true motives in the pursuit of its interests. But the question remains: can an African American truly represent the interests of the United States in foreign policy arenas when, in fact, those interests may be inimical to the interests of people of color around the globe?

The story of two early twentieth-century New Negro foreign policy thinkers suggests an answer: that the African American is perhaps the best representative of the nation's long-term foreign policy interests because he brings the potential for a synergy between the nation's domestic social reality and the nation's global reality that is ultimately healthful. Elite foreign policy thinkers are correct to suspect that lurking beneath the Negro mask is a black criticality that links the treatment of Negroes in America to the treatment of people of Africa and African descent globally. Canonical foreign policy managers worry that the Negro foreign policy thinker will reveal the secret of the West: that it is more in love with white supremacy than with the ideology of representative democracy and equality so widely advertised as the goals of America's foreign policy. Yet this criticality is precisely what American foreign policy desperately needs. We as a nation need to see ourselves as others see us, to see ourselves with a second sight, as W.E.B. Du Bois put it, that the American experience has taught the Negro to use when viewing the American project, for such critical vision is the only thing that will save us.[8]

Two men, Alain Locke and Ralph Bunche, who crafted what I call a *New Negro foreign policy*, exemplified this vision. In different ways, each tried to take a black criticality gained from years of observing and decoding the American domestic race problem into the "other room" of foreign policy in order to chart a new future for the world based on creating a viable future for Africa.[9] I call this a New Negro foreign policy not only because it emerged in the 1920s but also because these foreign policy thinkers sought to import the knowledge of race into the discussion of foreign policy and reframe race, power, and foreign policy thinking into a new ethic of internationalism and a global democratic approach to the African subject. These New Negro foreign policy thinkers were race men but also something more: people who saw themselves as citizens of the world, who brought the expertise of the college-educated, world-traveling, culturally sophisticated black cosmopolitan into the discussion of what kind of world we ought to live in. They sought to utilize black criticality as a lens for discussing what should happen in Africa between the world wars but also to hide it—to diminish the anger, sharp attacks, and murderous rage most people would feel as witnesses to what has aptly been called "the rape of Africa"—in order to try to sway opinion and shape a more progressive policy toward future Africa.

At the same time, New Negro foreign policy thinkers sought to break the Western intellectual tradition's habit of discussing the future of Africa without considering the people whose future was most centrally involved. They posed an uncomfortable question to American foreign policy thinkers: what does the African see as being in his or her best interest in the future? By lowering the temperature of racially motivated discussions about the future of Africa, but also placing the cognitive body of the African at the center of those discussions, a New Negro foreign policy elaborated on the argument Alain Locke made in *The New Negro: An Interpretation* emerged. The New Negro is a world-historical subject whose future is unfinished, undetermined, but incredibly important to the rest of the world. Like that book, Locke's and Bunche's writings on foreign policy sought not only to expose how race structured the relations of power in pre–World War II Africa but also go beyond a traditional "black" approach to create a new vision of what was possible for the rest of the world.

Because of space constraints, what follows is only the beginning of a fuller discussion of what the black embodiment of discourses of race, colonialism, and empire means for the history of modern foreign policy. My discussion is really a micro-study of how two men struggled differently with the benefits and detriments of being brilliant thinkers whose contributions are negotiated in terms of their embodiment of race. I call them exemplars of a New Negro approach to foreign policy because they embody the New Negro that emerged early in the twentieth century—the emergence of a Negro political subject who, despite the vicissitudes of racial domination, goes beyond dissembling to create a more cosmopolitan, more visionary approach to global affairs out of the experience of the Negro in America. Locke and Bunche represent, I believe, two different stages of development within the tradition of New Negro foreign policy thinking, even as they utilized similar approaches to bringing what later might be called a black consciousness into foreign policy thinking. Together they exemplify the essence of the New Negro foreign policy thinking: the capacity to call out racism but in a measured way. This approach was raised to the level of art and refined by Locke and Bunche. At the end of this chapter, I take the liberty of jumping ahead to theorize what this means to the foreign policy aspirations of another black subject, Barack Obama, who as president of the United States has enacted a New Negro approach to foreign policy.

The year 1929 began on a sour note for Alain Locke. That December he had learned that the Foreign Policy Association, to which he had submitted a report titled "The Mandate System: A New Code of Empire," was so displeased with it that they would not publish the work in its current form, as had been planned previously. The rejection of this major essay hit this African American intellectual like a blow in the stomach, so unaccustomed was he to having his writing rejected outright, especially by influential white people. Worse, over the previous year, he had peppered the press with notices of his trips to Geneva to conduct research on the report, thereby creating expectations that the finished project would appear in print. Now it would not, and its non-publication would heighten a perception he wanted to avoid—that as the heralded philosopher and promoter of the Negro Renaissance since 1925, when his epic anthology, *The New Negro: An Interpretation*, had appeared, he was now, four years later, slipping, having not published a book since *Four Negro Poets* in 1927.[10] Worried, perhaps overly, about the potential fallout from this failure, he chose his usual weekend visit with Mrs. Charlotte Mason, his millionaire Park Avenue patron, to pour out his frustration and seek consolation from a major personal setback. That his closest confidante with whom to discuss a New Negro foreign policy was an elderly wealthy white woman speaks volumes of the way this most independent of black thinkers embodied the discourse of dependency in his personal life.

As the diminutive, hypochondriac professor of philosophy at Howard University fidgeted nervously in the brightly lit drawing room of his psychic, overbearing matron, Locke, a man of almost clairvoyant personal diplomacy skills, confessed he had known something bad was going to come of the foreign policy project he had started researching years earlier. That had been a difficult time as well. Fired from Howard University in 1925 largely because its white president viewed him as a malcontent, Locke had searched for a new career, one that built on his reputation as editor of *The New Negro* and the first African American to obtain a PhD in philosophy from Harvard University to become a diplomat or diplomatic thinker, a role he had first imagined for himself after having been named a Rhodes scholar. He had become something of an intellectual celebrity in 1907 on the way to Oxford when, for the first time, he thought that a career as a diplomat would allow him to escape the limitations of race in America. In addition to his academic brilliance, Locke had mastered the interpersonal skills and professional diplomacy that were necessary to navigate his way through the most elite educational institutions in the world. But even with such skills at ingratiating himself to powerful academic patrons while maintaining his dignity as an upstart black Edwardian, Locke had found that a successful career as a diplomat was closed to him despite his being the second most educated black man—after W.E.B. Du Bois—in the world. In 1927, however, twenty years after his Rhodes scholar success, between jobs Locke had allowed himself to dream of the kind of cosmopolitan, transnational career he had always wanted. The time seemed right to strike and perhaps escape the stultifying racial and sexual environment of America that dogged him as a queer black man. He had thought he could take what was now his signature concept, the "New Negro"—the notion that a "new" kind of Negro had emerged from the Great Migration of hundreds of thousands of Negroes out of the South into the North and had changed the calculus of Negro-white relations in the 1920s—and make it the pivot of a new way of looking at the future of Africa and the African in the twentieth century. Now, barely two years after the first blush of that possibility, it was all in tatters. The question remained, why?

The specific target of his report—the League of Nations' administering of the fate of African colonies formerly held by Germany before its loss in World War I—had seemed quite promising. In Article 22 of the Covenant of the League of Nations, a plan was outlined as to what to do with those colonies Germany had to give up as part of the Treaty of Versailles.[11] The article stated: "To those colonies and territories which as a consequence of the late war have ceased to be under the sovereignty of the States which formerly governed them and which are inhabited by people not yet able to stand by themselves under the strenuous conditions of the modern world, there should be applied the principle that the well-being and development of such peoples form a sacred trust of civilization and that securities for the performance of this trust should be embodied in this covenant."[12] This "trust" would be exercised by putting these colonies under the administration and control of "advanced nations"—the French and the British—who "by reason of their resources, their experience or their geographic position, can best undertake" to provide the required "tutelage" of "such peoples" as a "responsibility" they exercised as "Mandatories on behalf of the League."[13] Of course, the "people not yet able to stand by themselves" were the Africans, since, from the social Darwinist perspective of Article 22, peoples who belonged to the "Turkish Empire" were deemed to "have reached a stage of development where their existence as independent nations can be provisionally recognized." By contrast, "those of Central Africa are at such a stage that the Mandatory must be responsible for the administration of the territory" to ensure "freedom of conscience and religion" and "prohibition of abuses, such as the slave trade," among others.

As a philosopher, Locke had seized on Article 22 for its moral language—that the mandatories had a "responsibility" for the "development of such peoples" toward a moment in the future when the existence even of the peoples of Central Africa "as independent nations" could "be provisionally recognized." Rather than attack its failure to live up to that "sacred trust," which the evidence of British and French mandatories seemed to suggest, Locke wanted to write a paper about the future—a vision of what the mandates tended toward even in their imperfect iteration in 1919 as documents and in 1928 as practices. As he had put it in his proposal to the Foreign Policy Association for the study, "The administration of mandates in the spirit of international guardianship of the rights of the undeveloped peoples and their preparatory tutelage for participation in government and constructive *self-adjustment* is one of the most important and progressive aspects of the work of the League of Nations."[14]

Locke had aimed for something higher than the Foreign Policy Association imagined a Negro scholar would produce, something more visionary than the typical foreign policy fact sheets with which they were familiar. Locke wanted to write something more farsighted, something that spoke to a higher consciousness of what was possible in the world of foreign affairs that could be revealed only if the document and its promise were liberated from the maze of facts and claims that dogged discussions of the League of Nations. As a philosopher, Locke was committed to doing something more, something different, something high-minded rather than self-interested, as most foreign policy papers were. In his doctoral dissertation on value theory, finished in 1918, Locke had argued that the key to humans' valuing something was their ability to transcend acting simply in their own naked self-interest to do what seemed designed to reach beyond the immediate gratifications of desire, to aim at what Aristotle called that for which other things are done.[15]

In the context of the League of Nations mandate system, a New Negro approach was more than simply acting out what would be an expected black response to the system—that is, simply to blister the League of Nations project as handing over the destiny of Germany's African territories to a patronizing band of thieves like the British and French imperialists after their victory in World War I. Something like that kind of "black" indictment of the mandates as a fig leaf of Western imperialism would be produced later by the Du Bois protégé Rayford W. Logan in *The Operation of the Mandate System in Africa, 1919–1927.*[16] And it meant producing something other than the liberal, empathetic, but largely acquiescent study of the mandate system that Raymond Buell, the white director of the research department of the Foreign Policy Association and an adjunct professor of international relations, had produced in his magnum opus, the two-volume study *The Native Problem in Africa* in 1928.[17]

But Locke had had problems finding his legs in writing his report, in part because he was not immersed in current foreign policy research, not trained in international relations, and not sure that his prescriptive, nonempirical thought piece about colonialism in general and the plight of Germany's former colonies in particular would find sympathetic ears at the Foreign Policy Association (FPA). Like so many of the ventures that this nervous, brilliant, but opportunity-seeking philosopher produced after *The New Negro*, the FPA report was not grounded in a firmly grasped intellectual trajectory that made sense to all of those around him. He sought something he believed was embedded in the current situation but largely unseen by the policy makers of the day. And like the New Negro positional itself, the report, even when finished, was an unfinished statement that reflected the unfinished nature of the New Negro, which was more than simply the latest iteration of race consciousness. In fact, it was a new, more cosmopolitan, more transnational notion of Negro possibility—what the New Negro could become, not what he or she currently was. And that "unfinished-ness" had crept into his writing of the report such that a lack of a firmness in his sense of where he was going with this project stole some of the energy from the argument he was making.

Locke was more than a year late in finishing the report, and when he did finally submit it in November 1928, after months of nagging by Raymond Buell, the director of research at the Foreign Policy Association, it was deemed inadequate by Mrs. Moorhead, the head of the FPA. The Foreign Policy Association considered itself a hardnosed research and policy entity, whose reports were incredibly detailed, case-by-case examinations of decisions by agencies like the Mandates Commission. In a sense the Foreign Policy Association represented the decadence of Progressive era advocacy, which by 1928 was a far cry from the broadminded engagement with construction of a new world order that had been implicit in the work of Walter Lippmann, Herbert Croly, and Colonel House, the latter serving on the first Mandates Commission.[18] Progressivism under the likes of the FPA now traded in passionate and visionary exposés on domestic and international crises, developed "reports," and used detail and "objectivity" to hide the international crimes that continued under the guise of their liberalism. By contrast, Locke's report spelled out a course of action and even intervention by the liberal West for the construction of a new future for the African and the West, by abandoning the style of writing that simply analyzed *right now.* No doubt what the FPA seized on to dismiss the report was that it was not based on detailed archival research, even though Locke had traveled to Geneva to do such work. It did not include ethnographic field research in Africa among the colonized. The report lacked the kind of specific recommendations that might increase the interest and participation of black Americans in the operation of the Mandates Commission, one of the main reasons the FPA had enlisted Locke to create the report in the first place. In his enthusiasm to put forward his intellectual reimagining of what the mandate system could mean to Africa, Locke had forgotten that to the FPA he was the embodiment of the black community in America, whose support the FPA believed would help its legitimacy as a broker in the field of international race relations. The FPA was not interested in a black intellectual's understanding of the mandates. What they wanted was a black political treatment that could be published, filed away, and quickly forgotten. Locke had not delivered that.

But the FPA underestimated the value of Locke's report. Taking Woodrow Wilson's insistence in Article 22 of the League of Nations' charter that set up the mandate system as his text, Locke argued that a policy of international restraint on the naked exploitation of Germany's former African colonies was the beginning of a "new code" of empire. Article 22, Locke argued, established a new ethical principle for the West in its conduct toward Africa—to wit, that the nations that seized the colonies of German, Turkish, and other Axis empires had to administer them as a "sacred trust of civilization." England, France, and even South Africa, which acquired South West Africa, were not to enslave the populations, not to exploit the land and natural resources to the point of ecological disasters, not to raise colonial armies for offensive military purposes, and, most important, not to look upon these colonies as their permanent possessions. Rather, Locke referenced Woodrow Wilson as declaring that the Allies should administer these colonies as a trusteeship that should help the inhabitants' transition, eventually, to self-government. This was the core outcome of a world war to make the world "safe for democracy."

Regardless of present abuses and violations of the charter, regardless of the timetable and the Allied manipulation of the oversight procedures, Locke argued that a revolutionary principle had been established: that empire was a temporary arrangement and that the colonized deserved freedom and self-government eventually. From his earlier study of imperialism in his *Race Contacts and Interracial Relations* lecture series given at Howard in 1915–1916, Locke had borrowed the concept that imperialism was nothing more than a power relationship of domination of one group of people over another. What the mandate system did was to suggest that the West was at a second stage of imperialism in which the world community had admitted the supposed "backwardness" of the colonized was temporary and that through education they could be prepared for self-government and self-determination. The mandates, therefore, had concretized that a qualitative change in the idea of colonies had occurred with World War I such that Africans were now seen as just as worthy as Europeans of the right to self-determination that Wilson said was the inherent right of all subject peoples. Wilson had updated and disseminated into the discourse of imperialism the principle that Thomas Jefferson had proclaimed to the soon-to-be American people in the Declaration of Independence as "self-evident"—that is, "that all men are created equal with the inalienable right to life, liberty, and the pursuit of happiness." The mandate system was, in effect, a declaration of independence for the African, even if it might not be seen as such by its current administrators.

Locke's report, therefore, was more innovative than the Foreign Policy Association gave him credit for when they rejected it. He pioneered a "third way" between criticizing the mandates for their ineffectiveness in restraining Western exploitation or total acquiescence to the current operation of that system as the best that could be had for colonized peoples. Avoiding a kind of criticism of the mandates that would be expected of a black radical critique like that authored by Logan in his detailed unpublished criticism of the mandate system, Locke sought to redefine the mission of the mandates as an institution evolving from a pretense for further imperial exploitation of the forfeited colonies to a path to self-determination and self-government for the colonized. What was needed, Locke argued, was a systematic strengthening of the Mandates Commission as an oversight agency so that it could expose, persuade, and, if necessary, twist the arms of those nations that violated the letter and the spirit of Article 22 of the League of Nations charter into moving Africans down the path to self-government. For in a way that anticipated the operation of the Federal Employment Practices Commission (FEPC), set up by FDR in his Executive Order 8802 in World War II, the Mandates Commission was most effective when it exposed to the light of international opinion and inquiry conditions that were racist and exploitative, even if the commission had no punitive power to force member nations to do its bidding. Here too was a place where strategic New Negro criticism of exploitative policies might aid the commission in restraining and reforming imperialistic practices by shaming rogue imperialists in front of the international community.

Locke went even further. He proposed that advocates of change capitalize on the Wilsonian aspects of Article 22 by demanding that European nations engaged in the Mandates Commission support a real process of education in the politics of self-government, the economic path to self-development, and the practices of responsible leadership among the colonized to prepare them for eventual freedom from colonialism. By holding back on enslaving, debasing, and raping the colonies for their raw materials, European powers might smooth the path to eventual freedom and engender a more harmonious postcolonial world. At the same time, Locke did not avoid detailing the abuses of the Americans or the Europeans in creating exploitative "closed door" colonial relationships through shady loans and pressured deals. But he was a pragmatist in suggesting that with the Mandates Commission already in existence, perhaps it made sense to strengthen its ethical authority and its mechanisms of constructive pressure to outline a third way to the options of continued and indefinite imperialist exploitation, on the one hand, and blind rage rebellion by the colonized, on the other. And the obligation of a New Negro foreign policy was, in effect, to find a way around the train wreck that was ahead: anticolonial violence; imperial counterinsurgency; and a spiral into an anarchic, postcolonial day of reckoning.

The only person on the research committee of the FPA who had liked the report, or at least had come to Locke's defense about the report, was Paul Kellogg, the editor of the *Survey Graphic,* who had brought Locke in to guest edit the special "Harlem: Mecca of the New Negro" issue of the magazine that had foregrounded the book version, *The New Negro.* Kellogg spoke up at a meeting to discuss the problems with the report and argued that perhaps there had been a misunderstanding between Locke and the committee as to the nature of the report. Kellogg's defense had not swayed the rest of the committee, but it had soothed Locke's hurt ego. He had written back to Kellogg thanking him and admitting that he was not good at the kind of detailed research work the FPA had expected. Now that the report would not lead out into the wider diplomatic world, he was content to try to make it the basis for a curriculum in the African studies program at Howard. "So, thank God, I won't have to go back to Harvard myself for re-boring," he wrote to Kellogg. "You see I think I know my role and appreciate its limitations—I'm a fairly good starting battery—not a magneto." That Locke, now forty-three, even contemplated a return to graduate work shows how much he had hoped this report would lead him out of his current segregated intellectual life at Howard and in Washington, D.C., and into the cosmopolitan lifestyle that a diplomatic thinker could imagine.

Locke's predicament was more than just personal. Elsewhere I have discussed how the New Negro was more than just a racialized subject that emerged into the American imagination in the 1920s.[19] There were at least two New Negroes—or two sides of the New Negro: (1) the mass movement of racially self-conscious working- and middle-class Negroes who began migrating north in the 1910s and constructed a new black world in the urban metropolises of Chicago, New York, Pittsburgh, and other cities; and (2) the intellectual migration of the educated black from a narrow, provincial, and claustrophobic life of the mind in segregated small-town communities into a more cosmopolitan and international lifestyle during the 1920s. The New Negroes like Locke, Langston Hughes, Claude McKay, Zora Neale Hurston, Richmond Barthe, and Howard Thurman were racially self-identified and not only advanced a new aesthetic vitality based on race but also grasped for a new, expanded notion of what it meant to be Negro: that it meant being a world-conscious and sophisticated people who could claim all of civilization as their estate. They traveled internationally, sometimes living abroad for months or even years, engaged in conversations and collaborations with white artists and intellectuals on a peer basis. They also saw themselves as the leading edge of a new wave of Negro consciousness that unshackled itself from the small-mindedness they perceived the previous generation of educated black people, even the likes of Booker T. Washington, Monroe Trotter, and Du Bois, had settled for—the role of merely being a leader of the Negro people, not the leader of the American world or even the world of people through their writings and work. As much as Locke defined the New Negro as a representative of the working- and middle-class Negroes who had constructed the convivial lifestyle of Harlem, there was always something more—that life laid the groundwork for the emergence of a racially proud but cosmopolitan Negro subject who would be at home anywhere in the world, and who would be known and valued for the cogency of his ideas more than for the color of his skin.

In the process of announcing this New Negro intellectual subjectivity, Locke had forgotten, just a little, perhaps, that the world of race politics had not changed as much as he wished it to. Powerful whites who valued him did so because he "represented" the black constituency, not because he had a "brilliant" mind. His white patron, Mrs. Mason, the real "magneto," seemed to grasp this better than Locke. The major fault, according to Mason, was his audience. "Extreme hostility" is all that they would like, she said. In her opinion, the Foreign Policy Association expected him to *play the nigger*—to attack the entire apparatus of colonial government and League of Nations sanctions through the mandate system. In that scenario they would then be able to use the report to attack their enemies while at the same time dismissing the report as hysterical and racially biased. Mason articulated his dilemma as an African American scholar working on this type of subject: "Alain, your not being ready to tell what you think is the exact truth about the mandate is the matter with your paper. It is not, of course, the *time* to do it."[20]

Close reading of the report reveals the truth of Mason's comment. Throughout the report, Locke wears the mask; his cautiousness, tentativeness, and self-consciousness pervade a report that is trying to put across what was at base a brilliant strategy for using the existing international apparatus to create a road map to freedom for colonized Africans. His tendency toward "natural diplomacy" had the effect of weakening his ability to convince his readers that he really represented the view of the Negro community. Absent was the essence of the New Negro as opposed to the old Negro: the ability to represent while mediating black anger. The report, in short, was not "black enough," especially for a progressive white audience that was now used to the harangue of a Marcus Garvey or a W.E.B. Du Bois but also willing to ignore such harangue because it lacked the power to persuade. As Mason explained, "They think your opinion is the best balanced of any among Negroes and that you won't go to an extreme about anything. That was why they asked you to do it. Not because you had written a fine article in the Survey."[21]

One can imagine how Locke felt hearing this in the drawing room of a powerful white patron whom he relied on to translate for him what the other white people thought of him. It must have left him no less defeated than when he arrived at her drawing room to discuss his "failure" and now hearing his life reduced to a formula by a powerful friend, whose cruel words were true. He knew he had spent much of his adult life twisting himself around a pivot of trying to use the black experience as a calling card to get in the door of white power brokers and gain attention for his views as an individual. Now, once again, he was reminded that he was not seen as a brilliant intellect, but as a little man who embodied the black problem, the black issue, to be managed, still, by powerful whites who continued to orchestrate world affairs themselves, despite it being the era of the "New Negro." He had spent his life placating whites who would listen to him but who wanted safe, optimistic, positive-thinking Negroes, every one of them said to his face. Yet when faced with one, they turned and laughed and treated him like a puppet and a fool. Inside, if only for a moment, largely through the promise to represent Negroes on the outside, he now heard from his white patron that those on the inside did not take him seriously because he was not "black" enough, not radical enough, for them to use.

Fortunately, 1929 ended more propitiously than it began. That fall, Ralph Bunche, newly minted with a master's degree in government from Harvard, arrived at Howard University, possibly the result of Locke's maneuvering. Since being hired back at Howard in 1927, Locke had been an unofficial adviser to its new president, Mordecai Johnson, a Baptist minister and visionary black college administrator, who had rehired Locke and sought his advice on how to recast Howard as a leader in modern higher education. Locke's recommendation was to build a powerhouse social science division by hiring the top Negro scholars from prestigious white universities like Harvard to come to the nation's capital and nurture a new generation of activist scholarship of disciplinary rigor and theoretical innovation. Bunche had already caused a stir at Harvard, impressing his professors in government to such an extent that they offered him a graduate fellowship to stay on campus. But a sixth sense in Bunche told him to come to Howard, the nation's most powerful Negro university, and join forces with Locke to remake the field of what today is called Black Studies.

Hired as a professor, and charged with starting a political science department at Howard as part of his job, Bunche was nevertheless relatively poor and after getting married took on additional work as an assistant to Mordecai Johnson, work that Bunche found challenging because of Johnson's mercurial and bombastic personality—a personality type that Bunche struggled with throughout his long career. Locke, too, found much to dislike in Johnson, even though Johnson had been the one who had brought him back to Howard. But

Johnson represented to Locke and Bunche the vagaries of the old-style Negro leadership, a leadership class that was disproportionately, in their minds, based in the black church affiliations of those leaders and the political connections to old-style Washington, where telling jokes to whites, currying favor, and scooping up money were key parts of the game of Negro-white "liberalism."

It is in this context that Bunche began to think seriously about what topic he would select for his doctoral dissertation at Harvard and that Locke likely suggested to Bunche that he take an African topic for his dissertation, one aligned with the research Locke had undertaken with Raymond Buell and the Foreign Policy Association. While the final topic came from Buell, as Bunche biographer Charles Henry suggests, the orientation toward Buell and the whole perspective of an African topic came from Locke.[22] Pearl Robinson asserts that in those early years of Bunche's residence as a professor at Howard, Locke mentored him on how to negotiate his way through the sometimes hostile and intrigue-based academic politics at Howard.[23] In Bunche, Locke saw an earlier version of himself, a rebel against the notion that Negro intellectual thought should be confined to the small, the narrow, and the segregated American mind-set, which Locke and Bunche saw as being co-constructed by whites and blacks in the American context. Africa allowed a way out of petty in-group Negro politics and into globalism, a larger and more capacious context in which the calculus of race was changed because globally black people were not only more of a majority but also in need of modernizing intellects like Locke and Bunche. A global dissertation opened doors for Bunche that Locke had wanted to open for himself in 1928 but that his limitations as a scholar and political scientist closed. Now, by putting Bunche in conversation with Buell, Locke achieved a kind of deliverance from the ghosts of his failed Foreign Policy Association paper by bringing African American eyes, a lived experience of colonialism at home, into the conversation about the future of Africa and global affairs. The point of view of the black American intellectuals was crucial not only because they were natural diplomats but also because by heritage and lived experience they embodied the discourse of racism.

But the road to approval of Bunche's final dissertation topic—"French Administration in Togoland and Dahomey"—would be a bumpy one. In a letter to Howard University dean E. P. Davis in December 1930 requesting a leave of absence, Bunche said the leave would be spent conducting research for a doctoral dissertation on "The League of Nations and the Suppression of Slavery."[24] But the matter was not settled even though Bunche asserted in that letter that the topic had been approved. Some of his advisers at Harvard wanted him to write a dissertation on the political activities of blacks in West Virginia, a relatively narrow topic. Most important, his dissertation director, Arthur N. Holcombe, favored another topic, a comparative study of race attitudes in Brazil and the

United States.[25] There was also the implicit problem of a study of slavery in Africa; while the project naturally flowed out of the League of Nations' demand that under the mandate system, the colonial powers would suppress slavery in Africa, investigation of such practices might expose Bunche to danger. In addition, Bunche did not want to disappoint Holcombe if the latter was set on having Bunche research Brazilian versus American racial attitudes. But a funny thing happened when Holcombe contacted Edwin Embree, the so-called liberal president of the Julius Rosenwald Fund, one of the few foundations that would fund overseas research by a Negro, about the research project. Embree expressed reservations about an "American" doing a comparative study of race attitudes in Brazil and America. According to Holcombe, Embree opined:

> The interracial conditions in Brazil are so different from those in this country that I wonder if much can be carried over from the experience in one country to that in the other. As I understand it, there is practically no racial discrimination as among the three bloods that comprise the population: Indian, Negro, and Latin. Might there also be some danger that an American student would really be led astray by the position of Negroes in public affairs in Brazil? Indiscreet utterances and reports on the basis of Brazilian experience might really do harm in this country.[26]

Bunche had not yet received Holcombe's letter with its information that as a Negro doing a comparative study of Brazil and the United States he might be "led astray by the position of Negroes in public affairs in Brazil" and make "indiscreet utterances" about the greater freedom of Negroes in Brazil to the embarrassment of the foundation and the racial hegemony in the United States. But as Bunche later confessed to Holcombe, Locke had known even before this confidence finally reached Bunche in a second Holcombe letter in February 1931 that the foundation would not support such a study.

> Your letter of February 17 is a very kindly one and has been of inestimable value in aiding me to map out a definitive course . . . for next year. The statement which you quoted from Mr. Embree's letter was a distinct surprise and somewhat of a shock to me. His statement is of no little significance in respect to the decision which I have made however. Dr. Locke in particular seems to feel that there is scant possibility of aid from the Rosenwald Fund for the Brazilian study. He thought so before he saw Mr. Embree's statement and is quite convinced of it now.[27]

Bunche was "shocked" because Embree's statements reminded him that as a Harvard scholar proposing to conduct comparative foreign-domestic policy research abroad, he still embodied the Negro problem at home. As an heir of slaves without inherited wealth, and proposing a dissertation topic in foreign affairs that required extensive travel, Bunche was "constrained to pursue whatever course promises the likeliest possibility of support."[28] Ironically, the African project, the more thoroughly "foreign policy" project, offered "far greater possibility of aid" if endorsed by his dissertation director "than the Brazilian question, which sounds, at least, much more 'dangerous' in its implications to the situation in this country."[29] Here, the greater "foreignness" of the Africa project—that it was less an embodiment of the American situation than the Brazilian—made it more acceptable. Here, therefore, was one of the benefits of the New Negro working on a foreign affairs thesis in Africa: it seemed to the conservative-minded white philanthropic community to be less relevant to the situation of the Negro in America and therefore less "dangerous" for Bunche to pursue. That America was not considered an official "imperialist nation" meant that pursuing a critical study of imperialism did not threaten elicit white philanthropic fears that their funding would be used to critique American racial practices. And the threat of no funding for the Brazilian project, ironically, freed Bunche from having to bow to his adviser's demand for a topic on Brazil. Racial hegemonic discourses could have unusual effects in the life of a young scholar!

Bunche flew to meet with Raymond Buell about his thesis topic, no doubt at Locke's suggestion, and Buell refined it and gave him a different one, although still on the subject of Africa and the mandates. Rather than try to document the elusive and dangerous practice of slavery under the mandates, why not do a comparative study of two colonies administered by one nation (France) in Africa to find out if the mandates proscription to rule in the former German colonies under the mandates was actually better than under traditional colonial rule? When Bunche informed Holcombe of this newly refined African mandates topic and the dilemma of funding, Holcombe allowed Bunche to choose whichever topic he wished. In July 1931 Bunche received the good news that the Rosenwald Fund had approved financial support for his dissertation research in Africa.

The resultant dissertation, "French Administration in Togoland and Dahomey," was a tour de force, thoroughly researched from years of combing the archives in Geneva and Paris, as well as on-the-ground research in Africa, and powerfully written. Finished in 1934, the dissertation won a prize for Bunche and led, some argue, to the establishment of the field of international studies at Harvard for the first time. The success of the dissertation was due not only to Bunche's obvious competence as a political science scholar but also because he added something new to the New Negro foreign policy paradigm: he brought a level of criticality to the study of colonialism that situated the particularities of the administration of Togoland and Dahomey in a larger narrative of the failure of imperialism. He brought something to the study of the mandates that had been lacking in Locke's Foreign Policy Association paper: the kind of critical assessment of the ideological fictions of race in justifying colonialism that Locke had articulated in his *Race Contacts* lectures but had silenced in *The New Negro* and his Foreign Policy Association paper. At the same time, Bunche preserved the New Negro impulse to avoid simply a doomsday assessment of Africa's future by suggesting that a way out could be on the horizon if Europeans approached Africa anew with a rational plan by which it, too, could partake of the democracy and self-determination that the West said was the self-evident right of all peoples.

Martin Kilson suggests that in Bunche's dissertation an almost schizophrenic tension exists between the Marxist voice of the Young Turk, who along with E. Franklin Frazier and Abram Harris would attack Du Bois and the NAACP for not pursuing a class analysis of American racism, and the Enlightenment voice of a young optimist who believed in the power of reason and intellect—especially his own—to bring more freedom and justice to the African.[30] I see it slightly differently. More than the typical Marxist analysis that race is a myth or illusion to distract the oppressed white and black from their solidarity, Bunche's dissertation shows that the racial dehumanization of the victims is what distinguishes colonialism from other forms of capitalist greed. Indeed, Bunche mentions the economic motive of imperialism as something obvious that does not need proving in the systematic way that Lenin provides it in *Imperialism: The Highest Stage of Capitalism*.[31] Rather, the drafts of the dissertation chapters in the UCLA archive do not so much advance a classic Marxist critique of French colonialism and mandates in Africa as provide an acid dismantling of the racist self-deception, overt manipulation, and denigration of the African by the European.[32] Indeed, the *self* in self-deception is perhaps Bunche's best arrow into the heart of imperialism, because he shows how imperialism is a mix of motives, sometimes humanitarian, sometimes naked greed, but always self-interested and self-congratulatory, so that even when helping the African, the European is really writing the history of Europe's glory in the African's mind. The consequence of this arrogance is not simply economic exploitation, but a warping of African minds such that they will find it difficult to properly value what is valuable in their own traditions after internalizing Europe's doctrines. In short, Bunche's dissertation is a great work because it brings forth a detailed black radical critique of colonialism that is far more nuanced and sophisticated than the narrower Marxist portrayal of how race functioned that he would fall back on in *A World View of Race*, published two years later.[33] What Kilson calls Marxian I call Bunche's criticality—a criticality emerging from his experience of race in the United States that frames the way he has assimilated the lessons of Marx so that the African empire emerges as not only a praxis of economic greed but a discourse of race as well.

What does this mean for a New Negro foreign policy? First, it seems that away from America, Bunche could allow a racial analysis to ground and contextualize his Marxian criticality so that something akin to the black radical tradition of imperialist analysis could emerge.[34] Second, his analysis was New Negro in that it placed the subjectivity of the African at the center of the foreign policy discussion. As Bunche put it, "Too often, however, in the earnest consideration of Africa and her myriad problems, sight is loss of the *African*."[35] But third, and just as important, the success that greeted his dissertation suggests that the intellectual conditions for New Negro scholarship had advanced so that whites in the academy in the United States could hear criticality of imperialism that was grounded in first-rate research. The Negro might be the ideal diplomat because of the ability to don the mask, but Bunche's refusal to do so here (at least in the first drafts of his dissertation) created a powerful exegesis of colonialism that was compelling because it was true. Locke had failed to realize that *his* white people were aware that Negroes were deeply critical of white imperialism, and any document that did not indict them for it was suspect. Bunche, not nearly as naïve as he sometimes wanted others to believe, knew that the whites he must please at Harvard were sophisticates and were quite aware of the crimes of the Western civilization they nevertheless wanted to preserve. Therefore, he knew that he must reveal his anger, his criticality, his sense of outrage at the "rape of Africa" if his dissertation were to have validity. And in this sense he was right; white people would distrust him if they suspected he was holding back.

Nevertheless, once Bunche turned in the drafts of the chapters, someone, most likely his senior adviser, marked them up with those sections that were most critical—and to be honest, those most *ad hominem* in their criticism—marked with "omit" at the top, while the other, less sweeping, more descriptive sections of the chapters were marked with "begin." It was as if now knowing the full extent of Bunche's indictment of French self-congratulatory colonialism, his advisers took him by the hand and showed him what not to say along the way to saying what was nonetheless true.

Here, then, was the tightrope the New Negro foreign policy thinker had to walk. As a diplomatic mind the New Negro must tell enough of the truth about white discourses of domination to be credible—and match the actual reality with analysis—yet also be measured in the indictment lest the leadership shut his mouth. That his dissertation was awarded prizes and opened up an area called "international relations" proved he had hit it just right—and been rewarded for having said enough but not too much about how the New Negro saw "imperialism." And this lesson was not lost on Bunche, who by 1934 seemed to have developed a strong criticality that was sweeping and indicting of almost everyone and yet a mind that already knew and calibrated that anger depending on the audience it addressed.

Of course, when that audience was a black one, Bunche was not as nuanced in his blending of class and race analysis. One problem with Bunche's analysis, which persisted throughout his career up into the 1960s, was his devaluation of the value of race as a tool of liberation for the oppressed. While the discourse of colonialism could be race—along with its economic ramifications—the oppressed were not to use race or any form of racial cooperation to forge their freedom. As Kilson notes, Bunche is particularly dismissive of African nationalists in his dissertation; they do not constitute the modernist African Bunche believes to be the way out for the continent politically. Here I am not talking about the issue of essentialism, that some black soul existed to be recuperated through political action, but the notion that solidarity among black people in economic and social struggle brought benefits. Indeed, Bunche's abhorrence of group politics extended beyond blacks to even Mahatma Gandhi and anti-imperialistic Indians; Bunche criticized Gandhi's nonviolent activism in his earliest writings as a mistake. Even nonviolent boycotts could not bring about change in a system in which the whites, in this case the British, held all the money and military power.

The other aspect of Bunche's perspective is his notion that real change could come only from the top down, not the bottom up. Bunche seemed as unsympathetic as Locke—indeed, in some ways, more unsympathetic—to the power of grassroots organizing to bring about substantive change. And this underestimation of what could be called the "power of the people" meant that Bunche's only alternative to complete defeatism and nihilism was a faith in technocratic rationalist political action, directed, of course, by academically trained and culturally broadminded elites like him and Locke. This points to a weakness in the New Negro formulation in Bunche: it was elitist in its belief that fundamental social change required the Negro (and the Indian and other colonized peoples) to give up those modes of organization and communitarianism that had sustained them under imperialist practices, even though the operation of those practices in different forms had not ended with the formal end of imperialism or segregation. Laudably anti-romantic, such a position tended to isolate the New Negro foreign policy theorist as an individual, if brilliant, thinker and expose him or her to the kind of vagaries that Locke experienced trying to lead the New Negro into the field of foreign policy studies without bringing the mass movement that had created the New Negro along with him. Criticality alone, detached from the social movements that spawned them, made the New Negro foreign policy thinker an easy target to take down.

Hence, the dichotomy that Kilson places between, let us say, the radical and the Enlightenment sides of Bunche is not an accident, but a kind of revolutionary elitism, since Bunche has no faith in the untutored people to bring about substantive change. This means that his doctoral dissertation is in sync with his political activity during the mid-1930s in Washington, D.C., when he criticized students and workers who were advocating in the New Negro Alliance a grass-roots boycotting of stores in the black community that did not hire blacks as workers.[36] Again, Bunche's disposition was against those who were the "people" served by these imperialistic institutions; he criticized such students for involvement in a race-based boycott, because that would alienate them from the white workers they would displace. While theoretically understandable, Bunche's position seemed not to recognize that for the starving black unemployed residents of Washington, the philosophical question of whether their self-activity to feed their families interrupted some future bonding with white workers was irrelevant. Bunche could not transfer the kind of nuance he allowed in foregrounding the discursive dismemberment of the African by the English and French colonizers to the white middle and working classes, who, in a different way—certainly to the black body—benefited just as inexorably from structural segregation of American employment as the British upper classes who pocketed the transcontinental wealth. With no real alternative to such race-based boycotting, since black-white worker solidarity was at best a work in progress, Bunche, in effect, left the black *lumpenproletariat* domestically with nothing to hope for in the matter of real change. In that sense Bunche could neither inject his own class position into his discussion of class solidarity politics in America nor see that his perspective as a professor at Howard University in a segregated school hierarchy gave him access to income in ways that complicated his authority to preach integration to working-class blacks in Depression-era Washington.

This theoretical dismissal of the functional workings of race as political practice also distorted *A World View of Race*, one of the few books produced by Bunche, and one wholly orchestrated by Alain Locke shortly after Bunche completed his dissertation. Here the conflict outlined was even more explicit. In what was a theoretical blueprint for global action, Bunche completely dismissed the role of race as an organizing principle of progressive political change. Indeed, the resultant pamphlet actually was toned down from the original version submitted to publication by the Associates of Negro Folk Education, since Locke debated Bunche on his dismissive attitudes about race as a factor in global self-organization among the oppressed. Bunche agreed to Locke's edits in part because Locke could argue with Bunche on the same level of analysis, but with one additional caveat: that Locke's own *Race Contacts* lectures argued that the truly Marxist approach to race was to treat race as Marx had treated class: as the vortex of social and economic relations, not as an epiphenomenal illusion. Race was the stand-in for power just as class was the stand-in for property, and to ignore that race also structured social relations was to miss the contribution that the American "experiment" had added to the history of capitalism in the West.

Perhaps here was the real "schizophrenia" Bunche struggled with as a New Negro foreign and domestic policy theorist. He had difficulty reconciling the efficacy of race as a tool of group organization and struggle with his desire for integration as the goal of all domestic and global progress. He could recognize how powerful the racial imaginary was in fueling European and American dominance while abroad, yet he could not see—until the end of his career, during the Black Power movement of the 1960s—how powerful some racial and ethnic collaboration was to those who resisted imperialism and segregation. In that sense the arc of New Negro foreign policy thinking in Locke and Bunche is limited by the range and trajectory of their domestic policy thinking on race. Bunche's New Negro, therefore, was a struggle to reconcile his training that class was the explanation of all things racial with his experience, in studying in Africa and in observing self-activity in the 1930s in India and America, that group struggle and bonding were key elements of transformation.

To his credit, Bunche allowed his debate with Locke over *A World View of Race* to amend his notion—seemingly stronger in his U.S. policy statements than in his dissertation—that class was the only thing that mattered, an intellectual trajectory that would eventually culminate in a much more sympathetic view of black self-organization based on race that appeared in Bunche's 1940s work with Gunnar Myrdal. There, as one of the lead social scientists on a project that excluded "old heads" like Locke, Bunche began to see the significance of self-organization among Negroes even as he decried the intellectual buffoonery and political crassness of many black political and social nationalist organizations. That movement toward greater sympathy toward the middle-class Negro leadership in the American community was not the only change in Bunche's posture in the 1940s. I use the term "posture" in response to what Jonathan Holloway calls the ambiguity of Bunche's revisionism in the 1940s, when the firebrand radical who could not stomach gradualism and liberalism suddenly dropped the fire and brimstone of socialist criticality from his speeches and writings and became, in effect, a liberal progressive himself.[37] The dualism that Kilson observes in Bunche's dissertation became a monism—pure Enlightenment, no longer Marxist, rationalism was the tool that the oppressed around the world needed to begin to free themselves from the yokes of imperialism and oppression. Of course, several factors probably accounted for this: Bunche's resignation from the National Negro Congress, which he had cofounded, because of its takeover, he asserted, by communists; World War II itself, which seems to have stunned Bunche into recognizing that the very existence of liberal democracy itself was not guaranteed in the face of mechanistic worldwide fascism; and his inclusion in the federal government intellectual apparatus to fight the threat of fascism to Africa and the Negro worldwide.

But I use "posture" to suggest, as Holloway hints at, that no one knows exactly whether this shift was a genuine change of ideological position or an adaptation to the changed political environment in which he had to survive as a policy wonk in the federal government. I suspect that the real Bunche did not change as much as he became more aware that his earlier views would get in the way of his being an effective steward of black interests in the 1940s. Here it is not so much opportunism that I want to get at, but rather something more fundamental: the way that the participation of the Negro in foreign policy in America requires, in effect, a deployment of masks in order to be taken seriously at all. Of course, earlier in his career, when he wrote his dissertation for Harvard, Bunche was able to bring his criticality to bear on imperialism in part because even liberals like Buell's and Bunche's professors at Harvard knew capitalism fused with racism drove imperialism. Even the untutored knew that the cause of imperialism was economic and the rationale was race. Not to foreground those elements had doomed Locke's treatise on a "third way" as much as the lack of detailed analysis from the archives in Geneva.

What Locke had struggled with was also something Bunche struggled with: how to elevate one's authority to propose and be taken seriously as an advocate of a "third way"—a progressive solution to the problem of colonialism in Africa—without having that position undermined by critiques of the bias attributed to any Negro who proposed a set of solutions about Africa. To be a radical was expected, almost a calling card to the conversation. But to remain a radical meant to eliminate oneself from the inner sanctum where the real decisions were made among the power brokers who did not look like him. And Bunche wanted to be in that room, wanted to be a player, not just an academic, and that is when he turned to the kind of New Negro vision Locke had advocated in his Foreign Policy Association paper, a visionary approach to solving thorny foreign policy and international conflicts that Bunche would adopt in the late 1940s and early 1950s.

I wonder, therefore, if Mrs. Mason's reflections on the dilemma of Locke in writing the Foreign Policy Association report are not also relevant to understanding the post-radical career of Ralph Bunche in the 1940s and perhaps the New Negro foreign policy paradigm more broadly. Recall that Mason said: "Alain, your not being ready to tell what you think is the exact truth about the mandate is the matter with your paper. It is not, of course, the time to do it." The report, she intimated, was not "black enough," especially for a progressive audience of white people now used to the harangue of a Marcus Garvey or a W.E.B. Du Bois but also willing to ignore such harangue because it lacked the power to persuade. "They think your opinion is the best balanced of any among Negroes and that you won't go to an extreme about anything. That was why they asked you to do it. Not because you did a fine article for the survey."

Was this not also true of Ralph Bunche? When Gunnar Myrdal asked Bunche to research and write analyses of Negro nationalist organizations and politics in America for the Carnegie Corporation–financed book *An American Dilemma*,[38] did he select Bunche, an Africanist, because he had written an award-winning dissertation on the mandate system in Africa, or because he was on record as critiquing Negro nationalism and being, in short, "the best balanced of any among Negroes," who would not endorse the "extremes" of Negro nationalist discourses, discourses that Myrdal was already critical of? When Bunche was selected by the American government to develop policy on Africa, was it because of the radical criticality in his doctoral dissertation or his Enlightenment faith in proper management, especially educational policy, to create an educated elite in Africa that the West could deal with? And when Bunche began his pivot away from radical socialist critiques of domestic and foreign policy, did he do it because of a real conversion experience, a fundamental renouncement of his earlier views, or because he knew that to continue to succeed, especially outside of a relatively harmless academic career available to him at Howard, he would have to be seen as one of those Negroes who "won't go to an extreme about anything"? Of course, on one level the decision, the transformation, was nothing so crass. Bunche was a principled man and would bristle at any idea that his was naked opportunism in the refinement of his views.

The point is really larger than any idea of personal responsibility narratives so frequent in critiques of whether Bunche or Locke or whomever was "black enough." Rather, I suggest that the very process of being welcomed into the realm of foreign policy discourse at the national level in the United States requires what we used to call in the 1960s "regrooving" if the Negro wants to be taken seriously. In American politics, after all, the proper place for the outspoken Negro according to the majority discourse is domestic policy making. If in fact the intellectual wishes to escape that policy ghetto and enter a new space of directing out loud the future of the world from a United States perspective, the calling card is a kind of erasure of race consciousness. And this was easier to accomplish for Bunche because from the beginning of his career he was skeptical of race consciousness as a political tool of liberation. All that was required, then, in the 1940s was to stop speaking about Marx.

Indeed, I conclude by arguing that the New Negro approach to foreign policy has roots in the intellectual tradition of the New Negro Renaissance of the 1920s, but it continues beyond that contextual frame. Its characteristics are familiar to us now. It emerges out of a criticality toward the exercise of white power as fundamentally imperialist—that race is fundamentally a power relationship, not a real cause of conflicts, but a kind of justification for what is really at stake: money and control of subject peoples in order to generate long-term profitability. But the concept of the New Negro is also a faith in Enlightenment blackness, involving self-conscious individuals who have internalized into their consciousness all of this knowledge about the function of race to justify exploitation as well as the freedom to pick and choose which aspects of that racial conundrum they will foreground in their public politics. In other words, the New Negro is always a cosmopolitan subjectivity who deploys race when it is convenient but holds it at bay when necessary to construct *a politics of the willing*, those who are willing to work for change in the quality of life for the oppressed.

The New Negro is also committed to a vision of change, an intellectual construct of what the world should look like in the future that is largely invisible to current players, but that the New Negro can gleam as the unrealized possibility pregnant in the moment that can birth through later if, and when, the right combination of right-minded people are in a position to *exercise power with vision*. And finally, and critically, the New Negro as operative in foreign policy debates is largely alienated from grassroots political struggles and committed to technocratic solutions to world problems, solutions that are generated by supremely rational and rationalizing black intellects who, in their conceit, believe they know what is best for the masses as well as the masters.

As for its current iterations, we can glimpse some of this New Negro positionality with regard to foreign policy in the presidency of Barack Obama. His Cairo speech, for example, at the beginning of his presidency and his Jerusalem speech, at the beginning of his second term, suggest that he carries forward some of the visionary thinking Locke outlined in his Foreign Policy Association paper, that a "third way" between violent reactionaryism on the part of the historically oppressed and hegemonic domination on the part of the historically privileged is possible if the Arab world chooses the path of enlightened reason and rationalistic pursuit of self-interest.[39] The Jerusalem speech offered the same kind of vision to young Israelis as twentieth-century New Negroes, who should break with the politics of the past and chart a new future that is not based exclusively on group predestination. But as a critical position on that positionality might also mention, there exists as well in Obama's approach a disposal toward technocratic rather than grassroots politics, a top-down approach built on the notion that having downloaded all of the radical politics of Chicago earlier in his career, he can, like Locke and Bunche before him, mask some of that criticality in trying to forge a "coalition of the willing."

The question that dogs this New Negro approach to foreign policy remains: Will a rationalist politics of the willing trump the politics of the will to power, which is still the dominant motivation in state-on-state and stateless struggles in the global landscape? And will an Enlightenment New Negro politics be able to escape the kind of historical determinism that the younger Bunche—no less than the younger Locke—recognized as the logic of power and capital in the world? And can that determinism be deterred without energizing grassroots progressive forces, however unpredictable or naïve they may be at times? We really don't have the answers to those questions. But so far the jury is out on how successful the New Negro foreign policy approach is in the world of realpolitik.

Notes

This chapter is dedicated to Pearl T. Robinson.

1. Paul Laurence Dunbar, "We Wear the Mask," in *The Complete Poems of Paul Laurence Dunbar* (New York: Dodd, Mead, 1913).

2. Alain Locke, ed. *The New Negro: An Interpretation* (New York: Albert and Charles Boni, 1925).

3. Jeffrey C. Stewart, "The New Negro as Citizen," in *The Cambridge Companion to the Harlem Renaissance,* ed. George Hutchinson (Cambridge, U.K.: Cambridge University Press, 2007), 13–27.

4. Alvin B. Tillery Jr., *Between Homeland and Motherland: Africa, Foreign Policy, and Black Leadership in America* (Ithaca, N.Y.: Cornell University Press, 2011).

5. Ibid.

6. Jeffrey C. Stewart, ed. *Race Contacts and Interracial Relations: Lectures by Alain Locke* (Washington, D.C.: Howard University, 1996). See Lecture 2: "The Practice of Race."

7. Brenda Gayle Plummer, *Rising Wind: Black Americans and U.S. Foreign Affairs, 1935–1960* (Chapel Hill: University of North Carolina, 1996), 1.

8. W.E.B. Du Bois, *The Souls of Black Folk* (Millwood, N.Y.: Kraus-Thomson, 1973), 3.

9. For a brief discussion of black criticality, see "Terms and Questions, 1968: A Global Year of Student Driven Change," Department of Black Studies, University of California–Santa Barbara, http://www.blackstudies.ucsb.edu/1968/terms_questions.html.

10. Alain Locke, ed. *Four Negro Poets* (New York: Simon and Schuster, 1927).

11. Article 22, "The Covenant of the League of Nations," December 1924, Yale Avalon Project, http://avalon.law.yale.edu/20th_century/leagcov.asp#art22.

12. Ibid. A typed copy of Article 22 is also located in the Alain Locke Papers, Moorland-Spingarn Research Center, Howard University.

13. Ibid.

14. "Memorandum: Foreign Policy Association; Alain Locke re: African Mandates Study Project," May 26, 1927, Alain Locke Papers, Moorland-Spingarn Research Center, Howard University. Emphasis added.

15. See Rose Cherubin, "Culture and the *Kalos*: Inquiry, Justice, and Value in Locke

and Aristotle," in *Philosophic Values and World Citizenship,* ed. Jacoby Adeshei Carter and Leonard Harris (Lanham, Md.: Rowman and Littlefield, 2010), 7–19.

16. Rayford Logan, *The Operation of the Mandate System in Africa, 1919–1927* (Washington, D.C.: Foundation Publishers, 1942).

17. Raymond Buell, *The Native Problem in Africa,* 2 vols. (New York: Macmillan, 1928).

18. See Christopher Lasch, *The New Radicalism in America, 1889–1963* (New York: Norton, 1971); and Robert Lansing, *Peace Negotiations: Personal Narrative* (Boston: Houghton Mifflin, 1921).

19. Stewart, "New Negro as Citizen."

20. Charlotte Mason to Alain Locke, [1929], Alain Locke Papers, Moorland-Spingarn Research Center, Howard University.

21. Ibid.

22. Charles P. Henry, *Ralph Bunche: Model Negro or American Other?* (New York: New York University Press, 1999).

23. Pearl T. Robinson, "Ralph Bunche the Africanist: Revisiting Paradigms Lost," in *Trustee for the Human Community: Ralph J. Bunche, the United Nations, and the Decolonization of Africa,* ed. Robert A. Hill and Edmond J. Keller (Athens: Ohio University Press, 2010), 73.

24. Ralph Bunche to Dean E. P. Davis at Howard University, December 22, 1930, Ralph Bunche Papers, Collection Number 2051, Department of Special Collections, Charles E. Young Research Library, UCLA (hereafter, Ralph Bunche Papers).

25. Arthur N. Holcombe to Bunche, August 7, 1930, Ralph Bunche Papers.

26. Arthur N. Holcombe to Bunche, December 11, 1930, Ralph Bunche Papers.

27. Bunche to Arthur N. Holcombe, Department of Government, Harvard University, February 28, 1931, Ralph Bunche Papers.

28. Ibid.

29. Ibid.

30. Martin Kilson, "African American Intellectual," in *Trustee for the Human Community: Ralph J. Bunche, the United Nations, and the Decolonization of Africa,* ed. Robert A. Hill and Edmond J. Keller (Athens: Ohio University Press, 2010), 3–9.

31. Vladimir Lenin, *Imperialism: The Highest Stage of Capitalism* (1917).

32. For example, in chapter 4 of Bunche's dissertation he writes: "The organized and official partition of Africa occurred . . . [and] . . . No single motive is applicable of course, but it is a safe assumption to make in a capitalistic, industrial world, the economic motive was the dominating one. The justification was easy to find. In the first place it was pointed out that no people have the right to isolate themselves (and their riches) from the rest of the world, while the world on the other hand has a superior right to take what it needs. (Footnote: Girault, *Principles de Colonization*). The creed of imperialism paraded economic necessity as adequate justification, which was simple enough—the raw materials of the 'backward regions' were necessary for a hungry and overpopulated world" (75). "French Administration in Togoland and Dahomey," 1934, Ralph Bunche Papers.

33. Ralph Bunche, *A World View of Race* (Washington, D.C.: Associates of Negro Folk Education, 1936; Bronze Booklet #4).

34. For more on this "black radical tradition," see Cedric Robinson, *Black Marxism: The Making of the Black Radical Tradition* (1983; Chapel Hill: University of North Carolina Press, 2000).

35. Bunche, introduction, "French Administration in Togoland and Dahomey," 1934, typescript, box 9, folder 1, Ralph Bunche Papers.

36. For more on the New Negro Alliance and Bunche's reactions to it, see Michelle F. Pacifico, "'Don't Buy Where You Can't Work': The New Negro Alliance of Washington," *Washington History* 6 (Spring/Summer 1994): 66–88.

37. Jonathan Holloway, "Responsibilities of the Public Intellectual," in *Ralph Johnson Bunche: Public Intellectual and Nobel Peace Laureate,* ed. Beverly Lindsay (Champaign: University of Illinois Press, 2007), 36–44.

38. Gunnar Myrdal, *An American Dilemma* (New York: Harper Brothers, 1944).

39. "Remarks by the President on a New Beginning," Cairo, Egypt: Cairo University, June 4, 2009, WhiteHouse.gov, http://www.whitehouse.gov/the-press-office/remarks -president-cairo-university-6–04–09; "Remarks of President Barack Obama to the People of Israel," Jerusalem, Israel: Jerusalem International Convention Center, March 21, 2013, WhiteHouse.gov, http://www.whitehouse.gov/the-press-office/2013/03/21/remarks -president-barack-obama-people-israel.

3

Carl Rowan and the Dilemma of Civil Rights, Propaganda, and the Cold War

MICHAEL L. KRENN

Anyone interested in the fascinating, convoluted, and intricately interwoven connections between race, the Cold War, and American foreign policy could do little better than starting with the career of Carl T. Rowan. Like many African Americans, Rowan felt himself constrained, constricted, confused, and pushed into any number of different corners during the Cold War. With any sort of domestic protest looked upon as suspiciously "un-American," participants in the civil rights movement came under the unforgiving glare of America's growing internal security system. Criticisms of U.S. policies, particularly those related to matters abroad, instantly brought forth the wrath of the American government and often resulted in the critics being painted with the broad and undiscriminating brush of "communist sympathizer"—or worse. Nevertheless, numerous black voices were heard during the height of the Cold War, protesting America's policies toward the new nations in Africa, criticizing America's reluctance to denounce the abhorrent apartheid regime of South Africa, and denouncing the last struggling remnants of colonialism around the globe. Indeed, a number of African American observers pointed out the distinct connections between America's domestic race problems and many of the issues facing the United States overseas: dealing with people of color revolting in Asia and Africa; its seeming acceptance, and even support, of South Africa's version of Jim Crow; and, perhaps most damning, the stark contradiction between America's proud acceptance of the mantle "leader of the free world," and the bias, segregation, and violence endured by millions of African Americans condemned to second-class citizenship in the land of the free.

Rowan, in his own fashion, understood the contradictions, confusion, and constrictions the Cold War created for both the United States and for much of its African American population. Yet for much of the 1950s and 1960s, Rowan— whether as a journalist or a member of the foreign policy–making bureau- cracy—relied on the same basic explanations when asked about America's race problem: that it was getting better, that it was largely a problem confined to a few ignorant and bigoted Southern whites, that the federal government was doing everything in its power to solve the problem, and that both communist propaganda and "irresponsible" African Americans at home were promoting a distorted and hateful portrait of the fate of African Americans. It was a stance that Rowan later regretted. In his 1991 autobiography he reflected on his State Department–sponsored trip to India in the mid-1950s. Not surprisingly, the African American journalist was bombarded with questions about his nation's race problem. At the time, Rowan recalled, "I simply went from Darjeeling to Patna to Cuttack to Madras, saying good things about my country because I believed that the society that had given me a break was in the process of taking great strides toward racial justice." Now, nearly forty years later, he realized that he had been "naïvely optimistic about the willingness of the South to accept the end of Jim Crow. It had not dawned on me that even Boston and Pontiac, Michigan, would become embroiled in violence as white parents sought to keep their children from going to school with black youngsters." As he concluded later in the book, "I know now that I was naïve, just plain wrong."[1]

Naïveté no doubt played a role in Rowan's overly optimistic appraisal of the civil rights struggle in the United States and his eagerness to share his opinions with a foreign audience during the 1950s and 1960s. As both a journalist during the mid- and late-1950s and a member of the foreign policy–making establish- ment during the Kennedy and Johnson administrations, Rowan reiterated a consistent story: the civil rights issue in the United States was being dealt with in an effective and speedy manner, amazing progress was being made, and the only obstacles were a minority of hateful and wrongheaded whites. Aside from naïveté there may have been other factors playing into Rowan's stance. Self-interest should never be underestimated. Rowan was an extremely ambitious individual.

Although he often chose to portray his career successes as simply a matter of dumb luck or being in the right place at the right time, no one—particularly an African American in the post–World War II period—could have experienced such a meteoric rise without an extremely aggressive approach to one's career. Rowan certainly would have realized that being too critical of America's race problems would effectively close off any government work during the height of the Cold War. This raises another possible explanation for his embrace of the official U.S. propaganda line on civil rights. Rowan was a witness to what happened to those African Americans who criticized U.S. policy too strongly: W.E.B. Du Bois, Paul Robeson, and Josephine Baker each felt the power of the U.S. government when their criticisms were perceived as "un-American."[2]

Closer scrutiny of Rowan's writings and speeches, however, reveals that another, more important force was at work molding his understanding of the race problem at home *and* abroad. The Cold War played a significant part in shaping his perceptions of the international implications of race and civil rights, the role of propaganda in dealing with those implications, and the domestic civil rights struggle. For Rowan, America's race problem and its struggle against communism in the Cold War were linked together in intricate and sometimes confusing ways, ways that served to strongly reinforce his "naïve optimism."

During the years from the mid-1950s through the mid-1960s, as both an unofficial and official spokesperson of the U.S. government, Rowan's understanding of the Cold War, civil rights, and propaganda led him to consistently underplay or ignore evidence that his optimistic appraisal of the progress in race relations in America was unfounded. One example was his failure to grasp the fact that America's propaganda concerning civil rights in the United States was denied not only by strong communist counterpropaganda, but also by the nearly implacable forces of bigotry and segregation in his own nation. In addition, and despite his repeated denials, Rowan's numerous appointments to foreign policy–making positions were not the harbingers of greater opportunities for blacks, but were, in fact, examples of a sort of diplomatic tokenism in which African Americans were placed in high-profile jobs not because they were qualified (although they were as qualified—and often more qualified—than their white peers), but because of their propaganda value. And finally, Rowan's Cold War ethos led him to downplay the suffering, stamina, and impact of the civil rights movement in the United States through a portrayal of the ultimate civil rights successes of the mid-1960s as simply the results of the natural evolution of American democracy.

Rowan's journey into the complex vortex made up of racism, civil rights, and Cold War diplomacy began with a trip to India. In 1954 Rowan was a journalist working for the *Minneapolis Tribune*. His writing was receiving some national attention, and he published his first book, *South of Freedom,* in 1952. In it he sharply criticized Southern politicians and officials who were vainly attempting to hold the line against the growing civil rights movement. Rowan's work brought him to the attention of the Department of State, which in 1954 asked him to go on a speaking tour in India under the auspices of the department's leader-grantee program, by which leading American figures were given grants to lecture abroad. Rowan quickly accepted and arrived in India in July 1954. For the next three months he traveled throughout India. (The State Department sent him on a speaking tour through other nations in South and Southeast Asia when his time in India ended, and he later attended the Bandung Conference in 1955 as a reporter for the *Minneapolis Tribune.*)[3]

The program Rowan participated in was part and parcel of America's Cold War propaganda effort. During the 1940s, 1950s, and 1960s, the United States mounted a wide-ranging propaganda effort in its battle against communism.[4] In this struggle for the "hearts and minds" of the world's people, American officials did their best to portray communist society, politics, and economics in the worst light possible. At the same time, they also undertook to illuminate other nations as to the strength and durability of the ideals that the United States stood for: democracy, free enterprise, justice, and equality. Yet, as an officer attending the Psychological Warfare School at Fort Bragg explained, America had an Achilles heel in its war of words with the communist world: segregation and racial discrimination against African Americans.[5] Not only did the civil rights situation in the United States make the nation's rhetoric about equality and justice ring hollow, but it also provided a readymade and easily exploitable subject for communist propaganda that was particularly effective in regions such as Asia and Africa.[6] One answer to the problem was for the U.S. government to feature African Americans as spokespersons for the American way of life. Sponsored trips overseas and interviews on the Voice of America were some of the means employed, and personalities such as Ralph Bunche, singer Marian Anderson, and author Richard Wright were some of those who participated.[7]

Rowan's invitation to lecture in India—a nation that was harshly critical of America's race problem—was part of these initiatives. With regard to his role, Rowan declared that "no one would have accused the State Department of sending a 'Red baiter' to India when it selected me. I considered myself politically independent—'liberal independent' my friends might call it."[8] Three months in India, however, had a dramatic impact on Rowan and his thinking about the Cold War, race, civil rights, and propaganda. The conclusions he drew about those issues would continue to help shape his thinking during the rest of the 1950s and, in particular, the early 1960s, when he served in several foreign policy positions in the Kennedy and Johnson administrations.

After his trip to India, Rowan wrote and spoke extensively about his adventure. He penned a long and detailed report to the Department of State. In 1956 he published *The Pitiful and the Proud,* which recounted his journey through South and Southeast Asia and his attendance at Bandung. In fact, his trip to India became one of the staple topics of the numerous speeches and articles he wrote during the late 1950s and into the 1960s. His main points did not vary much from medium to medium. First and foremost, his sojourn in India convinced him that "that race problem," as he referred to it in his report to the Department of State, was a volatile component of international relations. As he wrote in *The Pitiful and the Proud,* "almost every thinking Indian was seized by this consciousness of color. To many, this concern with color had become close to an obsession and I was convinced that for many years to come race would be an important factor in India's foreign policy." He was not completely surprised, therefore, to find that Indians had a "preoccupation with America's race problem," and that "I ALWAYS was asked questions about it."[9]

By the early 1960s Rowan was no longer a private citizen, but a full-fledged member of the foreign policy–making apparatus of the United States. His views on race and America's civil rights problems, however, had not changed. Speaking in 1961, he urged his audience to continue the struggle for civil rights not only because it was the right thing to do but also because of the international significance of that struggle. He argued, "Racial feelings, as much as any other single factor, will determine which way Asia, Africa and Latin America go in the mortal struggle in which the Western and Communist worlds are now engaged." A few years later, serving as director of the United States Information Agency (USIA), Rowan declared to a group of newspaper publishers: "I have concluded that if the Negro does not succeed in closing the gap and reaching the heights of absolutely first-class citizenship, then our country cannot succeed in its endeavors in the world. And if our country fails, Western society will have fallen, and perhaps we shall all be unequals in the purgatory of atomic conflict." "The Negro's struggle," he continued, "is important enough for what it means to the Negro himself . . ., but its international implications are also of the most compelling urgency."[10]

For Rowan, India's "obsession" with race was dangerously complicated by the communist menace he believed to be working so assiduously in Asia and elsewhere. He claimed that in India he "saw for the first time the shrewd workings of the international Communist conspiracy." Resorting to metaphor, Rowan recounted a conversation he had with a USIA officer about the vultures circling over a field in India. He exclaimed, "Always busy and waiting, aren't they?" To which the officer replied, "In Asia today vultures are very busy." Flying home, Rowan's plane encountered rough weather, leading him to muse, "Yes, I thought, there will be a lot of 'rough weather' out here in the years ahead. The Asian Communists will see to that."[11]

Rowan was not so shallow as to suggest that all of India's (and Asia's) problems were the "*product* of communism," but he was certain that India's internal turmoil was "the *vehicle* by which they hope to ride to power in Asia" (emphasis in original). A large part of that communist effort revolved around the issue of race, particularly the spreading of distorted and damaging stories about the civil rights situation in the United States. In India, Rowan observed, he saw "the limits to which the Communists will go in their efforts to spread dissension and chaos." The United States was "combating a world movement which knows no bounds of scrupulousness." This point was made clear after several encounters with audiences asking him uncomfortable questions about racism in the United States.

> I admitted, with some reluctance, that the deft fingers of international communism were manipulating my audiences, pushing hostility and disagreement to the surface where it burst forth in agitating accusations and tenacious suspicion. I had not been a witch-hunter in America; I had not come to India to search for the bones of Karl Marx; but now I was face to face with shrewd propaganda and artifice, inspired by the demonic dreams and illusions of the Lenins and the Stalins. Whether I willed it so or not, this was the big issue, the all-determining struggle in the India over which I traveled.[12]

According to Rowan, the communist propaganda was doing its work. He expressed "amazement at the bad press the United States is getting in India today." Amazement turned to anger "when I saw what appeared to be deliberate misstatements of fact or distortions" and "a deliberate selection of news which will embarrass the United States or prejudice her viewpoint in the eyes of the Indian people." The depth of the communist influence could be seen when "even the most honest, best-informed Indian who admits, for example, that racial prejudice is on the decline in the United States still pictures the situation as one in which bigoted whites are giving ground reluctantly under pressure from awakening Neg[r]oes backed by vast numbers of colored peoples of the world."[13]

After completing his trip through South and Southeast Asia, Rowan glumly concluded, "We are losing the propaganda battle in Asia. Many observers of the Asian scene . . . insist that the final question of whether democracy or Communism triumphs in Asia will be determined by this propaganda battle—the struggle for the hearts and minds of a billion human beings." Most Americans, unfortunately, were "woefully unaware of the fact that we fight a shrewd, dedicated enemy in the Asian Communist and that he will be beaten only by honesty, logic, and courageous action—and not by passion and emotion." Yet, Rowan was confident that the trend could be reversed: "We can make Asia's cocky Reds eat Lenin's words—but only if we realize the vitality of propaganda warfare and regard it as a technical, although human, thing instead of a guesswork game to be played by the curious and the disillusioned."[14]

Rowan's alarm over communist propaganda in India and the rest of Asia and his discouragement over the fact that even noncommunist Indians seemed to have a distorted view of America's race problem led him to conclude that propaganda was a vital and necessary part of his nation's Cold War arsenal. To be effective, however, Rowan was convinced that America's war of words concerning race and civil rights needed to undergo a dramatic revision. Shortly after returning from India, he decried the fact that "we are always on the defensive—we spend most of our time, energy and money trying to explain away our shortcomings, to rationalize our latest compromise with the principles supposedly inherent in democracy." Rowan, of course, realized there were often good reasons for that defensiveness. The criticisms of America's racial problems—whether communist-inspired or not—were very often based on a "large measure of truth and a great measure of injustice." As an example, he recounted an episode during his recent trip through India. After Rowan asserted that the United States was making great civil rights progress, one member of the audience passed him a newspaper clipping describing how a howling mob of whites in Philadelphia had tried to force a black family from the neighborhood. Rowan "gulped hot dry air with embarrassment" but countered with his own story about a similar event in a Minneapolis suburb. Here, however, most of the neighborhood rose up in support of the harassed black family, and the "Negroes stayed—in happiness." Rowan conceded that the second story did not make the first go away: "I could not whitewash all America." Nevertheless, he was "grateful that there had been courageous people" in the Minneapolis suburb. "They eased my embarrassment to the extent that I could indicate to Indians with good conscience that Reuter's Philadelphia story, true and sickening as it was, did not give a true picture of America."[15]

For Rowan this was the key to America's propaganda about the nation's civil rights problems: they simply needed to be put into perspective. Too much attention on "sickening" episodes such as the one in Philadelphia detracted from what Rowan saw as the *real* story: America's steady march toward racial equality. Even when subjected to the most heated and angry questioning about the treatment of African Americans in his own country, Rowan never lost his faith.

> Faith in the decency of mankind. Faith in a belief that all men need do is really to get to know each other. Faith that in the months ahead children white and black would join hands and play "ring around the roses" and the parents would

watch them, with reluctant, even happy awareness that contamination or "mongrelization" was not the fate of either group. Faith, after all, was what had made the Negro cling to democracy wasn't it? Yes, faith and the observation that he was moving, oh, so steadily, toward the goal of first-class citizenship.[16]

Rowan's views on race, communism, and propaganda matured during some of the hottest years of the Cold War—the mid-1950s through the early 1960s. It was clear that Rowan was a devoted advocate of civil rights for African Americans, and it was also clear that he recognized the damage done to America's reputation abroad by ugly racial incidents in the United States. However, during that time Rowan moved closer and closer to the position that communist propaganda, with its slanted, biased, and often misleading views of the civil rights situation in America, was the primary enemy. His answer was a deceptively simple one: simply take the "offensive" and show the world the kind of progress being made in America.

As a keen observer of America, however, Rowan must have been aware that such an approach had already been tried—and had dramatically and miserably failed. At the 1958 world's fair in Brussels, the United States took a novel approach to dealing with its race problem. Instead of the usual responses that had been forthcoming during the Truman years and most of the Eisenhower years—simply ignoring the problem or sending "representative" African Americans abroad (such as Rowan himself) to serve as examples of civil rights progress—American officials tried a different tack. At what came to be known as the "Unfinished Business" exhibit at the U.S. pavilion at the fair, visitors were confronted with three problem areas afflicting America. The first two—slums and urban decay and vanishing natural resources—were hardly likely to invoke much controversy or response. The section on civil rights, however, became a lightning rod for criticism in the United States. The exhibit was relatively simple and straightforward: one room showing newspaper clippings depicting in a no-holds-barred fashion the civil rights problem in America; a second room with pictures and charts suggesting the progress of African Americans in the economic, political, educational, and even social arenas; and a third room with a giant picture of white and African American children playing ring-around-the-rosy, suggesting the ultimate goal for American society. Even before it opened its doors, however, the "Unfinished Business" section dealing with race came under fire. Southern congressmen pilloried the exhibit. Senator Herman Talmadge (D-GA) expressed his utmost "shock" that an exhibit sponsored by the American government would dare to "apologize for racial segregation." The Eisenhower administration caved in to these criticisms, first forcing dramatic revisions of the civil rights section of "Unfinished Business." The newspaper clippings were crumpled and crushed to decrease their impact; in the second room a picture of a young African American man dancing with a white girl was removed; and in the final room the picture of the children playing was reduced in size. This did nothing to placate the objections of Talmadge and others, and eventually Eisenhower (whose own record on civil rights was ambiguous, to say the least) ordered the entire exhibit closed. When it reopened some time later, the section on race was gone, replaced by an exhibit on public health. This change did not go unnoticed. African Americans, supporters of civil rights in Congress, and some of the young guides (many of them African American) at "Unfinished Business" decried the closure, but to no avail. The Eisenhower administration stood firm, and the most public and daring propaganda attempt by the United States to face its civil rights problem head-on was defeated, not by insidious communist propaganda, but by the forces of racism and bigotry in the United States.[17]

By the early 1960s Rowan was in a position to put his faith in American democracy and his belief in the efficacy of propaganda into practice. In 1961 he was named deputy assistant secretary of state for public affairs; two years later he was made ambassador to Finland. In 1964 Lyndon Johnson appointed Rowan director of the USIA.[18] At each step Rowan hammered away at the idea that America's progress in race relations was both noticeable and noteworthy. In March 1961, just a short time after accepting the position of deputy assistant secretary of state for public affairs, Carl Rowan addressed the Washington Urban League. "I confess," he began, "that had I come to speak before your members eight years ago, I would have spoken only of the injustices and humiliations meted out to Negroes, but the day is long since past when I, or any other American, could afford to think of the social problems that beset us in any such narrow terms."[19] One of his first duties as deputy assistant secretary was to explain to a meeting of U.S. chiefs of mission from Latin America how to cope with the "distortions" of America's race problem. Rowan admitted that "there will continue to be race incidents in the U.S." The problem was to "put it in perspective. We must show that the picture is not one of whites vs. Negroes, as our enemies would depict it, but of the vast majority of whites and Negroes striving together for progress." In August 1961 he used his recent appointment to the Department of State as a perfect example of that progress. African Americans, he declared, should recognize the "really fantastic progress that is possible because of appointments and executive decrees." Rowan congratulated the Kennedy administration for undertaking "a little forced feeding of Negroes into the higher jobs. The assumption is that if you get the upper levels properly integrated the lower levels will take care of themselves."[20] Speaking at a luncheon given in his honor in Finland in 1963, Ambassador Rowan warned those in the audience that they might "assume from reading the press that what occurs today in Birmingham and Mississippi is merely white majority against Negro minority. Actually it is the Negro and the Government and the majority of the people against custom and a powerful, unenlightened minority." The battle against that custom would be hard, he said, but, "We *will* break it in the United States. Our President, our Federal Government and the great mass of our people are committed to it" (emphasis in original).[21]

Rowan often used his own success in achieving high-ranking foreign policy positions in the U.S. government as an example of the progress being made on the civil rights front. He was hardly unaware of the State Department's reputation among African Americans as being the "lily-white club." Black newspapers and spokespeople had been criticizing the department (and particularly the prestigious foreign service) as bastions of white racism, where African Americans had little or no chance for success. Years later Rowan recalled, "I learned quickly that the State Department was a virtual plantation." There were few blacks in the upper echelons of State's bureaucracy, and in the foreign service "too many were southern elitists who in 1961 still carried the mental baggage of the Civil War era." He was convinced, however, that his appointment to a higher-ranking job would act as a sort of "'trickle-down' theory" wherein the naming of an African American to a supervisory position would result in the "fruits of fairness" falling to those "people below who had suffered through years of discrimination."[22]

Rowan fought hard to dispel any notion that his successive appointments were not merely some sort of diplomatic tokenism; that his success was an indication that the walls of segregation were breaking down not simply at the Department of State but in America as a whole. Here again Rowan's Cold War thinking acted to blind him to the reality. In fact, as the evidence makes clear, nearly all appointments of African Americans to high-profile positions in the State Department and the foreign service contained aspects of tokenism. This is not to detract from the talents and qualities of the black men and women who were named to these posts, but merely to face reality: that most of the appointments were made with the race of the candidate in mind. In addition, the idea that such appointments would lead to greater opportunities for African Americans in the State Department and foreign service was not something that suddenly occurred with Rowan's appointments in the early 1960s.[23]

The idea of African Americans serving as token appointments in the U.S. foreign policy bureaucracy during the Cold War took hold early on and continued at least through the 1960s. A May 1949 State Department report laid out the scheme in no uncertain terms. Titled "Countries to which an Outstanding Negro might Appropriately be sent as an Ambassador," the report was clear about the number one priority. Bulgaria or Romania were the first choices, primarily because "the appointment of an outstanding Negro as Ambassador to one of the iron curtain countries should serve to counteract the communist propaganda that Americans are guilty of race discrimination." From there the choices narrowed considerably, since the other countries mentioned in the report would "resent" having a "Negro" as U.S. ambassador; other nations simply were not "evolved enough socially to overcome race prejudice" (apparently the irony of this assessment coming from one of the most racially segregated societies in the world was lost on the report's author). The notion that African Americans could serve as largely symbolic diplomatic appointments continued throughout the 1950s. When the Dwight D. Eisenhower administration was considering people for the U.S. delegation to the United Nations, one adviser moaned that "what we really are stuck on is a negro." The issue was primarily "political," since Eisenhower had been "criti[ci]zed for not having appointed a negro to high office." Secretary of State John Foster Dulles remained unmoved, however, arguing that only "qualified" individuals should be considered. In an extraordinarily telling turn of phrase, Dulles also worried that few if any African Americans could "come through an FBI check lily white, because all of their organizations had been infiltrated at one time or another [by the communists]."[24]

Dulles need not have been terribly concerned. Racism in the Department of State proved stronger than Cold War demands, and most African American appointees continued to toil in out-of-the-way places. Even when an African American finally succeeded in being named a chief of mission to a nation outside of Africa in 1958, the appointment was another example of tokenism in action. Clifton Wharton Jr. (who had struggled to make use of his talents in the Department of State for more than three decades) was named minister to Romania—one of the Iron Curtain nations named in the 1949 memorandum. Wharton no doubt deserved the honor, but the symbolic nature of his appointment was explained by a story in *U.S. News & World Report*: Romania, an Eastern Bloc nation that had been "sharply critical of the U.S. for 'suppressing' Negroes," was "in for a surprise," since "Mr. Wharton is a Negro."[25]

Beginning with the naming of Edward R. Dudley as the first African American ambassador in 1949 (to Liberia), many African American newspapers and supporters of civil rights outside and inside the U.S. government hailed the development as one that would finally break down the wall of segregation in State. And so it continued with each new appointment: the African American press greeted each one with the expectation that, finally, the "lily white club" was opening its doors to blacks. Those hopes reached a crescendo during the Kennedy and Johnson presidencies. Surely these presidents, committed to racial equality, would provide the final push. By 1969, however, the results were meager indeed. As one article summed up the situation, during the past eight years there had been "three Negro ambassadors, two in Africa; two Deputy Assistant

Secretaries of State, none in African areas, nineteen Foreign Service Officers; eleven Junior Foreign Service Reserve Officers; and twenty-four Foreign Service Reserve Officers—a drop of twenty-seven since 1967. This picture is a disgrace, a monument to bureaucratic rigidity and an embarrassment to the United States everywhere in the world, especially in Africa and Asia." Rowan's optimistic hopes for any sort of "trickle-down" effect generated by his own appointments ignored both the history of African American involvement in the Department of State and the dismal situation he himself witnessed during his years in office.[26]

More than a decade after his trip to India, Rowan, now a full-fledged member of the American foreign policy bureaucracy, was pounding away at the same points he had stressed in the 1950s. The "opposition—particularly the Soviet and Chinese Communists—have waged and continue to wage a vitriolic campaign against us on the issues of civil rights and race in an effort to scar our international face beyond repair." In particular, "The Chinese made abundant use . . . of racial violence and discrimination in the United States. Peking ridicules the Civil Rights bill as a 'deceitful trick,' a 'cheap hoax' and a 'legislative fraud' designed to break up the Negro's civil rights movement." It alarmed Rowan that the "Chinese claims fall on sympathetic ears in many parts of the world, the result being that our racial problems continue to be our biggest burden in trying to assert the U.S. claim to moral leadership."[27]

When Rowan became America's chief propagandist in 1964, he accelerated his efforts to put the proper spin on America's civil rights progress. In an interview shortly after his appointment as director of the USIA, Rowan was asked if he was "embarrassed or bothered when somebody abroad asked him about racial incidents in the United States." He responded, "The questions were sometimes ugly and sometimes quite embarrassing to the country, but when put in proper perspective they tell a pretty interesting and remarkable story about the kind of country this is." In a speech later that year to the National Urban League, Rowan proudly declared, "Since World War II we have gone through a phenomenal period in American race relations." Though the progress was not "as fast as I desired," he admitted, "there could be no doubt that there was great progress, no doubt as to the course America had chosen. She had chosen to prove that the ideals of our Declaration of Independence could also be a reality; she had chosen to show a hate-scarred world that it *is* possible to create a multi-racial society in which there is genuine equality of opportunity and mutuality of respect" (emphasis in original). To the Harvard Law Forum, Rowan announced, "We don't try to hide or alibi away our faults and blemishes; we speak of our unsolved racial problems but at the same time emphasize how the vast majority of our people are striving to obtain a greater degree of social justice for all Americans." And he made the same point at an awards banquet in 1965, noting, "We in USIA have not denied our racial *problems*—for they are there for all to see—but what we have done is to underscore the racial *progress*—which is unhappily something the world often does not see" (emphasis in original).[28]

In order to get the proper perspective out to the world's people, Rowan suggested that the federal government would require some help from the nation's newspapers. He gently chided his former colleagues of the press in 1965 when he noted, "Too often in the past the spectacular and sensational aspects of this struggle for equality and equal opportunity have overshadowed in the public prints of all countries, including the United States, the quiet accomplishments and steady progress that has been won on many fronts of this battle."[29]

Yet, Rowan was not always so circumspect in his criticisms of the U.S. press and its reporting of the civil rights issue. At various gatherings during the early 1960s, he strongly suggested that the press should engage in a form of self-censorship. Being a government official brought him to the realization that "while the public does have a right to know, it also has a right *not* to know." Unfortunately, he concluded, "the complications of being part of a terribly complex world society imposes obligations of restraint and responsibility on the free press." It was a fact that "we face certain disadvantages because ours is an open society while the Sino-Soviet bloc which confronts us can operate under conditions of complete secrecy." That being the case, Rowan considered it "essential that we endeavor as a people to agree as to what it is we seek to communicate" to the world. A year after leaving his post with USIA, Rowan was still pressing his message. In an article in *Reader's Digest* he declared that he was disturbed by both "the extent to which the American press is relied upon to supply items damaging to the United States" and the "cleverness with which the communists exploit racial conflicts in the United States." For the communists, "the choicest tie-in of them all these days is racial unrest in the United States." He recounted a conversation he had with a Russian journalist, with the latter charging, "The same bullets that shot James Meredith on the highway in Mississippi are the same bullets that kill Vietnamese. It is this racist attitude that makes you wage the war on Vietnam." Rowan was incensed; after all, "The Vietnamese we are defending are just as dark as those we are opposing. How do you reduce that to a race war?" The exchange led Rowan to suggest, "We shall be increasingly pressed to decide whether our cherished freedom of press and speech can continue unrestrained." He cautioned the reader that he was "not advocating abolition" of either right, "but I do want to remind Americans that today's careless column or reckless Senate speech may constitute a heavy mortgage on America's future."[30]

Rowan could be particularly harsh on the African American press. In 1961 he urged the Department of State to subscribe to more black newspapers, many of which made extra efforts to establish close contacts with African diplomats in

Washington and understood the "frustrations and resentments" of these officials in dealing with racial bias in the nation's capital. However, he warned that the "articles and cartoons appearing in these newspapers often have the effect of aggravating the problems by making these diplomats feel that they have far greater reason to feel offended than they originally had thought." In a 1962 speech he said he was "appalled week after week by the amount of misinformation funneled out to the Negro public through the Negro press—most often through columnists and pundits with personal political axes to grind or who are eager to establish themselves as foremost Messiahs of Negro freedom."[31]

Rowan also asked his fellow African Americans for help in the propaganda war. In particular he pleaded for an end to street protests and demonstrations and issued a call for what he referred to as "responsible militancy." He also suggested that African Americans begin to give credit for much of the progress on the civil rights front where credit was due: to the federal government (particularly presidents Kennedy and Johnson) and the majority of white Americans who supported those actions.

In numerous speeches in the early 1960s, Rowan set the tone for his criticisms and suggestions. African Americans, he declared, "have got to learn the art of the possible and stop wasting energy and emotions in useless complaints." His own appointment to a high government position indicated the "fantastic progress" being made. While he admired "those youngsters who prefer jail to the indignity of segregation . . . we must also keep before them, the realization that there is an intellectual side to dignity, too." It was now time to "shift from a program of constant protest that was necessary when there were few or no allies in high places to one of co-operation wherever feasible." There was far "too much protest that is based on ignorance—protest by people who don't even make a minimum effort to get the facts."[32]

He continued the theme when he became director of the USIA. He cautioned that "the Negro dare not concentrate so exclusively on street demonstrations that he forgets other fields of battle." He lashed out at individuals such as Malcolm X "and his roamings about Africa where he poured forth a steady stream of hate, of illogical venom." It was clear to Rowan that "many of our northern cities experienced bitter racial strife this summer [1964]—and largely because so many of the present generation are vulnerable to demagoguery." The black masses in the inner cities (somewhat like the poverty-stricken masses of the Indian cities Rowan visited a decade before) were particularly susceptible to the siren's song of protest and violence; they were "easy prey for the Black Muslims and the other peddlers of disillusionment and hatred."[33]

It was in a speech to the National Urban League in August 1964, however, that Rowan most forcefully enunciated his position. He began by reasserting his belief that terrific progress had been made on the civil rights front. Turning to "my fellow Negroes," Rowan let his anger flare: "The hour has come when bold, uncompromising efforts must be made to free the civil rights movement from the taint of street rioters, looters and punks who terrorize subways." He believed that "the only effective way to achieve the things we really want is to call off those street demonstrations which unfortunately have come to serve as little more than a fuse to ignite the tempers of the ignorant and irresponsible and as a shield behind which they can hide." Rowan declared that "demonstrations—with possible rare exceptions—have served their purpose for the time being. They serve today, for the most part, only to becloud the real issues of the Negro's legitimate grievances and to raise a bogeyman of supposed excessive, unreasonable desires on the part of the country's colored citizens." Comparing the leaders of these street demonstrations to medical quacks, he charged that they would "kill the hopes for total freedom of many a Negro with their nostrum of endless and often pointless demonstrations."

While Rowan agreed that protests had served some purpose in the past, he proceeded to undercut that assertion. To the argument that the end of protests would mean an end to civil rights progress, he responded, "Nonsense." He went on to say, "Nothing could be more foolhardy than for Negroes to proceed on the assumption that progress has not flowed, and will not continue to flow, from the rulings of our courts, from the power and prestige of the executive branch of government, from the personal and social pressures exerted by workers such as you in the Urban League movement, and now, from the Civil Rights Act of 1964." He referred to the Montgomery bus boycott as an example, for as "dramatic and courageous" as it was, "the issue was finally resolved only by a ruling by the United States Supreme Court." And although the "March on Washington surely played a role in producing passage of the Civil Rights law, . . . certainly *some* of the credit for the success of that demonstration must be given to those Washington officials—the late John F. Kennedy, President Johnson, Washington police officials—who gave it their blessing because they saw it as an expression of one of the most noble rights enshrined in our Bill of Rights."[34]

In another speech given at about the same time, Rowan called on African Americans to cease their protests and let the Civil Rights Act of 1964 do its work. The act, he argued, "must be considered the symbol of white America's conscience at work." Though that conscience had indeed been "prodded and jarred" by a "new Negro militancy," it was also true that "*it is* the conscience of white America which has helped to spell out this new standard of our society. And I say that before we rush rashly and irresponsibly into any adventures to prove what the new law does or does not mean, we ought to see how far this conscience of America will go in producing compliance with the new standards" (emphasis in original). In short, "We ought to let white Americans themselves show who intends to honor America and her new expression of ideals and who intends to dishonor this country by assuming the role of outlaw."[35]

Rowan also acted to make sure his views made their way into U.S. propaganda. When criticisms were raised by some USIA posts overseas that the agency-produced film *The March* "failed [to] make clear [that] demonstration took place with [the] support [of] top U.S. officials and in no way was protest against federal government," Rowan immediately "filmed a brief introductory statement covering this point which should help put into perspective THE MARCH's place in [the] U.S. civil rights movement."[36]

Rowan's naïve optimism, his "faith in the decency of mankind," was obviously at work in his speeches and actions, but so, too, were the necessities of America's Cold War propaganda. A 1964 USIA summary of its "worldwide themes" for U.S. propaganda suggested that on the issue of racial minorities the message should be that "the U.S. democratic social, political, and economic system has provided a means for them to join and be absorbed into the main stream of American life." African Americans, it should be emphasized, "are now actively in this process of full integration. Progress will not always be easy, but, with the support of the Federal Government and a majority of the citizenry, will continue until the process is complete." In a report published just a few months after Rowan stepped down from the directorship in July 1965, the USIA indicated that one of the goals of its propaganda on race relations in America had been to ensure that recent civil rights legislation was not seen to be simply the result of "Civil Rights movement and Negro leadership." That, unfortunately, would "suggest that what has occurred or is occurring in the US is a successful War of People's Liberation" (hardly a pleasing prospect as the United States stepped up its involvement in the Vietnam War). It was necessary, therefore, that U.S. propaganda put "Negro progress in the context and framework of normal American life, rather than within the civil rights movement. The Negro needs to be perceived within a pattern of acceptance, rather than as conducting a separate social movement." In future propaganda, USIA would "keep our emphasis on the response of the white community, not the fate of the Negro. We should avoid, in short, the black-and-white treatment, prefer[ring] the low key, mulatto, as it were coverage. And we should not dwell on the past; it probably serves better to remind of an unfavorable situation than to point up a more favorable one."[37] Obviously, internal divisiveness and references to racial schisms did not serve U.S. interests in the war of words with communism.

With the passage of the Civil Rights Act of 1964, Rowan seemed to believe that the struggle for equality—and the propaganda war on that subject—was as good as won. As he had always expected it would, America had rallied to the side of decency. In a speech shortly after the passage of the act, Rowan told his audience, "I've traveled all over this country and have been in contact with many thousands of white Americans these last several months. I remain convinced that there has been a genuine general enlightenment on racial matters." In a series of reports to Johnson, Rowan explained how the news of the civil rights legislation was being greeted in the foreign market. In Africa the bill was seen as "a great tribute to President Kennedy." Africans saw the act as "giving the Federal Government power to enforce the Constitution and as guaranteeing to Negroes the legal rights hitherto guaranteed only to whites." Overall around the world, "Non-communist editors universally and extensively acclaimed the event as marking an historic advance. . . . Tribute is paid to your skill, courage, and authority in bringing about the bill's passage." The passage went far toward "reinforcing the moral authority of the United States and its dedication to freedom and social justice." The Soviets, for their part, were left nearly speechless and merely "sought to downplay the importance of the Senate's action."[38]

Satisfied that the civil rights issue—in both its domestic and international contexts—had been settled, Rowan stepped down as director of the USIA in July 1965. Less than one month later, one of the largest and most destructive race riots in the history of the United States left more than thirty people dead, nearly one thousand people injured, over four thousand arrested, and nearly forty million dollars' worth of damage in its wake. In that same month the Johnson administration made the momentous decision to commit U.S. troops in South Vietnam to full offensive operations. By the end of the year, African Americans were furious to discover that black servicemen made up nearly one-quarter of the combat deaths and injuries suffered by U.S. forces. Martin Luther King Jr. declared in 1967 that he could no longer "be silent in the face of such cruel manipulation of the poor." By then, however, the USIA had made the decision that "preoccupation" with civil rights in the nation's propaganda was probably "more damaging than helpful to our cause." Even the assassination of King in 1968 did little to change that perception. The "race problem" in the United States was viewed, so the agency declared, as a "wart, so to speak, on the face of America rather than the image as a whole." It was likely that the "race problem with all its current very negative aspects will be perceived in correct perspective as only a partial element in the American image."[39]

Speaking to the national conference of the Urban League in August 1964, Rowan admitted that he faced a trying task in discussing the racial violence that had swept through America during the past few weeks. In Mississippi the bodies of three young civil rights workers had been discovered, murdered by white terrorists; in Harlem, destructive riots took place during the first of the long, hot summers of the 1960s. As Rowan explained,

My task is difficult, not merely because of the tenseness of the situation, but also because of what I am and what my responsibilities are: on the one hand, I am a Negro with a vital desire, indeed a fierce determination, to see that my children escape the degrading shackles of racism; on the other hand I am a public official whose job it is to help protect this country's reputation abroad, and an American citizen eager to see his country bind up wounds and wipe out scars of a conflict that should have been forgotten decades ago.

Fortunately, he concluded, "My difficulty is not that there is any conflict of interest in being all these things. Indeed, what is good for America and its reputation abroad is also good for my children."[40] In part, Rowan was correct: there was certainly no conflict between his color and his ability to serve in the foreign policy–making apparatus of the United States. Perhaps displaying the naïve optimism he would ruefully comment on decades later, he did not see the conflict between trying to "protect" America's "reputation" abroad and effectively and realistically dealing with America's very real racial divisions at home. Rowan, however, faced a dilemma. To criticize U.S. civil rights problems too harshly, to agree with foreign critics that the situation was terrible, to suggest that only aggressive protest by African Americans could push the American people into reluctantly accepting civil rights legislation would play into the hands of communist propagandists. To remain silent about such matters was equally problematic, for Rowan was undoubtedly a strong supporter of civil rights. In attempting to meet the demands of America's Cold War propaganda and the needs of the civil rights movement at home, Rowan found himself in a predicament, one in which his understanding of "that race problem" was partially obscured not only by his innate optimism and faith in mankind but also by his Cold War fears and mentality.

In 1996, with the Cold War already a distant memory for some Americans, Rowan published his last book before his death in 2000. Titled *The Coming Race War in America: A Wake-Up Call,* the volume shocked many of Rowan's devoted readers. It was a fiery condemnation of the growing white supremacist movement in America, but Rowan also turned his vivid anger against the U.S. government for doing nothing to stop what he perceived as a growing cancer. He warned America that "a terrible race war is coming in the United States. It is coming fast." Proclaiming to have little faith in the U.S. government or law enforcement agencies to stem the rising tide of racial hatred and violence, Rowan concluded his preface as follows:

I will remind readers of this book that nowhere, on any page, do I say that a ghastly race war was/is *unavoidable.* We can help to avert what the bigots call "Armageddon," but only if we stop denying that a grave threat exists and move with resolve against the most dangerous of the self-styled revolutionaries. In the final chapter I have spelled out the steps of wisdom and justice that are necessary to keep us safe and free. But in one more moment of candor, let me say that I am not optimistic that this society is up to the challenge before it. [emphasis in original][41]

There is a certain tragic and touching quality to reading these words, written by an individual who spent so much of his time during the 1950s and 1960s publicly declaring his faith that America would do the right thing concerning civil rights and race relations. It would, of course, be far too simplistic to suggest that Rowan, with his Cold War blinders now removed, was suddenly able to perceive a very different racial reality in America. Yet it is also apparent that with the fall of the Berlin Wall, a mere seven years before the publication of his last book, Rowan now felt no compunction to paint an optimistic appraisal of race relations in the United States, no necessity to mute his public criticisms, no overwhelming urge to portray the current crop of white supremacists as simply a misguided minority fighting against the tide of the majority of both the black and white public striving for racial equality. Perhaps, free from the stifling intellectual and political constraints imposed by the Cold War mentality that shackled America in the 1950s and 1960s, Rowan was finally able to see America's racial problems in a new—and not terribly optimistic—light.

Notes

1. Carl T. Rowan, *Breaking Barriers: A Memoir* (Boston: Little, Brown, 1991), 124, 370.

2. Gerald Horne, *Black and Red: W.E.B. Du Bois and the Afro-American Response to the Cold War, 1944–1963* (Albany: State University of New York Press, 1986); Martin Duberman, *Paul Robeson: A Biography* (New York: New Press, 2005); Mary L. Dudziak, "Josephine Baker, Racial Protest, and the Cold War," *Journal of American History* 81 (September 1994): 543–70.

3. Rowan, *Breaking Barriers*, chs. 7–8.

4. For studies of U.S. propaganda efforts in the Cold War, see Nicholas J. Cull, *The Cold War and the United States Information Agency: American Propaganda and Public Diplomacy, 1945–1989* (Cambridge, U.K.: Cambridge University Press, 2008); Laura A. Belmonte, *Selling the American War: U.S. Propaganda and the Cold War* (Philadelphia: University of Pennsylvania Press, 2008); Edward W. Barrett, *Truth Is Our Weapon* (New York: Funk and Wagnalls, 1953); Robert H. Haddow, *Pavilions of Plenty: Exhibiting American Culture Abroad in the 1950s* (Washington, D.C.: Smithsonian Institution Press, 1997); Walter L. Hixson, *Parting the Curtain: Propaganda, Culture, and the Cold War, 1945–1961* (New York: St. Martin's, 1997); Robert D. MacCann, *The People's Films: A Political History of U.S. Government Motion Pictures* (New York: Hastings House, 1973); and Thomas C. Sorenson, *The Word War: The Story of American Propaganda* (New York: Harper and Row, 1968).

5. Captain John D. Silvera, "Color—A Factor in U.S. Psychological Warfare: An Appraisal and Approach to the Use of the Negro as PsyWar Themes," White House Central Files, official file 142-B, box 673, Dwight D. Eisenhower Presidential Library, Abilene, KS.

6. Analysis of U.S. propaganda dealing with race and civil rights is found in Michael L. Krenn, *Black Diplomacy: African Americans and the State Department, 1945–1969* (Armonk, N.Y.: M.E. Sharpe, 1999), chs. 2, 5, 7. For the U.S. propaganda effort in Africa, see Donald Culverson, "The U.S. Information Agency in Africa," *TransAfrica Forum* (Winter 1989): 61–90.

7. See Krenn, *Black Diplomacy*, 37–39, 74–76; Horne, *Black & Red*, 280–81; Brenda Gayle Plummer, *Rising Wind: Black Americans and U.S. Foreign Affairs, 1935–1960* (Chapel Hill: University of North Carolina Press, 1996), 212. An interesting analysis of how African American jazz musicians played a role in America's propaganda campaign is found in Penny M. Von Eschen, *Satchmo Blows Up the World: Jazz Ambassadors Play the Cold War* (Cambridge, Mass.: Harvard University Press, 2004).

8. "A Report by Carl T. Rowan on Three-Month Lecture Tour in India," September 27, 1954, Papers of Carl T. Rowan, subgroup II, series 1, box 1, Africa Report folder, Archives of Oberlin College (AOC), Oberlin, OH.

9. Carl T. Rowan, *The Pitiful and the Proud* (New York: Random House, 1956), 144; Rowan, "Report on Three-Month Lecture Tour."

10. "Address by Carl T. Rowan, Deputy Assistant Secretary of State for Public Affairs at the Golden Anniversary Conclave of Omega Psi Phi Fraternity, Sheraton Park Hotel, Washington, D.C., Tuesday, August 15, 1961," August 15, 1961; "Address by Carl T. Rowan, Director, U.S. Information Agency before the National Newspaper Publishers Association Convention, Louisville, Kentucky, Thursday, June 17, 1965," Rowan Papers, subgroup III, series 2, box 1, Speeches, vol. 1 (1–45), 1960–1963 folder; vol. III (93–105), 1965, AOC.

11. Rowan, *Pitiful and the Proud*, vii, 417–18. It is interesting to note that a similar book by Saunders Redding, an African American educator, titled *An American in India* (New York: Bobbs-Merrill, 1954) reached many of the same conclusions. Like Rowan, Redding had been invited by the U.S. government to give a speaking tour in India. In his book he used the same type of metaphors, replacing Rowan's vultures with wild dogs circling around many Indian cities.

12. Rowan, *Pitiful and the Proud*, 418, 66; Rowan, "Report on Three-Month Lecture Tour."

13. Rowan, "Report on Three-Month Lecture Tour"; Carl T. Rowan, "We Can Lick the Reds in Asia," n.d., subgroup VI, series 4, subseries 2, box 1, "We Can Lick the Reds in Asia, 1954" folder, AOC.

14. Rowan, "We Can Lick the Reds."

15. Ibid.

16. Rowan, *Pitiful and the Proud*, 150.

17. This summary of the "Unfinished Business" exhibit at the 1958 world's fair is taken from Michael L. Krenn, "'Unfinished Business': Segregation and U.S. Diplomacy at the 1958 World's Fair," *Diplomatic History* 20, no. 4 (1996): 591–612; Robert W. Rydell, *World of Fairs: The Century-of-Progress Expositions* (Chicago: University of Chicago Press, 1993);

Haddow, *Pavilions of Plenty*; and Hixson, *Parting the Curtain.* Talmadge quote is found in Talmadge to Secretary of State John Foster Dulles, March 16, 1958, General Records of the Department of State, Record Group 59, file 855.191-BR/3–2658, National Archives, College Park, Maryland.

18. Krenn, *Black Diplomacy,* 123–24.

19. "Address by Carl T. Rowan, Deputy Assistant Secretary of State for Public Affairs, at General Membership Meeting of the Washington Urban League, Baldwin Hall, Howard University, Washington, D.C., Sunday, March 5, 1961, at 5:00 P.M., E.S.T.," March 4, 1961, Rowan Papers, subgroup III, series 2, box 1, Speeches, vol. I (1–45), 1960–1963 file, AOC.

20. Rowan, "Address to Omega Psi Phi"; remarks by Carl T. Rowan, "Fourth Regional Operations Conference," Lima, Peru, October 10, 1961, Papers of John F. Kennedy, President's Office Files, Departments and Agencies, box 88, State 10/61–12/61 file, John F. Kennedy Library, Boston, Massachusetts.

21. "The Incomplete Revolution," remarks by Ambassador Carl T. Rowan at a luncheon at the Pohjanhovi Hotel, Rovaniemi, Finland, June 26, 1963, Rowan Papers, subgroup III, series 2, box 1, Speeches, vol. I (1–45), 1960–1963 folder, AOC.

22. Rowan, *Breaking Barriers,* 173–74.

23. To understand the background of the Department of State and the more exclusive foreign service, particularly their biased hiring policies, see Robert D. Schulzinger, *The Making of the Diplomatic Mind: The Training, Outlook, and Style of United States Foreign Service Officers, 1908–1931* (Middletown, Conn.: Wesleyan University Press, 1975), chs. 1–3; and Martin Weil, *A Pretty Good Club: The Founding Fathers of the U.S. Foreign Service* (New York: W. W. Norton, 1978), chs. 1–3. For a more specific focus on the struggles of African Americans to find a place in the U.S. foreign policy bureaucracy, consult Jake C. Miller, *The Black Presence in Foreign Affairs* (Washington, D.C.: University Press of America, 1978), and Krenn, *Black Diplomacy,* chs. 1, 3.

24. Christian Ravndal to Mr. Peurifoy, May 23, 1949, State Department Correspondence, box 35, folder 1948–49, no. 16, Confidential Files, Papers of Harry S. Truman, Harry S. Truman Library, Independence, Missouri; "Telephone Conversation with Gov. Adams," July 17, 1953, 1:56 P.M.; "Telephone Conversation with Gov. Adams," July 17, 1953, 5:25 P.M., Papers of John Foster Dulles, Telephone Calls series, box 10, White House Telephone Conversations—May to December 31, 1953 (2) file, Eisenhower Library.

25. "Clifton R. Wharton Gets Ready for Rumania," *U.S. News & World Report* 44, no. 22 (1958): 22. For more on Wharton's career, see Michael L. Krenn, "Clifton R. Wharton, Sr.," *Notable U.S. Ambassadors since 1775: A Biographical Dictionary,* ed. Cathal J. Nolan (Westport, Conn.: Greenwood, 1997), 365–69.

26. Krenn, *Black Diplomacy,* particularly chs. 6–7; John A. Davis, "Black Americans and United States Policy toward Africa," *Journal of International Affairs* 23, no. 2 (1969): 238.

27. "Address by Carl T. Rowan, Director, U.S. Information Agency at the 1965 UCLA Foreign Journalism Awards Banquet, Los Angeles, California, Friday, May 14, 1965"; "Address by Carl T. Rowan, Director, U.S. Information Agency before the Harvard Law School Forum, Cambridge, Massachusetts, October 9, 1964," Rowan Papers, subgroup

III, series 2, box 1, Speeches, vol. III (93–105), 1965 folder; subgroup III, series 5, box 3, 1964–1965 USIA Addresses, etc. folder, AOC.

28. "The Carl Rowan Story: The Voice of America Abroad," *Sepia* (June 1964): 10; "Address by Carl T. Rowan, Director, U.S. Information Agency at the National Conference of the Urban League, Sheraton Hotel, Louisville, Kentucky, August 5, 1964"; Rowan, "Address before the Harvard Law School Forum"; Rowan, "Address at UCLA Foreign Journalism Awards," Rowan Papers, subgroup III, series 2, box 1, Speeches, vol. II (46–92), 1964 folder; subgroup III, series 5, box 3, 1964–1965 USIA Addresses, etc. folder; subgroup III, series 2, box 1, Speeches, vol. III (93–105), 1965 folder, AOC.

29. Rowan, "Address at UCLA Foreign Journalism Awards."

30. "Remarks by Carl T. Rowan, Deputy Assistant Secretary of State for Public Affairs, at the Panel Discussion of Government Press Relations, New York University, New York, New York, Friday, September 29, 1961, 8:15 P.M., E.D.T.," Rowan Papers, subgroup III, series 2, box 1, Speeches, vol. I (1–45), 1960–1963 folder, AOC; Carl T. Rowan, "We're Helping the Communists Win the Propaganda War," *Reader's Digest* 89, no. 535 (1966): 106–10.

31. Rowan to Roger Tubby, February 3, 1961, Rowan Papers, subgroup III, series 1, box 1, Personal Correspondence folder; Carl T. Rowan, draft of speech, Association of Marketing Specialists, New York City, September 27, 1962, Rowan Papers, subgroup III, series 2, box 1, Speeches, vol. I (1–45), 1962 folder, AOC.

32. Rowan, "Address at Omega Psi Phi"; "Excerpts from Remarks by Carl T. Rowan, Deputy Assistant Secretary of State for Public Affairs, at the Annual Meeting of the Chicago Urban League, Wednesday, November 15, 1961"; Rowan, draft speech to Association of Marketing Specialists, Rowan Papers, subgroup III, series 2, box 1, Speeches, vol. I (1–45), 1960–1963 folder, AOC.

33. "Commencement Address by Carl T. Rowan, Director, U.S. Information Agency, Howard University, Washington, D.C., June 5, 1964"; "Address by Carl T. Rowan, Director, U.S. Information Agency before the American Civil Liberties Union, Chicago, Illinois, October 23, 1964," Rowan Papers, subgroup III, series 5, box 3, USIA Addresses, etc. folder, AOC.

34. Rowan, "Address to Urban League," August 5, 1964, Rowan Papers, subgroup III, series 2, box 1, Speeches, vol. II (46–92), 1964 folder, AOC.

35. "Address by Carl T. Rowan, Director, U.S. Information Agency at the NAACP Annual Convention 'Youth Night,' Washington, D.C., June 24, 1964," Rowan Papers, subgroup III, series 2, box 1, Speeches, vol. II (46–92), 1964 folder, AOC.

36. Rowan to All Principal USIS Posts, 1964, Rowan Papers, subgroup III, series 5, box 4, "The March" (Civil Rights Film) folder, AOC.

37. USIA, Document 5–3: Worldwide Priority Themes, 1964, 6 April 1964, Papers of Lyndon Johnson, Special Files, 1927–1973: Administrative Histories, Administrative History of the USIA, box 2, vol. II: Document Supplement [2 of 2], Lyndon Johnson Library, Austin, TX; "Racial Issues in the US: Some Policy and Program Indications of Research," 14 March 1966, Record Group 306, Records of the USIA, Office of Research, Special Reports, 1964–1982, box 2, S-3-66 file, National Archives, Washington, D.C.

38. Rowan, "Address to Urban League," August 5, 1964, Rowan Papers, subgroup III, series 2, box 1, Speeches, vol. II (46–92), 1964 folder, AOC; Rowan to Johnson, July 21, 1964, Papers of Lyndon Johnson, National Security File Country File: Africa, box 76, Africa-Gen. Memos and Misc. [1 of 2], vol. 2 (7/64–6/65); Rowan to Johnson, June 29, 1964, Papers of Lyndon Johnson, White House Central Files, FG 296, box 314, FG 296-USIA (5/22/64–6/30/64), Johnson Library.

39. For African Americans and the Vietnam War, including the King quote, see Michael L. Krenn, *The Color of Empire: Race and American Foreign Relations* (Washington, D.C.: Potomac Books, 2006), 93–97; "Report to the Director from Lawrence H. Rogers II: USIA-Tropical Africa, April 15, 1967," Leonard Marks Papers, Box 28, Report: VOA Operations in Africa file, Johnson Library; "Reactions to U.S. Race Relations and General Opinion of the U.S.," April 12, 1968, RG 306, Office of Research, Special Reports, 1964–1982, Box 4, S-20-68 file, NA.

40. Rowan, "Address to Urban League," August 5, 1964.

41. Carl T. Rowan, *The Coming Race War in America: A Wake-Up Call* (Boston: Little, Brown, 1996), preface.

PART II

African American Participation in Foreign Affairs through Civil Society

Religious, Military, and Cultural Institutions in Foreign Policy

4

Reconstruction's Revival

The Foreign Mission Board of the National Baptist Convention and the Roots of Black Populist Diplomacy

BRANDI HUGHES

In May 1899 Reverend Emmanuel K. Love stood before a state-wide coalition of black Georgians in Atlanta's Mount Zion Baptist Church. Like many of the black women and men gathered before him, Love had been born enslaved. He had witnessed the tumultuous years of the Civil War, and when the war ended, the Reconstruction Acts for black emancipation, equal protection, and suffrage guided his path from a farm in Marion, Alabama, to Augusta Institute, a freedmen's school in Georgia. After graduating from the institute in 1877, Love became a leading representative for black Georgians. He worked as a state missionary through 1879, and in 1885 Savannah's historic First African Baptist Church elected him pastor. For many of the congregants assembled in 1899, Love's prominence surely offered a measure of emancipation's promise. But the convention members knew the years that launched Love's leadership as a time of tremendous onslaught against black Georgians in the Reconstruction state.[1]

In 1867 African American delegates participated in Georgia's constitutional convention in Atlanta. Thirty-two African American men won elections to the state legislature in 1868. By the close of the year, a counter-Reconstruction had overtaken black elected office. An alliance of white Democrats and Republicans in the statehouse unseated Georgia's black legislators. In response, African American congregations helped organize black civil and political rights associations throughout the state.[2] Their mobilization compelled an 1870 U.S. congressional order to restore African American representation to Georgia's state legislature. Yet in the process of petitioning the federal government, black Georgians had to recount the brutal and systematic acts of violence that preyed on their claims to citizenship. As black petitioners in Camilla, Georgia, testified in 1868, "The same crouching servility required of us as slaves [is] now exacted of us as free people." Although the Freedmen's Bureau neglected consistent reporting, the petitioners knew "from personal knowledge" that "several hundred" black Georgians had been murdered, and the government had held no one accountable.[3]

The black Baptists who joined Reverend Love in the spring of 1899 could add their own testaments of black lives menaced and destroyed without state redress. During his convention speech, Love acknowledged that "lynching, jim-crow cars, and other injustices" had undone the interracial alliance of Republicans envisioned in Reconstruction. Black children born in the first decades of freedom were in danger of becoming "perpetual consumers and wards" of a Southern caste, and Love assured that hope for federal or state intervention was wholly misplaced. Southern black Americans had to "launch out" boldly for their own defense and communal progress.[4] The arguments Love delivered from Mount Zion's pulpit reflected the central debates that drew black Baptists to the state convention. In the late 1860s, as African American men entered and were expelled from Georgia's statehouse, hundreds of black Baptist congregants laid the foundation for the Georgia Missionary Baptist Convention. From 1870 the faith coalition met annually to identify the needs of local black Baptist churches and to define the congregations' responsibilities to impoverished black communities in Georgia. Against the retreat of the Freedmen's Bureau, members of the convention organized farming cooperatives, built schools, and led campaigns to address the imprisonment of black children.[5] Winning souls for Christ was central to the convention's founding, but its evangelicalism required a spirited, and often divisive, confrontation with the legal and economic practices that kept free black citizens in bondage.

The convention's meeting in 1899 offers an important place to reconsider the political strategies of Southern black evangelicals living through the turn of the twentieth century. Love's exchange with black Baptist delegates in Atlanta was an integral moment in the historical process that helped black communities make their independent church polities a vital counter-public for African American claims to citizenship. In 1895 the Georgia Missionary Baptist Convention joined fellow state conventions of black Baptists throughout the South and border states in the West to form the National Baptist Convention, USA (NBC).[6] With more than three million African Americans counted as Baptists in the 1926 U.S. census, the NBC has been recognized as the largest religious body of African Americans formed through the post-emancipation era.[7] Against a lingering impression of a constrained black Baptist bourgeoisie, historians have looked to the turn of the twentieth century to explain how the grassroots mobilization of black Baptist churches negotiated racial matters of gender, class, and region with progressive insight in the political order of the post-Reconstruction U.S. nation-state.[8] We can find the conservative and subversive viewpoints that shaped that insight in the annual minutes of convention meetings.

At the Atlanta state convention in 1899, for example, black Baptist delegates debated plans for a black institution of higher learning that rivaled the vision of white trustees at Spelman Seminary and the Atlanta Baptist College (the institution later renamed Morehouse). They argued over an independent publishing house and its ability to provide their children with literature that affirmed black Christian identity. From the pulpit, ordained men offered sermons on collective responsibility, and the black women who directed many of the funding drives expanded the vision of black leadership in their reports from temperance and missionary societies. The diverse perspectives that competed and allied at the meeting represented a mutual endeavor to cultivate a black leadership class and to advance a practice of black statecraft that could defy the civic exclusions of Jim Crow. Scholarship on the deep roots of black civil rights activism in the United States offers an interpretive context in which these broad contours of black Baptist organizing seem familiar. But our understanding of freedmen's political praxis—within and beyond the U.S. state—has much to gain from contexts that unsettle the familiar narrative. When Reverend Love encouraged black Baptists to embolden their faith in 1899, he offered a list of scriptural queries: "Why didn't Almighty God send some of those learned Egyptians to emancipate Israel? Why did he send an Israelite? Why did not Jesus Christ select Gentile apostles to go to the Jews? Why did he choose Jews as his apostles?" The rhetorical questions supported Love's position on African Americans' institutional independence. He reasoned that "heaven's plan" had always been to "send members of the race to be redeemed to redeem them." And he closed his address with a striking plea: "Nothing must get in the way of our giving Africa the Gospel. Divided on whatever subjects may be, we must be united on this. Let us bury all our differences in the desire to preach Jesus to the perishing millions in Africa."[9]

With so many perishing in Georgia and with so few resources in Camilla, Appling, and Atlanta, why would Love speak of African Americans' evangelization of Africa? As the terror of white supremacy overwhelmed the post-Reconstruction South, how could Southern African Americans imagine a calling to "preach Jesus" in the African continent? In the 1880s and 1890s hundreds of Southern black emigrants left the United States with hope for a better life in Liberia. By the end of the nineteenth century, a majority had returned from West Africa with reports of sickness and poverty that unraveled the populist back-to-Africa movement. How was it possible to extract a counter-witness of black redemption from those reports? These questions unsettled the resolutions of black Baptist conventions across the turn of the twentieth century, but they were continually posed—in Georgia, across the black belt, and in many of the Northern and Western states represented in the NBC.

Love's plea for Africa joined a collective forum on black rights and international relations that black communities developed through slavery and the collapse of Reconstruction. In their Sunday services, Bible study meetings, and later conventions, black Baptists learned to relate reports on the colonization of Africa with their interpretations of the Old and New Testaments. Their readings of the scriptures offered a way to debate their diasporic affiliation with the African continent, and across the nineteenth century they tried to redirect the recurring controversy of African American emigration to West Africa to a collective vocation for African mission work. From Liberia's colonial settlement in the 1820s, black Baptists came to see the interdependence of U.S. debates on African American freedom with the international campaign to suppress the transatlantic slave trade in the colonization of Africa. Through their local missionary societies, black Baptists made the appointment of black missionaries in Liberia a means to advocate for the civic standing of black Americans. When African communities confronted black Americans with the limits of Christian theology, black Baptist missionaries were among the first African Americans who grappled with the nexus of African and African American coloniality in Anglo-American empire. After the U.S. Civil War and the end of Reconstruction, the suppression of black political representation compelled black Baptists to test their accumulated literacy in empire. When Reverend Love advised the Georgia convention to unite in African mission work, he invoked a generational discernment that the domestic contexts of U.S. Jim Crow were related to the collusion of empires that colonized Africa. To save African Americans from white supremacy, African Americans would have to advocate through (and, at times, against) the imperial policies enacted on Africans. At the turn of the twentieth century, black Baptists debated and implemented their most expansive vision of African American advocacy in the organization of mission stations in South, West, and Central Africa. Their mission work was fraught with the racial and religious bias of colonialism, and it often eluded description as anti-imperialism. But the historical practice of black Baptist missions in Africa was integral to the ways black American communities learned how to identify and relate their commonality with African communities in colonization. The mission practice was also central to the process that allowed African communities to revise the political platform of black diaspora.

Histories of African American internationalism have often undervalued the role of black Baptist organizing, but black Baptists' African missions enabled a radicalizing mode of populist diplomacy.[10] Before the Pan-African conventions and labor movements of the World War I period, black Baptists in the United States and Africa crafted a form of transnational alliance and a method of intervention orchestrated beyond the bounds of state. What follows in this chapter is a closer accounting of the ideas and practices that made African missions central to black Baptist debates on strategies for civic protection and political influence. The cross-generational perspectives that framed Reverend Love's 1899 address are traced from black Baptists' abolitionist mission in colonial Liberia across the first decades of the NBC Foreign Mission Board—an administrative body incorporated in 1895 to extend African American efforts to reclaim rights and protections in the United States with the support of mission work abroad. I examine the forum on Africa that was created by the Foreign Mission Board's *Mission Herald,* an instrumental, and largely understudied, repository of black religious and political perspectives on the parallel status of black communities living in the Jim Crow United States and colonized Africa. The insights, questions, and contradictions raised in the *Mission Herald*'s forum cultivated a populist mode of diplomacy for African and African American Christians living at the nexus of empire.

African Missions and the Origins of the African American Baptist Convention Movement

The Richmond African Baptist Missionary Society (RABMS) helped pioneer the movement for African American missions to Africa. In 1815 free and enslaved black women and men founded the society through their Bible study group at the First Baptist Church in Richmond, Virginia. Lott Carey, a self-manumitted tobacco factory worker and literate lay preacher, was a leading member of the society. When letters from black American emigrants living in Britain's colony in Sierra Leone reached Richmond, Carey helped the study group organize its support of West African colonization. Repatriation, Christianization, and freedom were themes that helped Richmond's black Baptists see a relationship between their faith and the colonization schemes that moved formerly enslaved and exiled black communities to Freetown and Sherbro Island. When the American Colonization Society (ACS) formed in 1817, the RABMS had already begun to imagine a movement of African Americans to West Africa.[11]

The ACS originated in a fraught alliance of white politicians and reformers who feared the fate of the slaveholding U.S. republic. Abolitionism exposed deep ideological fissures in the roots of republicanism, and African American rebellion against slavery—like Gabriel thwarted uprising in Richmond in 1800— reminded Americans that contending ideas of rights and freedom could have devastating consequences. The proximity of Haiti's free black state and vivid accounts of the bloody revolution from which it emerged haunted legislators, slaveholders, and church societies in the United States. When the ACS formed, it proposed plans for a colony of free and emancipated African Americans in West Africa to channel anxiety about black revolution and the nature of U.S. dependence on enslaved labor. A number of African American leaders discerned that the ACS's affiliation with slaveholders made its proposed colony a project of black removal that secured the U.S. slave-based economy. Resettling free and emancipated African Americans along the western coast of Africa worked to destabilize the foundation of a collective movement for black freedom and emancipation in the United States.

But members of the RABMS made a mission of the removal scheme. By 1818, the year the ACS sent its first agents to survey West African land for colonization, the RABMS had raised nearly seven hundred dollars to support missionary work in West Africa.[12] The society petitioned the Triennial Convention—the predominantly white American Baptist assembly for foreign missions—to appoint Lott Carey as a missionary to the settlement that would become Liberia. Both Carey and Colin Teague, a black preacher affiliated with the RABMS, received foreign missionary appointments to West Africa. They were among the first of more than one hundred African Americans who worked as foreign missionaries during the nineteenth century.[13] Carey and Teague established a church charter with seven black Baptist emigrants who joined them aboard the Nautilus, which departed for West Africa on January 23, 1821. The small church was among the second company of African American emigrants to arrive in the fledgling ACS settlement at the southern edge of Sierra Leone. In 1822 the church established the first black Baptist congregation in the coastal settlement renamed Liberia.

The missionary project envisioned through the RABMS helped found Liberia's Providence Baptist Church in Monrovia, and it supported a day school for the sons of Africans and African American emigrants. As the pastor of Providence Baptist Church and the director of the day school, Carey became a pivotal mediator in the colonial administration of Liberia.[14] In 1826 he was appointed the first African American vice agent in the colony, but he died two years later. His death—in a fight to prevent African communities from entering an African American emigrant storehouse—was indicative of the religious and interethnic conflicts aggravated by efforts to enforce a Christian mission in a land already ordered in diverse systems of faith and governance. Sixteen ethnic communities lived in the region taken to create the colony of Liberia.[15]

The contentious relationships of ACS officials, African American emigrants, and indigenous communities persisted and often intensified as "recaptured" Africans—enslaved men, women, and children removed from illegal slave ships—were transported to Liberia by the U.S. Navy. A number of the merchant and military ships that carried emigrants and supplies to Liberia returned to the United States with letters and reports about the status of life and Christian ministry in the colony. U.S. abolitionists circulated news of rampant sickness and death in Liberia to discredit West African emigration as a movement for black freedom. Opponents of the ACS used reports of languishing agriculture; the exploitation of Liberian women and children; and the prominence of "gin, Mohammedism, and fetishism" to challenge claims of Liberia's Christian governance.[16]

Yet there were a number of African American congregations who received the news from Liberia through different frames of interpretation. Many of the black Baptist societies who heard of Lott Carey's leadership in the Liberian colony perceived a significant path to black emancipation. The international affiliations that enabled the RABMS's early vision to take form in Monrovia's Providence Baptist Church came to represent a network of resources and ideas that could transform the status of African American lives in the United States and redefine the relationship of African Americans to Africa. In 1847 Providence Baptist Church was the site of the constitutional convention that authorized the ruling elite of Liberian emigrants to declare the independence of the Republic of Liberia. The black state that was formed through Providence Baptist Church encouraged African American Baptists to imagine a broad sphere of political influence that could be developed from foreign missions to Africa. While West African emigration and colonization remained divisive subjects in U.S. abolitionism, black Baptist congregations continued to devise institutional strategies for freedom through support of foreign missions in Africa. Providence Baptist Church and its affiliated school offered comparative models for independent black churches and schools in the United States, and the history of their founding helped African Americans consider the ways that coordinated church and school building in the United States and Africa could critically advance black literacy and world regard for the disciplining capacity of Afro-Christianity. The legacy of Lott Carey also raised a standard for the political role an African

American foreign missionary could achieve. Across the nineteenth century, Carey's memorialization as a pastor, colonial official, and diplomatic mediator associated foreign missionary service with a range of political power that was routinely denied to free black men living in the antebellum United States.

This way of thinking about the role of foreign missionaries and the promise of foreign mission work in Africa became instrumental to the regional and national organization of African American Baptists in the United States. Unlike the black Philadelphian Methodists who incorporated the African Methodist Episcopal (AME) Church in 1816, African American Baptists were unable to rely on a denominational structure to guide the union of black Baptist churches. The local congregation—rather than the order of bishops, dioceses, and conferences—is the central polity in Baptist tradition, and the affiliation of Baptist congregations is voluntary. In the early nineteenth century it was difficult to direct the voluntary union of black Baptists toward a national convention or association. There was neither a centrally recognized leader nor a concentrated population of free African American Baptists to support the organization of a racially autonomous black Baptist denomination in the antebellum period. Yet the idea of African missions helped draw black Baptist churches together in regional conventions.

The Providence Baptist Association of Negro Churches of the West formed in 1836, and it offered a model for the American Baptist Mission Convention (ABMC) established at New York's Abyssinian Baptist Church in 1840 and the Western Colored Baptist Convention (WCBC) founded in St. Louis in 1853. These early black Baptist associations generally joined the African American national convention movement in opposition to the ACS and the emigrant-colonization plans that directed Liberian development. But the black Baptist associations did combine their endeavors to strengthen the influence of independent African American Baptist churches with support of foreign missionary service in West Africa and the Caribbean. In 1858 the ABMC appointed Rev. William John Barnett as a missionary representative to Sierra Leone. During the U.S. Civil War the WCBC supported Rev. William P. Newman as a foreign missionary to Jamaica and Haiti.

In the years that followed the Civil War, African American Baptists measured initiatives to expand their independent conventions against resources they could access through affiliation with the predominantly white American Baptist Home Mission Society (ABHMS). In 1865 the ABHMS established its Freedmen's Fund, and the mission society helped lead the movement for freedmen's education by establishing North Carolina's Raleigh Institute (later Shaw University) and Wayland Seminary in Washington, D.C. Black Baptist leaders who were prominent in the earlier independent convention movement warned fellow African American Baptists that overreliance on the ABHMS, like dependence on the

Republican Party, could undermine the fulfillment of black emancipation. In his 1866 presidential address before African Americans' Northwestern and Southern Baptist Convention, Reverend Newman, the former foreign missionary, advised: "The professed friends of God and man, for the most part, are unwilling to accept the truth of human brotherhood, and the equality of men's rights. . . . The Republican party has never done any more for us than it was compelled to do, to save its life. God emancipated us by the selfishness of our oppressors, and to him be the glory."[17]

Newman's pointed critique of the racial politics that governed the post-emancipation United States inspired support for the Consolidated American Baptist Missionary Convention (CABMC), which formed in Nashville in 1867. Although short-lived, the CABMC was the first nationally oriented black Baptist association of the postbellum era. It also helped shift the locus of the African American Baptist convention movement to the South. When the CABMC splintered in 1879, a fractured conception of African American Baptists' local, regional, and national affiliation was exposed. But what remained was a formative vision of black diaspora that had advanced from the early history of the RABMS. This diasporic imagining helped revive a unifying objective for African American Baptists' national alliance.

In November 1880 more than one hundred African American delegates gathered at the First Baptist Church of Montgomery, Alabama, to found the Baptist Foreign Mission Convention (BFMC) of the United States. The Montgomery gathering emerged from the call and response of African American emigrant and missionary ventures across the shores of the Atlantic. With the demise of U.S. Reconstruction, hundreds of Southern African American laborers, church leaders, and politicians renewed their hope for black emancipation in plans for Liberian emigration. Yet, through the late 1870s and 1880s, African American dreams of land ownership, protection from racial terror, and economic prosperity in West Africa confronted reports of hunger, poverty, disease, and violence across the southern and western regions of the African continent. The fragile stability of Liberia and the rampant expanse of Europe's colonization of Africa stemmed the tide of populist back-to-Africa movements at the close of the nineteenth century. For a pivotal time, however, the collapse of U.S. Reconstruction realigned a vision of African American political autonomy with foreign mission work in Africa. As Southern African Americans pondered the possibility of a better life in Liberia, a public forum on Africa expanded. The testimonies of African American missionaries who served in Africa were integral to this forum and shaped the ways African Americans came to believe that building churches and mission schools in Africa could strengthen the fight for African American rights and protections in the post-Reconstruction United States.

The black Baptist delegates who gathered in Montgomery in 1880 arrived at their convention through the organizing efforts of William W. Colley, a black Virginian who worked as a missionary in Nigeria. In 1875 the predominantly white Southern Baptist Convention (SBC) commissioned Colley to serve as an assistant at its Yoruba mission in southwestern Nigeria. Working as an intermediary between British, white American, and Yoruba leadership, Colley was forced to ponder the intersecting spheres of racism that colonized African and African American lives. When Colley returned to the United States, his account of the Yoruba mission compelled black Virginia Baptists affiliated with the RABMS to recruit him as a promoter of foreign missions in the U.S. South. Colley's charge was to present evidence that the color line in Baptist mission stations abroad was integrally related to African American struggles to secure racial and denominational autonomy at home. For nearly a year, Colley toured Southern black Baptist churches and state conventions to explain why African American Baptists should unite nationally. A national body of African American Baptists, Colley argued, would allow African Americans to direct foreign work independently and to advance the campaign for black civil rights through foreign mission stations. Colley's lecture circuit helped persuade black Baptist state conventions to join in the formation of the BFMC in 1880.[18]

In its constitution the BFMC affirmed African American Baptists' commission to carry the gospel into all the world, but the workings of race and empire fixed the convention's focus on the continent of Africa. For a brief time the BFMC co-sponsored Rev. James O. Hayes as a missionary to Liberia, and in 1883—just a year before the Berlin Conference on Africa—the convention commissioned Colley and his wife, along with Harriette and Rev. Joseph Presley, to establish the Bendoo Mission near Grand Cape Mount. The board named Rev. John J. Coles and Rev. Henderson McKinney preparatory missionaries and provided for their training at Liberia College before they directed the Jundoo and Mafa missions near the Bendoo station. In 1886 the BFMC commissioned four additional missionaries—Rev. J. J. Diggs and his wife, and Mattie Topp and her husband, Rev. E. B. Topp—to support the Baptist missions in northwestern Liberia.[19] Lucy Henry Coles, the wife of Rev. John Coles, joined the mission work in 1887. By 1892 Lucy Coles and her husband were the only remaining BFMC missionaries in Grand Cape Mount, and the BFMC had learned a number of difficult lessons about the ambition of its foreign mission work. The endeavor to demonstrate African Americans' civic capacity through African missionary service exacted the physical toll of adapting to a tropical environment. The work required more expansive lines of communication between foreign missionaries in Africa and black Baptist churches that raised missionary offerings in the United States. And as BFMC missionaries struggled in relations with Liberia's Vai communities, the convention learned that Africans and African Americans had to develop new ways to see the possibility of alliance.

While the BFMC grappled with a challenging first decade, new initiatives developed to organize African American Baptists nationally. In 1886 black Baptist delegates met in St. Louis to establish the American National Baptist Convention (ANBC). In 1893 another delegation formed the Baptist Educational Convention in Washington, D.C. Although distinct in leadership, the conventions shared a mutual concern for the domestic focus of African American activism and sought strategic cooperation with the ABHMS to improve African American schools and black ministerial leadership. In 1894 the conventions were compelled to rethink their strategy. The majority white ABHMS and the SBC organized a conference to discuss freedmen's education, but African Americans were excluded from the meeting. The insult compounded a growing tally of racialized offenses, and African American Baptists renewed their efforts to establish an independent national convention.

In September 1895 more than five hundred African American Baptist delegates gathered in Atlanta, Georgia, to restore faith and to deliberate the nature of their communion. This Atlanta gathering is remembered for creating the National Baptist Convention (NBC). But in the fall of 1895, the will and collective vision to form the organization was uncertain. Black Baptist delegates arrived in Atlanta with the varied interests of their state conventions and the multiple objectives of the BFMC, the ANBC, and the Baptist Educational Convention. No single initiative guided their effort to define a consensus across congregational, state, and regional associations. Yet, by the close of the first day's meeting, missionary work in Africa reemerged as the "nucleus" around which a national polity of African American Baptists was defined.[20]

During the convention's first evening session in Atlanta's Friendship Baptist Church, Rev. Elias Camp Morris, the president of the BFMC, offered remarks on African American missions in Africa. After reviewing the challenges of the BFMC's early work in Liberia, he recalled the restoration promised in the Old Testament story of Job, and he read aloud a letter sent from Rev. R. A. Jackson, a BFMC missionary working in Cape Town, South Africa. Jackson, a black minister from Mississippi, was among the first missionaries affiliated with the BFMC to direct a mission station within the jurisdiction of a British colony. In 1894 Jackson and his wife, Emma, were among the first African American Baptists in South Africa. The religious Ethiopian movement that emerged from South Africa's independent African churches influenced the Jacksons' mission work in Cape Town, and the letters Reverend Jackson sent to the BFMC introduced African American Baptists' most pronounced indictment of European empire. The letter Reverend Morris read to the Atlanta meeting began: "The native policy of the colony and imperial government is more destructive than slavery. The laws are made to demoralize, degrade, degenerate, expel and annihilate the natives." Jackson's letter explained how the "subtle cunning fraud" of British colonial administrators enlisted "white missionaries" whose "so-called Christian" works "daily made the Dark Continent Darker." The letter ended with an appeal to the African American Baptists who were convened in Atlanta: "If you, brethren of the [convention], could hear the native South African praying in his own tongue, that God may open your hearts to help them, I am sure you would do more for them."[21]

This missive from Cape Town prompted African American Baptists to contemplate the symmetry of "laws made to demoralize, degrade and expel" black life in the Jim Crow United States and in British-occupied South Africa. The letter also provided vantage points from which African Americans could imagine how a mission to "do more for" colonized Africans could also be a way to do more to save themselves. Across the spectrum of perspectives debated in Atlanta, Jackson's appeal surely registered unevenly, but after six days of prayers, sermons, and committee deliberations, the Atlanta assembly voted unanimously to form the racially autonomous National Baptist Convention of the United States of America. The NBC incorporated an Education Board, a Home Mission Board and publishing committee, and a Foreign Mission Board that continued the work of the BFMC. The Atlanta delegates elected Reverend Morris, presiding director of the BFMC, as the first president of the National Baptist Convention.

Black Baptists formed the NBC with a political vision that aspired for a middle ground between Booker T. Washington's platform for interracial cooperation in the United States and the black nationalist call for West African emigration that was issued by AME bishop Henry McNeal Turner. Both Washington and Turner addressed the black Baptist convention in Atlanta, and across the convention's first decades the NBC's attempts to balance Washington and Turner's activist strategies were a source of persistent dissent among convention members. Yet the political balance the NBC strived to reach also provided African American Baptists a reason to regularly engage, debate, and adapt the work of the Foreign Mission Board incorporated in the NBC. Five years before the inaugural Pan-African Congress in London, and nearly two decades before Marcus Garvey began his lecture tour in the United States, the Foreign Mission Board's effort to align African American Baptists' denominational stand in the United States with the "evangelization of Africa, the West Indies, and Latin America" cultivated a global vision of racial, religious, and political kinship that helped produce diplomatic affiliations in the African diaspora.[22]

Testimony and Diplomatic Sensibility in the
Foreign Mission Board's *Mission Herald*

Money, trust, and geography were central to the work of the NBC Foreign Mission Board (FMB), and they were also the board's recurrent source of discord and frustration. When African American Baptists incorporated the FMB in 1895, the headquarters of the former BFMC were relocated from Richmond to Louisville, Kentucky. The move unsettled the regional legacy of the early RABMS, and in 1899 Virginia Baptists formed a separate organization for foreign missions that was named the Lott Carey Foreign Mission Convention. The institutional division complicated the already difficult endeavor of persuading black Baptist churches to raise Sunday offerings in support of foreign mission work. In 1896 Rev. Lewis G. Jordan, the corresponding secretary of the FMB, reported that only twenty-five dollars had been raised for foreign missions in the year following the Atlanta convention. The very limited resources of so many black American Baptists troubled Jordan's campaign for greater support of foreign missions. His leadership was also compromised by rumors that the FMB was stealing church offerings and leaving its foreign missionaries to starve in the field.[23]

The distance between African American Baptists in the United States and FMB mission stations abroad further challenged the coherence of the board. Through its first decades the FMB sponsored missionaries in Guyana and Cuba, but its primary work established churches, missionary schools, and farms in Liberia, South Africa, and Nyasaland (Malawi). Persuading African Americans to give the little they had to Africa was an uneasy task. As Reverend Jordan acknowledged, even the most educated NBC members "had been taught that all Africa was one great wilderness with a desert, where man ate man."[24] In order to sustain its foreign mission work, the FMB had to span the ideological and geographic gulf that stood between African Americans' self-conception and their projected image of Africans and the African continent. The FMB had to initiate a process of reteaching African Americans how to see Africa, how to care for the lives—as well as the souls—of potential African converts, and how to trust that an investment in the religious and political well-being of Africa was also an investment in the well-being of African Americans. The process became the central work of the FMB's *Afro-American Mission Herald,* a newspaper whose ambition arguably spanned the work of the AME *Christian Recorder* and the UNIA's *Negro World.*

The FMB first circulated the monthly newspaper in 1896, with hopes that the publication would "act as a stimulus" for foreign missionary donations. The *Mission Herald* was distributed and read in congregations affiliated with the NBC, and the paper became an essential public forum for black internationalism. This forum was a study in contradictions. The FMB issued the *Mission Herald* to demonstrate its racial independence from predominantly white publishing boards, but its editorials often depended on the racial logic of white dominance. Anglo-American values associated with Christian civilization formed the FMB's standard of evaluation, and across the pages of the *Mission Herald* various aspects of black identity and culture—at home and abroad—were marked as matters that needed reform from deviance and lack of discipline. The *Mission Herald* regularly denounced the Jim Crow system of exploitation, mob violence, and segregation, but its columns were often reluctant to denounce the similar system of European colonial administration in Africa. The FMB's faith that Africa could be redeemed—and in return, redeem the racial and civic identity of African Americans—drew inspiration from a colonizing imaginary. Although the *Mission Herald* strived to bring African communities closer to African Americans' empathetic view, the paper framed the FMB's terms of Christian fellowship in ways that routinely positioned Africans and African beliefs in a netherworld of "heathen thralldom."

And yet the stories that accumulated across the *Mission Herald*'s columns also enabled an exchange of ideas and testimonies that reorganized the paper's conflicting framework. From its earliest issues, the *Mission Herald* published the letters and reports missionaries sent from FMB missions in the Caribbean and Africa. Like the letter Reverend Jackson sent from Cape Town in 1895, the missionaries' correspondence urged NBC members to develop a diplomatic care to "do more for" colonized black communities and to appreciate broader claims of racial and religious kinship. The published letters from Africa varied in tone, subject, and intent, but they offered collective instruction in how to see African and African Americans' related subjectivity. As the *Mission Herald*'s forum offered a platform to contemplate foreign missions as a coordinated response to "Jim Crow colonialism,"[25] the published missionary correspondence offered African Americans three essential lessons: (1) sustaining partnerships with African Christian intermediaries could better inform African American analysis of the intersections of race and empire; (2) attention to compulsory labor and methods of disfranchisement could bridge the presumed divide between African and African American experience; and (3) concern for the status of black women could cultivate a deeper commitment to Pan-African alliance.

These three themes were key aspects of the FMB's reporting from its Providence Industrial Mission in Nyasaland. In 1900 the FMB helped establish the Ajawa Providence Industrial Mission (PIM) in the Chiradzulu district of present-day Malawi. The PIM's directing missionary, Rev. John Chilembwe, was a Yao man who was born and baptized in the region. In 1897 Chilembwe arrived in the United States as an assistant of Rev. Joseph Booth, an English missionary who directed the Zambezi Industrial Mission in Nyasaland. Chilembwe and Booth came to the United States in search of American Baptists who would support the development of an African Christian Union in Central Africa. The FMB decided to sponsor Chilembwe's missionary training, and black Baptist state conventions in Pennsylvania and Virginia provided for his education at the Lynchburg Theological Seminary, a freedmen's school in central Virginia. In 1899 Chilembwe was ordained and the FMB appointed him its supervising missionary in Chiradzulu.[26]

Of the several African ministers the FMB commissioned as missionaries in Africa, Chilembwe was the most acclaimed. The *Mission Herald* faithfully recounted the development of the PIM from its first church meetings to its work with Ngoni, Lomwe, and Yao families who cultivated coffee plants and cotton at the mission. To establish the PIM, the NBC provided Chilembwe power of attorney to purchase ninety-three acres of land from British colonial officials. In 1900 the FMB commissioned Rev. Landon Cheek, a black Baptist minister from Mississippi, to help Chilembwe improve the land with agricultural training and lessons in brick masonry for African men at the mission. When Reverend Cheek departed for Nyasaland in 1901, the newly established Woman's Convention of the NBC had begun a campaign for the appointment of an African American woman missionary at the PIM. State conventions of black Baptist women had been the most consistent allies of the FMB.[27] When the national Woman's Convention (WC) formed as the largest organization of African American women in the United States, WC president Sarah Willie Layten and Nannie Helen Burroughs, the secretary and bookkeeper of the FMB, helped direct considerable resources to foreign mission work. With their support, Emma B. Delaney, a graduate of Spelman Seminary, received an FMB missionary appointment to Nyasaland. Delaney was the first unmarried woman commissioned by the FMB, and she arrived at the PIM in 1902 to begin the FMB's first directed mission to African women and children.

Through the missionaries' published letters and reports in the *Mission Herald*, the PIM provided African American Baptists a model of Pan-African alliance. Chilembwe, Cheek, and Delaney supported a community built across African ethnicity and African American nationality. Bible study and African conversion to Christianity directed the vision of community building, but as the mission's correspondence explained, daily activities at the PIM had to address the material needs and political vulnerability of African communities living in the region. The PIM began a decade after the British Foreign Office declared the central African region of the "Makololo, Yao, and Machinga countries" a protected territory of Great Britain. The mission station witnessed the often devastating consequences of the British Protectorate's campaign against Portuguese colonial officials and Arab slave traders vying for regional control. Hundreds of displaced African families sought refuge at the PIM, and the FMB's appointed missionaries had to forge an interethnic cooperative that tended to African hunger and sickness, protected women and children from kidnapping and assault, and provided men labor to alleviate the colonial hut tax and military conscription.

The *Mission Herald* encouraged African American Baptists to imagine their place in the PIM's diasporic community. By 1907 both Cheek and Delaney had returned to the United States, but the letters and photographs Chilembwe continued to send the FMB helped sustain African Americans' connection to the mission. Chilembwe's published letters detailed how mission offerings raised in African American churches supported six hundred African children in the mission's affiliated schools and three hundred African Christians who worshipped at the PIM's chapel.[28] On the eve of World War I, the *Mission Herald*'s featured reports from Chilembwe and Ida, his wife, strengthened the FMB's effort to persuade African American Baptists that their missionary donations were critical acts of intervention in a shifting world order. While John Chilembwe's letters drew attention to the famine exacerbated by colonial administration, Ida Chilembwe issued an appeal for NBC members to devote their prayer and resources to the impoverished state of African women and girls. In 1913, shortly after Ida Chilembwe's letters appeared in the *Mission Herald,* the FMB designed lesson plans that paired Mrs. Chilembwe's appeal with maps of the African continent and a lecture outline titled "Is the Cause of Missions Worthwhile?"[29] Chilembwe's intimate view of the plight of Central African mothers and children resonated with African American Baptists' concern for their own domestic sphere. The FMB hoped the ideological link would convince NBC members of the tremendous cause of African missions.

In 1915, however, the public forum sustained through *Mission Herald* reports on the PIM nearly imploded. During the last week of January, Reverend Chilembwe directed an attack against white planters' estates that bordered the PIM. Within a few weeks Chilembwe was killed and the black Baptist mission station was razed. When news of the uprising reached the United States, the FMB took great effort to denounce Chilembwe's leadership and to withdraw the board's affiliation with the mission in Chiradzulu. The May 1915 *Mission Herald* announced Chilembwe's death with the headline "Rev. John Chilembwe Is No More among the Living—In the Midst of Life We Are in Death." The article that followed named Chilembwe a "religious maniac" and a "Nat Turner" whose desperate response to "wrongs, real or imagined," led him to a wicked end. The *Herald* column asserted that the only "warfare" the FMB engaged in was spiritual, and the newspaper helped the board craft a strategic narrative of pacifism that protected its missionary interests in other regions of Africa and the Caribbean.[30] In effect, the FMB's remarks on Chilembwe's armed struggle and subsequent death established the viable limits of black American Baptists' intervention in African foreign affairs. They also enabled African Americans' retreat from the vexing contexts that incited Chilembwe to attack. What the *Mission Herald*'s obituary withheld from view was Chilembwe's understanding of the imperial consolidation that conscripted African labor for world war defense and consumed African lives for colonial profit. Chilembwe plotted an armed struggle against the planter class and the colonial state, because he perceived the "warfare" they had already waged on colonized African communities.

Although Chilembwe's perceptions of power were too incendiary for the FMB's cause, his underlying analysis of empire and caste reached African American Baptists in a modified form. In May 1913 the front page of the *Mission Herald* featured an editorial on "The Color Line in South Africa." A. W. Baker, an African lawyer and founding director of the South African Compounds and Interior Mission, provided the article for the FMB's publication. He hoped African American congregations would use his testimony to better understand the similarities of black status in the recently united South Africa and in the segregated United States. "As in the United States with the Negro," Baker explained, "so also with us in South Africa." In Baker's worldview the future existence of black populations was the "vital question" before both unions.[31]

Baker's editorial turned to recent history to frame an outlook on the potential future of black life in South Africa. He reviewed the native policies that regulated the labor and settlement of African communities in the Transvaal, the Orange State, Natal, and the Cape Colony. He explained that the Cape Colony had once led the region in the resources and opportunities it offered select members of the native community. Unlike Natal, which was known to confine Zulu communities to "a state of menial servitude," Cape Colony had allowed black men of "certain educational status" to acquire the franchise. As Baker recalled, the modest concessions in Cape Colony had drawn from an alliance with missionary schools and churches, but the policies developed through the alliance were among the first casualties of the South African Act of Union. Since 1909 the unification of South Africa's four colonial states had virtually nullified black men's access to political representation. Baker's article paused to note: "Rev. [Walter B.] Rabusana, a native, [was] lately returned to represent one of the districts." Yet Rabusana's exceptional status in the provincial assembly underscored how deeply the process of South African unification had overwhelmed the Cape Colony's tentative vision of black political integration. Recent native policies required "millions of [African] people to pay hundreds of thousands of pounds in direct taxation" and considerably more in "indirect contributions" to South

Africa's railways and customs. In return, native Africans were given "not even the semblance of a shadow of representation or voice in the laws by which they were governed." As Baker told his African American audience, the union of South Africa had arrived at a "state of things which [was] a disgraceful scandal to a so-called Christian Government of a professedly liberty-loving nation."[32]

The final remarks of Baker's essay looked from the recent past to troubling events unfolding before the South African parliament. A "Squatter's Bill" was awaiting ratification by the union government. The bill proposed a system of classification that identified African families as servants or squatters. According to the bill, servants lived and worked on owner-occupied land and paid the required taxes. Squatters lived on land that the government claimed for the Crown, or they settled, without mandated permits, on land privately owned by a non-African landholder. The bill and its likely passage worried Baker. He confided in his editorial, "If this is not perilously like compulsory labor and a mild form of slavery, I do not know what is." The "illusory privilege" of African servant status thinly veiled a scheme to supply black labor to Boer farmers. And the category of squatters justified the process of removing, dividing, and resettling black families away from their homelands.

Baker's editorial closed with a parting admission that it hardly seemed possible that legislation of this kind could be proposed. But he encouraged his readers to take account of the strength of "color prejudice" that "enslaved party politicians" and threatened the future sanctity of countless of black homes. Notably, Baker's call for more "pressure brought to bear" on a Christian "sense of justice" appeared just above the *Mission Herald*'s column on the sin of neglecting foreign missions.

As African American Baptists prepared to celebrate the fiftieth anniversary of the Emancipation Proclamation in the United States, Baker's remarks offered the FMB's forum critical themes for comparative reflection. His description of African possibilities opened, briefly, in Cape Colony and foreclosed, rapidly, in South African unification surely reminded African American Baptists of the promise of Reconstruction and the failed civic integration they had experienced in the United States. The account of South African families evicted from their land and subjected to compulsory labor on Boer farms recalled the systematic exploitation that overshadowed African Americans in the sharecropping economy of the rural American South and abetted the racialized wage caste encountered in African Americans' urban migration. Moreover, Baker's concern for the solitary position occupied by Reverend Rabusana offered a reminder of the political reasons why foreign mission work had become an important project for African Americans. As African American access to political office and the franchise receded, foreign mission work provided an alternative sphere of political representation and influence. How that sphere should adapt its evangelical response to the testimonies offered by Reverend Chilembwe and Reverend Baker remained an unresolved question. Missionary correspondence affirmed the importance of black-directed mission stations in colonial Africa, but it also highlighted symmetries in U.S. racism and African colonization that the FMB struggled to engage. If the administration of colonies in Africa looked like Jim Crow administration in the United States, how should African American Baptists realign their missionary work in Africa as a direct confrontation with empire? The political consequences of World War I compelled a closer view of the question.

Mapping Ways Forward

A short time after Germany's surrender in World War I, the African maps used in the Foreign Mission Board's education programs took on new significance. A carefully scaled map of the African continent was the central feature of the January 1919 edition of the *Mission Herald*. Reprinted from the *Philadelphia Evening Bulletin*, the map was filled with dots, slanted lines, blank spaces, and black shapes. An accompanying legend explained how the varying shades corresponded with colonial territories claimed by Britain, Italy, Belgium, France, Portugal, and Spain. The blank, or white, regions represented the independence of Liberia and Abyssinia. The black zones represented the protectorates in German East and Southwest Africa and Germany's West African colonies in Togo and Cameroon. As a small column at the left of the map indicated, these were colonies that Germany would likely lose to Great Britain at the close of the Paris Peace Conference.

In a number of ways this map marked a significant turn in the exchange of ideas administered through the FMB. Since the early nineteenth century, the work of promoting black Baptist missions to Africa had depended on a popular lore that colored the entire African continent black. The colonizing insistence that African people worshipped devils, that they were unprepared for free labor economy, that they lacked the discipline for self-rule, and that they were prone to the savagery of cannibalism had produced and maintained the mythology of the "Dark Continent." In its first decades the FMB relied on this mythology to explain the significance of its work. The board had often incorporated African maps in denominational literature that acquainted NBC members with the convention's African mission stations and appointed missionaries. These maps usually appeared as an outline of Africa's external borders, with small rays of light and missionaries' profiles pictured against a black background. The maps intended to persuade black Baptist churches that their missionary offerings were a tremendous investment in bringing the gospel light to the darkness of heathen Africa. The *Mission Herald* map of 1919, however, represented a shift in the kind of narrative that the FMB circulated. As the map of Africa turned from undifferentiated blackness to varying shades of gray—and as the interior boundaries of Europe's colonial claims replaced the shining lights of NBC mission stations—the FMB helped train African American focus on the political dimensions of a shifting world order.

The map the FMB published in 1919 circulated in a time when the relationship between the United States' domestic policies and the peace plans concerning Europe's colonies was a matter of deep contention. The U.S. senatorial opposition that refused to ratify the Treaty of Versailles and blocked American participation in the League of Nations presented a view of U.S. political order that was bounded and contained. The presentation of the FMB map suggested otherwise. When readers found the map on the front page of the *Mission Herald,* they also encountered an unsettling account of the segregated order in Washington, D.C. The left column of the January 1919 *Mission Herald* reported: "Colored Women Clerks Served Food by Restaurant for Employees in U.S. Government Building—Told This Is 'Dual Government' and Colored Really Separate—On to Versailles." The article that followed described the experience of a young black woman who clerked in a governmental office and had regularly taken her lunch in a cafeteria for department staff. One day she was unexpectedly refused service in the dining room. When she questioned why, the chief clerk of her department told her that the United States was a "dual government." As the clerk reasoned, "colored people," who had "separated themselves into churches and schools of their own," should understand segregated service in the restaurant. The editor of the *Mission Herald* offered a pointed rejoinder to the chief clerk's explanation. The column declared it shameful that "here at the Nation's capital, in a government building of a nation, proclaiming that it is making the world safe for democracy . . . the people denied service represent the truest type of Americans doing their 'big,' not only their 'bit' in the recent war, [yet] are forced the inconvenience of no service in the lunch room unless accepted from the kitchen window." As *Mission Herald* readers pondered the recounted experience, the final remarks of the column offered another rejoinder: "Go to Africa? Yes, my Lord commands, and I am afraid not to go."

The critique issued from this edition of the *Mission Herald* was not especially heavy-handed. There was no additional commentary to connect the rebuke of D.C.'s segregated dining with the depiction of colonial territories in Africa or to explain why increased African American missions to Africa related to the hopeful outcome of the peace convention in Versailles. Yet as the layout of the paper's front page asked its readers to look upon the map of colonized Africa and to witness a black woman's experience of segregation in the U.S. capital, the editors enabled an important perspective on the simultaneous ordering of race and power across the Atlantic world. The relational proximity of the African map and the column commenting on U.S. segregation underscored the broader relationship between the colored lines tracking the realignment of empires in Africa and the color lines enforcing the rule of white supremacy in the United States. The relationships outlined in the paper's editorial design encouraged a worldview that challenged an isolationist perception of the United States' domestic policies. The paper also asserted, once again, that African American support of missions in Africa was a pivotal response to the international matrix that segregated and exploited black labor.

The FMB's use of the colonial African map extended the process of cultivating a diplomatic sensibility among black American Baptists. Yet in early 1919 the function of the map remained constrained by the close affiliation of evangelicalism and the political belief that tools and methods of racial uplift could be extracted from Africa's colonial administration. The same *Mission Herald* edition that paired the African map with an indictment of the color line in D.C. published a front-page report from Rev. Donald Fraser, a Scottish missionary in Nyasaland. Titled "The Changes in Central Africa," the report took up the full length of the right-hand column that bordered the map of colonial territories in Africa. Fraser's review of recent history in the British Protectorate in Nyasaland surely brought to mind the testimonies that John Chilembwe had provided years before. But the article overshadowed Chilembwe's critical account of colonial rule with a glowing tribute to economic and religious progress. Fraser offered a captivating tale of the transformation of Central African lifeways. As he recounted, African wives and slaves were no longer "massacred" to accompany a departed chief's soul to the afterlife. Villagers who lacked "two coppers to rub against one another" forty years ago could now pay sixty thousand francs in "hut taxation." Fraser assured his readers that the promise of future railways and plantations in the region could not eclipse the present glory of black Christian congregations gathered in the foothills and valleys of Nyasaland. While praising British officials for bringing prosperity to a "once lawless land," Fraser's account informed NBC members that foreign missions in Nyasaland were doing the work of the Christian kingdom. The maiming, murders, sexual assaults, and deep impoverishment that Fraser repressed and hid from view allowed the FMB to use his report as another endorsement of mission work in Africa. It also enabled the narrative framing of the *Mission Herald* to imply that the methods and outcome of social reform in Nyasaland were a reason to be hopeful for the transitions of power that were re-shading the map of Africa and paving the path to Versailles.

The hopeful implication blunted the analysis the FMB drew from the political map of Africa. In the narrative line extending from the column on D.C. segregation to the African map, African American readers were invited, again, to ponder how a racial caste governed in domestic U.S. policy paralleled the position of African colonies claimed by Europe. Many questions could be derived from the pairing of the left column and the map: if the color lines in the U.S. capital had some resemblance to the shadings of African colonization, in what ways did African American citizenship resemble colonized African subjectivity? If "dual governance" and racial segregation were shameful in the United States, how should they be named in the administration of colonies in Africa? How did U.S. democracy relate to European imperialism? If African Americans noticed the symmetries of racial exploitation in the United States and in colonial Africa, how should they mobilize against the color line? How should African American kinship with African communities be defined? And who should assume leadership of enacting the definition? Each of these questions had been raised by the FMB's efforts to sustain mission stations in Africa. From the 1880s through the first decades of the twentieth century, the questions recurred in the personal letters and mission reports sent from South Africa, Liberia, and Nyasaland.

In the public forum organized by the FMB, the most frequently recorded responses to these questions aligned with two contending points of view. A number of black Baptist ministers claimed that the urgency of African American struggles against U.S. peonage and lynching demanded a more localized frame of concerns and commitments. Elected officials in the FMB and their allies in the Woman's Convention argued that the commission of Christianity—and the special calling of African American Christians—demanded simultaneous ministry to the needs of black communities in the United States and in the continent of Africa. In the often polarized debate, the FMB used the *Mission Herald* to valorize the ways that missionaries and the building of churches and mission schools in Africa kept the commandments of the gospel. As in the case of Reverend Fraser's published report in 1919, the FMB's efforts to vindicate the costs of African missions in a time of tremendous African American needs depended on accounts that overshadowed ambiguity and doubt with assurance of progress and triumph.

Consequently, when African American readers surveyed the featured articles of the *Mission Herald* in January 1919, the uneasy contemplation of U.S. segregation and the rise and fall of empires in Africa was eased, for a time, in Fraser's article. The questions about analogous political subjectivity and uncertain strategies for defense were muted in the reporting of the right-hand column. But much like the missionary reports that exceeded the framing of the FMB's forum before the war, these questions lingered, and black Baptists' efforts to make better sense of them reformed their geopolitical view of Africa and African Americans.

In January 1921 the *Mission Herald* featured "The New Map of Africa." Printed in the lower right corner of the paper's front page, the "new map" offered a striking contrast to the map of 1919. The earlier map had been typeset and accompanied by the *Philadelphia Evening Bulletin*'s brief editorial remarks on expectations for the peace conference in Paris. Published after the Treaty of Versailles, the new map of 1921 was hand-drawn, with a carefully labeled, if unevenly scaled, legend that indicated the European colonies that remained on the African continent. This handmade map focused attention on the wide expanse of territory claimed by France and Great Britain. The independence of Liberia and Abyssinia was represented in a considerably smaller scale, but most noteworthy was the caption the *Mission Herald* provided. It began: "A continent containing nearly one-quarter of all the land on Mother Earth, with a population of more than 200,000,000 souls has been taken over by European Powers. It has been dissected, its people outraged and robbed all without 'self-determination.'"[33] As the editorial lines that followed described the complicity of "Christian nations" that dumped shiploads of rum on the continent, the FMB issued its most explicit indictment of Europe's colonial authority in Africa. The map's critique recalled the letters of R. A. Jackson, John and Ida Chilembwe, and A. W. Baker. It also brings to mind the geographic conceptions of race and empire that guided W.E.B. Du Bois's penetrating analysis of the "The African Roots of War."[34] Few of the black Baptist missionaries or church members who were affiliated with the FMB had opportunities to study the depth of political theory, world history, and economic systems that produced Du Bois's treatise on the origins and prospects of the First World War. But black Baptist congregants had long been engaged in a similar endeavor to understand how international relations organized through Africa's colonization shaped a world order and structured the condition of black lives in Africa and across the African diaspora. Although dislocated from recognized state power, the FMB and its affiliates mobilized networks of faith and political alliance to contemplate and to respond to the continuum of domestic disfranchisement in the United States and imperial colonization in Africa.

In honor of the one hundredth anniversary of Lott Carey's departure for Liberia, the *Mission Herald* published the new map of Africa with a column that featured excerpts from Carey's early letters from Monrovia. It was a fitting tribute to the century of accumulated insight, contradiction, and persistence that helped reframe African American Baptists' relationship with the geopolitical map and diverse communities of Africa. The routes leading from the mission Carey directed in Monrovia are uneasy to plot in a linear mapping of the genealogy of Pan-African conferences and labor organizations that challenged state departments' foreign policies for Africa. But the routes are highly indicative of the ways African Americans cultivated a vision and a method of advocacy for a world of linked fates.

Notes

1. E. K. Love, *History of the First African Baptist Church* (Savannah, Ga.: Morning News Print, 1888), 85–90; "Historical Account," *Minutes of the Thirtieth Annual Session of the Missionary Baptist Convention of Georgia* (1901). The annual convention reports are part of the microfilm collection "African American Baptist Annual Reports, 1865–1990, Georgia," from the American Baptist Historical Society Archives.

2. Edmund Drago, *Black Politicians and Reconstruction in Georgia: A Splendid Failure* (Baton Rouge: Louisiana State University Press, 1982), 35–65.

3. Robert Crumley and Philip Joiner, "The Memorial of the Colored Men of the Second Congressional District of Georgia, Setting Forth Their Grievances, and Asking Protection," reprinted in Lee Formwalt, Robert Crumley and Philip Joiner, "Petitioning Congress for Protection: A Black View of Reconstruction at the Local Level," *Georgia Historical Quarterly* 73, no. 2 (1989): 305–22.

4. E. K. Love, *Annual Address to the Missionary Baptist Convention of Georgia* (Nashville, Tenn.: National Baptist Board, 1899), 9, 19.

5. *Proceedings of the Consultation Convention of Leading Colored Men of Georgia* (1888); *Minutes of the Twenty-Sixth Annual Session of the Missionary Baptist Convention of Georgia* (1896); *Minutes of the Tenth Annual Session of the General Missionary Baptist and Educational Convention of the State of Georgia* (1902), all in "African American Baptist Annual Reports, 1865–1990, Georgia," American Baptist Historical Society Archives.

6. The collective state histories of the African American Baptist convention movement are subjects of James Melvin Washington's study *Frustrated Fellowship: The Black Baptist Quest for Social Power* (Macon, Ga.: Mercer University Press, 1986), 47–159. See also Sandy Martin, *Black Baptists and African Missions: The Origins of a Movement, 1880–1915* (Macon, Ga.: Mercer University Press, 1989).

7. The 1926 U.S. census of religious bodies reported roughly 3.2 million African Americans affiliated with predominantly black Baptist denominations. The number included members of the NBC and members of organizations that split from the NBC, including the Lott Carey Foreign Mission Convention and the National Baptist Convention of America, Inc. For extended reflections on this census accounting, see Milton Sernett, *Bound for the Promised Land: African American Religion and the Great Migration* (Durham, N.C.: Duke University Press, 1997), 4–7.

8. See, for instance, Washington, *Frustrated Fellowship*; Elizabeth Higginbotham, *Righteous Discontent: The Women's Movement in the Black Baptist Church, 1880–1920* (Cambridge, Mass.: Harvard University Press, 1993); and Bettye Collier-Thomas, *Jesus, Jobs, and Justice: African American Women and Religion* (New York: Alfred Knopf, 2010), 57–138.

9. Love, *Annual Address*, 41.

10. The African Methodist Episcopal Church has been the more frequent subject of study. Consider James Campbell, *Songs of Zion: The African Methodist Episcopal Church in the United States and South Africa* (New York: Oxford University Press, 1998); Brenda

Gayle Plummer, *Rising Wind: Black Americans and U.S. Foreign Affairs, 1935–1960* (Chapel Hill: University of North Carolina Press, 1996), 9–36; and Alvin Tillery, *Between Homeland and Motherland: Africa, U.S. Foreign Policy, and Black Leadership in America* (Ithaca, N.Y.: Cornell University Press, 2011), 14–42.

11. J. B. Taylor, *Biography of Elder Lott Cary, Late Missionary to Africa* (Baltimore: Armstrong and Berry, 1837); Baptist Board of Foreign Missions (U.S.), *Second Annual Report of the Baptist Board of Foreign Missions for the United States* (Philadelphia: Anderson and Meehan, 1816), 74; *Latter Luminary*, February 1819, 2. Lott Carey's surname is also spelled "Cary" in historical documents. I spell the surname "Carey" in the model of the Lott Carey Foreign Missionary Convention that black American Baptists organized in his name at the turn of the twentieth century. Paul Cuffee's 1815 resettlement project in Sierra Leone preceded the work of the RABMS and the ACS.

12. The missionary commission and the instructions given to Carey and Teage are recounted in Taylor, *Biography of Elder Lott Cary*, 20–23. See also, Miles Fisher, "Lott Cary, the Colonizing Missionary," *Journal of Negro History* 7, no. 4 (1922): 386–87.

13. African American foreign missionaries were affiliated with a broad range of Protestant denominations—Baptist, Methodist, African Methodist Episcopal, American Methodist Episcopal Zion, Presbyterian, Episcopalian, and Seventh Day Adventist included. The rough approximation of more than one hundred African American foreign missionaries is an effort to account for the less clearly documented number of black lay missionaries who departed the United States before the Civil War and for the number of black missionaries who served in the Caribbean and South America. For a useful provisional roll of foreign African American missionaries, see Walter Williams, *Black Americans and the Evangelization of Africa, 1877–1900* (Madison: University of Wisconsin Press), 184–90.

14. See, for example, Lott Cary to Mr. Crane, January 16, 1825, republished in *Latter Day Luminary*, April 1, 1825; Cary to Crane, June 10, 1825, republished in *Columbian Star*, December 31, 1825; Cary to Norfolk, April 24, 1826, republished in *American Baptist Magazine*, August 1826.

15. The West African communities identified by political scientist J. Gus Liebenow include the Vai, Dey, Bassa, Kru, Grebo, Krahn, Gio, Mano, Kpelle, Loma, Belle, Kissi, Mende, Gbandi, Gola, and Mandingo. Liebenow's designations draw from a synthesis of prior linguists and missionaries' accounts and the Liberian Census of 1962. See J. Gus Liebenow, *Liberia: The Evolution of Privilege* (Ithaca, N.Y.: Cornell University Press, 1969), 32. See also, Ayodeji Olukoju, *Culture and Customs of Liberia* (Westport, Conn.: Greenwood, 2006).

16. Consider Carey's republished letters in Adelaide Cromwell Hill and Martin Kilson, eds., *Apropos of Africa: Sentiments of Negro American Leaders on Africa from the 1800s to the 1950s* (London: Frank Cass and Co., Ltd., 1969), 82–85. See also Fisher, "Lott Cary," 396–402; and Tom Shick, *Behold the Promised Land: A History of the Afro-American Settler Society in Nineteenth-Century Liberia* (Baltimore, Md.: Johns Hopkins University Press, 1980), 10–30.

17. The Northwestern and Southern Baptist Convention was the postbellum successor of the WCBC. *Northwestern and Southern Baptist Convention Minutes* (1866), 31. A fuller excerpt from these minutes is offered in Washington, *Frustrated Fellowship*, 77.

18. Colley worked in cooperation with the RABMS and the broader affiliation of the state convention of Virginia black Baptists. Additional details are offered in Leroy Fitts, *A History of Black Baptists* (Nashville, Tenn.: Broadman Press, 1985), 74–75; Edward Freeman, *The Epoch of Negro Baptists and the Foreign Mission Board* (New York: Arno Press, 1980), 70–71; Lewis G. Jordan, *Negro Baptist History, USA, 1750–1930* (Nashville, Tenn.: NBC Sunday School Publishing Board, 1930), 114–17; Martin, *Black Baptists and Foreign Missions*, 49, 54–56; and Williams, *Black Americans*, 18.

19. NBC records from the turn of the twentieth century are inconsistent in reporting the names of black women appointed as foreign missionary wives. The first names of Mrs. Colley and Mrs. Diggs are difficult to locate in the existing board reports.

20. *Atlanta Constitution,* September 26, 1895, 5. "Nucleus" was the term used by the *Constitution* reporter who covered the events of the Baptist convention.

21. E. C. Morris, *Sermons, Addresses, and Reminiscences* (Nashville, Tenn., 1901), 65–66.

22. The quotations here are taken from the NBC's ten-point organizational charter that was drafted in 1895 and from the convention's annual report in 1904. Jordan, *Negro Baptist History,* 118–22; and *Journal of the 24th Annual Session of the National Baptist Convention* (1904): 14–19, "African American Baptist Annual Reports, 1865–1990," American Baptist Historical Society Archives.

23. Jordan succeeded Rev. L. M. Luke, who died in office. L. G. Jordan, *Up the Ladder in Foreign Missions* (Nashville, Tenn.: National Baptist Publishing Board, 1903), 106–8.

24. Ibid., 109.

25. The term "Jim Crow colonialism" is borrowed from Peter Schmidt's study of the Southern roots of U.S. imperialism. See Schmidt, *Sitting in Darkness: New South Fiction, Education, and the Rise of Jim Crow Colonialism, 1865–1920* (Oxford: University of Mississippi Press, 2008).

26. "Rev. John Chilembwe Is No More among the Living," *Mission Herald,* May 1915, 2; Jordan, *Up the Ladder,* 129–30; Desmond D. Phiri, *John Chilembwe* (Lilongwe: Longman Ltd., 1976), 6–10; Thomas Price and George Shepperson, *Independent African: John Chilembwe and the Origins, Setting, and Significance of the Nyasaland Native Uprising of 1915* (Edinburgh, Scotland: University Press, 1958), 83–124.

27. Jordan, *Up the Ladder,* 146–48; *First Annual Report of the Executive Committee of the Woman's Convention, Auxiliary to the NBC* (1901), 4–5, 11, "African American Baptist Annual Reports, 1865–1990, American Baptist Historical Society Archives; E. C. Morris, "President's Annual Address" (1901), in *Sermons, Addresses, and Reminiscences,* 138–39.

28. *Mission Herald,* January 1911, 1.

29. *Mission Herald,* May 1913, 2; *Mission Herald,* June 1913, 1.

30. "Rev. John Chilembwe Is No More among the Living," *Mission Herald,* May 1915, 2.

31. Baker, "The Color Line in South Africa," *Mission Herald,* August 1913, 1.

32. Ibid.

33. *Mission Herald,* January 1921, 1.

34. Du Bois, "The African Roots of War," *Atlantic Monthly* (May 1915): 707–14.

5

White Shame/
Black Agency

Race as a Weapon
in Post–World War I
Diplomacy

VERA INGRID GRANT

On October 5, 1920, an American military policeman arrested a British subject "(negro)" in a café in Antwerp, Belgium, believing he was an African American soldier at large. Containing the presence and activities of African American soldiers in Europe during and after the First World War was an unspoken yet urgent preoccupation of the military. The desire was that the practice of race in Europe look and feel like that in America, a system known as Jim Crow. In this racial system African American soldiers did not casually sit in cafés and enjoy the company and civil graces of larger society.[1] The soldier was not American, however, and the misidentification, occurring midway during the American occupation of the Rhine, from 1918 to 1923, led to international complications. It was a confusing affair and provoked an American military investigation and correspondence between the United States and Great Britain's consulate although it occurred on Belgian soil. The case received singular mention in the seven-volume *American Forces in Germany, 1918–1923,* published by the U.S. government, in a section titled "Operation of American Military Police Outside American Area." The story appeared under a chapter listing "miscellaneous policies."[2]

Although an African American soldier did not directly figure in this matter, I argue that it was the presence of African American soldiers and bodies in Europe that disturbed, confused, and confounded U.S. foreign policy regarding race directly before, during, and after the Great War. In the situation described above it was the misidentification of a *black* soldier that exposed an uneasy juncture of the usually codified material practice of American race once it ventured overseas. The difficulties intrinsic to asserting the visual indexicality of the black race in America brushed up against a gamut of European national black belongings and posed a new problem for the American military. The case illuminates the limits of American foreign policy as it converged with domestic American military racial expediency regarding African American soldiers. I excavate it in this chapter as a signal case where the theoretical intersections of race, gender, and nation, as understood and expressed by American military discourse, resulted in an extraordinarily pulverized mix. While it ballooned into an international incident at the time, it drew no attendant media attention, and it lingered only briefly as a diplomatic embarrassment subsequently buried in the appendixes of American military history. Racial encounters during the Great War usually remained within the national borders of history; and the experiences of African American soldiers strained these national categories as if when they traversed the Atlantic they wreaked havoc on European and American attempts to contain their colonial legacies and adjust and shape their postwar maps of empire.

This chapter examines the role of race in the transformation of the former German enemy into an American friend that took place in the Rhineland occupation zone between 1918 and 1923. I propose that in the crucible of the occupation zone, dissimilar and heightened American and German understandings and practices of race converged with usual postwar indignities of brutality, revenge, and survival. What emerged was a transformed global pattern of racial perspectives and reconciled alliances. W.E.B. Du Bois named this reorganization of racial discourse "the discovery of personal whiteness among the world's peoples."[3] I propose that another stream of interactions bound the two national groups—Germans and Americans—together: they grappled with their perceptions of interior "racialized" enemies, deepened their crafting of white supremacy, and expressed similar interior visions while at work on their world visions. Although Germany had suddenly lost her colonial empire, some of the ramped-up effects of that adventure had reverberated back home. I would further argue that *a gap exists between the representations and practices of nationalism and racism.* It is a fluctuating gap between the two poles of a contradiction and a forced identification, and it is perhaps when this identification is apparently complete that the aperture is most visible. The gap is not a contradiction between nationalism and racism as such, but a slippage between these determinate forms, between the political objectives of nationalism and the crystallization of racism on a particular *object* or "(negro)," when they converge at a particular moment. Étienne Balibar discusses this suggested lacuna as a gliding or slipperiness of discourse when "a racial signifier has to transcend national differences and organize 'transnational' solidarities so as to be able, in return, to ensure the effectivity of nationalism." Balibar includes European national identity formations in his analysis and the slippage contained within the discourse of anti-Semitism, however he reaches a similar notion of global white consciousness that was defined before the First World War by W.E.B. Du Bois: "At the same time, the European or Euro-American nations, locked in a bitter struggle to divide up the world into colonial empires, recognized that they formed a community and shared an 'equality' through that very competition, a community and an equality to which they gave the name 'White.'"[4]

If we use the occupation of Germany as a staging ground—this specific Allied occupation turf of the Rhineland that went from Allied turf occupied by the French to the American zone—as an alternate site of inquiry from which to examine the trajectories of racial history, we may examine anew how race operated in the occupation zones after the Great War. I suggest this approach instead of looking at particular explosions of race—in the instance of the propaganda war around the use of colonial troops in the French zone, for example. I see the two approaches—strategies of occupation and strategies of racial subjection—as intricately entwined and interdependent. And if we may envision an occupation after a conflict as the necessary codicil of war to determine or ensure the negotiated peace, then we may see "race" brandished as a weapon of war. If we examine the experiences of African American soldiers in the First World War through a disciplinary lens as a significant historical narrative, we can tease out the tensions of the American national story of race as a predominant social vector in a domestic and imperial policy of American white supremacy, a policy growing in virulence after the war. Within Germany the everyday citizen's experience of race was most often an indirect experience of empire discourse—both the overly harsh or bleak actual colonial encounters described in press and public forums and the strange adventures and dreams of story, novels, transforming popular visual culture. "In the course of the twentieth century, American racial classifications tended to become more rigid. . . . Ironically, the scientific community moved in the opposite direction by refuting previous assumptions of significant biological differences."[5]

In the twenty-first century the concept of race itself is undergoing a metamorphosis; an unraveling of the discourse found at the dawn of the twentieth century when "race" referred to both black and white pseudo-scientific and national categories that together formed a crowded and seemingly rigid hierarchy. Whether we discuss one more ethnic history of the Great War, usually a domestic "other" than one of the prime national actors in the conflict and most often a contributory narrative excavated at considerable expense and difficulty by their authors, we are presented with teleological highlights and insights offered for present-day consumers who are content with victories of our "post-racial" society or otherwise we support in heroic-history those seeking valorous and exemplary support to those still in the struggle. If we look at how race *works* in this first major conflict of the twentieth century, perhaps neither consumer is sated, but we may gain additional and crucial insights and contend with our current preoccupations of nation building, violence, and entangled racial legacies. I consider a further interrogation of race relations in Europe immediately after World War I and, in particular, examine the discourse of and about American soldiers in that period, both white and black, along with the culture of the American military government in the occupation zone. The Great War and its postwar discourse on race was crafted and shaped by the development of what Du Bois called "a white global consciousness." I suggest it was an uneasy formation, and this new awareness of a possible white racialized and globalized solidarity included its own exclusions and reconciliations. I argue that not only had the recently vanquished Germany used race in this period as a weapon of war—in the colonial outpost of German East Africa, for example—but also that an American lesson in racial mores and strategies of subjection was now at hand for Germany, in the occupation zone. This was a lesson to be learned as part and parcel of the reconciliation of Germany as a white civilized nation. It included racial games of subjection along with temporary and fluid inversions of the hierarchies. These games of race were historically woven into the social fabric of the United States and its expression in the larger world; its threads still entangle us.

In this chapter I present a gathering of ephemera—inventions and exertions of "America" as revealed in small acts of song, recollections, and movable practices of "home"—to make visible the practice of race in the Rhineland occupation zone. I juxtapose the performance of blackface variety shows by American soldiers (and other racialized moments within the zone) alongside the American occupying regime's often brutal encounters with German civilians and demobilized German soldiers. What emerges from this repositioning of historical narrative is a fresh glimpse into the utility and subtle craft of how race worked as a pivotal linchpin of American hierarchical societal patterns. Yes, we know of the deliberate darkness thrust upon African Americans in its lasting formations of legalized segregation after *Plessy v. Ferguson* (1896). Yes, we know of the shunting of north-migrating Southern multitudes into ghettos and exclusionary practices of work and pleasure in the urban landscape of the North. Yes, we know of the terror, of the lynching, and of the white supremacist practices. We know of and continue to reveal, examine, and explain the overt practices and consequences of race in America. We also know that American racial practices walked up the ramps of ocean liners crammed with departing American troops bound for the European theater of war and that these practices went along.

African American soldiers were not just a singular minority group experiencing survival under the pressures of the U.S. racial system, in which military service was a paradoxical moment of enduring racism, while disproving the stereotypes and contributing a laudable record of service to the country. In addition, how race operates within the U.S. racial regime as it brushed up against the various European powers' systems of race became an additional and unacknowledged force field in which power was not only exerted but also used to diminish the experience of African American soldiers. Connecting seemingly disparate narratives into one field of consideration may change the perception of significance and relevance of race once taken as a whole cloth. In this way the minority narratives of war, service, and valor are not relegated to the margins of a dominant narrative, but may be seen to feed into the upholding of the main narrative. Another way of considering this perspective is that of revealing the necessity of race and the racial system of hierarchy to both dominant and minority positions. While these theoretical positions and frameworks for understanding the practice of race in this world, by nation, globally, or transnationally, the theory is often held in a separate discourse while the practice of race stories or histories continues the narratives of dominance and marginality. Similarly, narratives around black Europeans and their historical experience often begin with World War II or the rapidly changing population dynamics in Europe after the war. Colonial legacies are acknowledged as formative of the social legacies of race inside the "mother" countries of various empires or viewed as tales of the homeland—the margins where these dynamics played out. In the metropole race is a different story and practice that not only has its roots within the area's history but also involves a practice that has a past, present, and continued operation between the European nations and their Western offspring. This dynamic of entering a racialized zone has been well told in U.S. history in the discourses on whiteness, but that narrative may also describe how many immigrants negotiate the U.S. racial system on their way to assimilation and may be applicable to Europe as well.

As historian David Blight has noted, "Traditional historians' treatment of the black experience . . . was a conscious and deliberate manipulation of history and the *stakes* were high." He goes on to explain that "the question of stakes involved in struggle over rival versions of history leads us not only to the political and social meanings of what historians do; it also provides an angle of understanding about the confluences of history and memory for intellectuals and for the larger society." I suggest that it is not only the filling in of missing histories that may illuminate the context of the African American experience in the military but also how that experience is still written about as supplementary to the dominant context. Another approach may be to look afresh at the entire social history simultaneously and see how American structures and practices of race dismissed and concealed the experience of African American soldiers, and how the shaping of American military experience and war memories was dependent upon the suppression and diminishment of the African American narratives in the very same military organization. For World War I and its aftermath there are a few examples that may tease out the varying dynamics when these stories are told in tandem.[6]

Black Doughboys: Real People or Just a Specter?

By the time any American soldiers arrived on the war scene, both European and colonial soldiers were exhausted, depleted, and imbued with a weariness described succinctly by the various war poets. And although African American troops had been the first to aid the European Allies directly, the American army sent them home directly after the war, with only a few battalions remaining behind in France to rebury the dead on the battlefields. The literature on the Rhineland occupation zone, where a quarter of a million white doughboys marched and took possession of territory in December 1918, makes no mention of these African American troops. In *From Harlem to the Rhine*, Arthur W. Little narrates his adventures with the 369th Infantry, known as the "Men of Bronze" or "Harlem's Hell Fighters." They served with the French, not the American, army in Europe. They marched to the Rhine first, arriving on November 20, 1918, and remained for three weeks: "The period of the occupation of the towns of Blodelsheim, Fessenheim, Balgau, and Namsheim, and of the West bank of The Rhine along the area of those towns, by the 369th Infantry, passed uneventfully. We remained about three weeks, when, upon December 9th, we received the welcome orders to start immediately for the west, to prepare to leave the French Army, as the first step towards going home."[7]

During the war the presence of African American troops in Europe presented problems for the American racial regime. General John J. Pershing's office had sent out a memorandum titled "To the French Military Mission—Secret Information Concerning Black American Troops." This memorandum stated in part: "1) prevent the rise of any 'pronounced' degree of intimacy between French officers and Black officers; 2) do not eat with Blacks, shake hands, or seek to meet them outside of military service; and 3) do not commend 'too highly' Black troops in the presence of white Americans."[8] In spite of these American military instructions, of the four African American "regiments, the 369th, 370th, 371st, and 372nd," attached to French command, "three were awarded the *Croix de Guerre* by France."[9]

The African American soldier experienced and expressed multiple identities in the Great War that wound up in varying personal, historical, and institutional narratives. The most intriguing of the entries in terms of the conflicted national belonging of the African American soldier is in the title of Frank E. Roberts's monograph *The American Foreign Legion: Black Soldiers of the 93rd in World War I*.[10] Roberts discusses how this division was broken into several regiments and "attached" to the French army during the war and asks: "How did these men come to be serving under the command of a foreign army?" His answer is that "Pershing used an obscure clause in the formal policy statement to dispose of four regiments of the American infantry troops that neither he nor his corps or division commanders wanted. Pershing decided that the 371st Infantry and its sister regiments—the 369th, 370th, and 372nd—which made up the 93rd Division and were composed of black enlisted men and black and white officers, were undesirable and not essential to the AEF [American Expeditionary Forces] and quietly ceded them to the French Army."[11]

In addition to the 93rd Division, other African American soldiers served most often as laborers and supply chain recruits. However, in what is usually mentioned as an aside or marginal issue, they joined other African American soldiers or "colonial troops" in Europe, each of which was affiliated with a different and particular nation. In addition, controversy and propaganda on the appropriateness and danger of armed troops from the African diaspora on European soil was a hefty and paradoxical discourse in its own right. Typically all of the troops from the African diaspora—no matter their colonial origins— received incomplete training and insufficient equipment before and during the grand conflict. Chad Williams offers this description of *les soldat noirs*: "Unable to master the complexities of modern warfare, such as use of the machine gun, the Tirailleurs Sénégalais were 'particularly apt for attack and counter-attack,' a euphemism for their crude battlefield utilization as shock troops."[12] However, a vastly different and contrasting image appeared in the *Chicago Defender*, a weekly periodical aimed at African American readers. In this medium the audience was offered an image of French colonial troops "Picking Off Germans." Williams explains that while the editors pursed their discursive strategies to celebrate "blackness" at war and grasped at opportunities to display colonial troops as bastions of modernity and prowess, they may not have known of the disparaging propaganda regarding the French colonial soldiers.[13]

One example of the cultural artillery launched in racial skirmishes is the Bert Williams song "You'll Find Old Dixieland in France," which includes the line *They're pickin' Germans off the Rhine* directly after the line *Instead of pickin' melons off the vine.* A host of imagery and popular culture visuals presented this simultaneous nostalgic and degrading imagery—a ridiculing and assertive projection of a happy and inept "Negro" soldier figure of the Southern imaginary—who could ludicrously be found *"playin' blues upon a Gatling Gun."*[14]

> You remember Dancin' Mose?
> Folks all called him "Tickle Toes,"
> You'll find him "Over There" in France,
> Alexander's Band, left old Dixieland,
> They used to play the "lovin' blues" for ev'ryone,
> Now they're playin' blues upon a Gatling Gun;
> Don't forget "Old Shimme Sam,"
> Famous boy from Alabam,'
> He marched away in khaki pants,
> Instead of pickin' melons off the vine,
> They're pickin' Germans off the Rhine,
> You'll find old Dixieland in France.[15]

These visual and sonic cultural attacks on black military manhood and prowess became more insistent and prolific as the war continued. Anxiety-filled white citizens may have consumed them with lumps in their throats as countervailing images from personal photographs, portraits, posters, even military panoramic documentation of troop formations and movements proclaimed otherwise. However, the photographic image in "Four Soldiers Reading" (fig. 1) does not depict confusion, servility, or a desire to entertain. If anything, the men seem to entertain *themselves* in their pose, poise, and pseudo-reading stance. The image also projects a performative moment: a subtle parody of the multiple posters and American ephemera of the white doughboy soldier "reading."

Maurice O. Wallace interrogates the photography of African American soldiers during the Civil War. He concurs that "photography pictured war" and that war, "in turn, pictured photography as an instrument of national fantasy," as revealed in the work of William A. Frassanito, William C. Davis, and Alan Trachtenberg. But he further suggests that pictures were used to formalize "for the public imagination the picturable prospect of a new national subject, one fully assimilable into the imagined body politic: namely, the African American male as soldier and, thus, would-be citizen."[16] Fathoming the paradoxically revealing power of the photograph, Wallace demonstrates how the "popularity and proliferation of the black soldier portrait" visually imagined a black manhood and identity for post–Civil War society. However, by the time of the First World War, the national imaginary objective had changed to eliminate the full participation

FIGURE 1. "Four Soldiers Reading," France, spring 1918.
Stanley B. Burns, MD, and the Burns Archive.

of the African American soldier from the national family. Juxtaposed to examples
of national military images of white-bodied warriors set into panoramic frames
of rows and rows of the willing and able soldier were the separate groupings of
African American soldiers. Here the division of separate and unequal took on
its ominous meanings when juxtaposed with those of laboring black bodies as
being supportive to the white troops.

The reading soldier was one of the main tactical promotions and consequent
provisions made to educate and entertain the soldiers both domestically and
away from home during the war and the American occupation of Germany.
Literary offerings and persuasions were often brokered as part of multitiered
disciplinary measures to counteract boredom and prankish behavior. Especially
after the armistice in Europe, libraries for the doughboy were one solution among
many others to address the extreme concerns of the occupying doughboys'
violence and animosity toward the Germans. Poster campaigns featuring the
reading white doughboy littered the American cultural landscape. As Martin
Andresen of the U. S. Army Military History Institute notes in his review of
National Library Week, annually sponsored by the American Library Associa-

FIGURE 2. A World War I–era poster from Bertrand Patenaude's
A Wealth of Ideas, a book released in conjunction with the 2006
exhibit at Hoover Memorial Exhibit Pavilion. Poster Collection,
Poster ID #US 656, Hoover Institution Archives.

tion (ALA), "Secretary Baker kept 'a room full of senators and diplomats and
other dignitaries waiting' while he developed plans to provide adequate library
facilities for the Doughboys."[17] However, the separate accommodations the U.S.
Army provided for African American soldiers meant less adequate facilities: "The
largest Y.M.C.A. hut in France was one built at Camp Lusitania, St. Nazaire, for

FIGURE 3. An American domestic promotional poster.
Poster Collection, Poster ID #US 715, Hoover Institution Archives.

the use of colored soldiers. . . . It did service for 9,000 men, and had, in addition to the dry canteen, a library of 1,500 volumes."[18] (See figs. 2 and 3.)

African American soldiers had been welcomed by most of the French as the first American soldiers to aid them, and some contentment emanates from the four faces in "Four Soldiers Reading" that may not have survived the ensuing conflict. This parody of the reading soldier is part of a psychological "flip the switch" strategy that African Americans who were employed in the face of the boundless racial animosity endured in the homeland and now carried along overseas. A key feature of the racial mores of white American soldiers was the projected and grotesque double-edged specter of blackness: the foolish bumbling child-man indicated in the Bert Williams song discussed above, coupled with a monstrous projection of danger, along with supposed inappropriate social tendencies and animalistic responses to human relations—mainly heightened violence, criminality, and unbounded sexuality. All of these expanded and ever more delusionary depictions of African Americans had sharpened the psychic racial burdens of life in America and within its colonial expansion landscapes since the late nineteenth century; they were now unleashed anew in the European theater of war and occupation.[19]

The seriousness of expression evoked in the photograph (fig. 1) resonates simultaneously with a performative parody of soldier-hood and the new vulnerabilities that all African diaspora combatants experienced in Europe. The tale of the arrested black Belgian points to this assumption of criminality on the part of American military police that synergized with their confusion on *blackness* in Europe and an arrogance of global *whiteness*. These confusions and anxieties prompted the frequent arrests that African diaspora soldiers were subjected to in Europe. However, the parody performed in the image also points to the enduring tradition of blackface performance within the military by white soldiers and inverts it. In his paradigmatic analysis of blackface minstrelsy in nineteenth-century American culture, *Love and Theft: Blackface Minstrelsy and the American Working Class,* Eric Lott emphasizes that "blackface acts did not merely confirm an already existent racism—an idealist assumption that ignores the ways in which culture is reproduced. Social feelings and relationships are constantly generated and maintained, regulated and fought over, in the sphere of culture and elsewhere, and . . . they began to ease the friction among various segments of the working class, and between workers and class superiors, by seizing on Jim Crow as a common enemy."[20]

What role did blackface minstrelsy play in the tumultuous landscape of the American occupation zone in Germany after the Great War? I propose it shaped the discourse of the invisibility of African American participation and presence in an extended theater of war while easing overall doughboy anxiety overseas. Blackness is invoked as a derogatory specter both comedic and grotesque. The practice and ideology of race *work* in its form of blackface minstrelsy performances in the occupation zone helped occlude actual black experiences of victory and contribution. Furthermore, trajectories and formations of racial games and mockery with intertwined strategies of subjection helped to resolve conflict between Americans and Germans. I propose that the *work* of race helped to redistribute the role of enemy and ally in the occupation zone, and racial *acts* in the occupation zone eased the friction between Germans and doughboys. There was a lot of friction. German complaints against American troops in the occupation zone highlight the feelings of humiliation and outrage in the face of doughboy arrogance, violence, and abuse.

The choices made by various actors in the post–World War I assessment of the performance of African American soldiers during the war reflected the complicated domestic space—a multivoiced nexus of practical action, dissenting voices, compromise, and at times complicity. In the preliminary draft for *The Wounded World*, Du Bois would sum up the perfidy of the army high command in four terse phrases: "First, was the effort to get rid of Negro officers; second, the effort to discredit Negro soldiers; third, the effort to spread race prejudice in France; and fourth, the effort to keep Negroes out of the Regular Army."[21] The wonder was that there were four African American units that had performed outstandingly—the 369th, 370th, 371st, and the 372nd of the never completed 93rd Division. These were the infantry regiments that Pershing had hurriedly sent abroad to fight alongside the French. In addition to the American military high command's promise to immediately lend a number of units to the French while the American Expeditionary Army was being assembled, the escalating racial friction in towns and cities near the camps of the African American units had led Scott to also urge their relocation. It was a mere two months after the Houston or Camp Logan Riot—a mutiny by 156 African American soldiers of the Third Battalion of the all-black Twenty-fourth United States Infantry Regiment in August 1917. So while in Houston in December of that year, 13 court-martialed African American soldiers were hanged in unison for their part in the riots, the men of the 369th, the former New York National Guard regiment, arrived in Brest to support the French. It was among the first American fighting units in France. Desperate for manpower, the French high command pounced on the unit. Its uniforms, weapons, and order of march suddenly became French.

The Rhineland Occupation Zone:
Reconsidering Race in a Colonizing Space

Immediately after the armistice that ended World War I on November 11, 1919, African American troops serving under French command marched into the Rhineland. It was significant to them that they were the first to arrive—as occupiers. They commented sympathetically on the state of the fallen German citizen. They gave the title to their entire wartime adventure "Harlem to the Rhine." Just days later, however, they quit the Rhineland and reversed their journey, calling it

"Rhine to Harlem." These departing soldiers were then quickly replaced by white American doughboys when the territorial zones of the Western occupation of Germany were reconfigured during quick and terse diplomatic negotiations in Paris. The land they had marched upon and occupied had been the French occupation zone for the better part of a month, and now it became the American zone. New American soldiers entered the Rhineland as occupiers. They sang "Dixie" as they marched. They also commented on the state of the German citizen, but in more disparaging ways.

"To the Rhine" was a major propaganda phrase of the American military. It appeared on posters and was used in talks and pep rallies within the military and without in broader society. However, the American soldier did not accomplish this goal of making it *to the Rhine*. Or did he? The African American soldier did. His story, embedded ethnic accounts of valor and racial progress, is not mentioned in our major histories of the Great War, because he wore the French uniform. Three weeks after the armistice more than a quarter million white American troops marched into Germany to occupy the Rhineland. Representing roughly a third of the total Allied occupying forces, they were joining smaller contingents from France, England, and Belgium. The French forces did include up to forty thousand of their colonial troops, including a large component of African soldiers, whose deployment would come to draw criticism not only from the outraged Germans but also from some French critics at home.[22] Units had "cheered when informed they were to participate, and soldiers talked with eagerness of the 'party.'" Initially "they saw this as the long-awaited chance to get even with the foe."[23] Six months later, when Maj. Gen. Henry T. Allen took command on July 2, 1919, he found a disturbing development in the relations between American soldiers and German civilians: "the moment the Germans showed an insubordinate spirit, the troops reacted violently." The problem, it seemed to Allen, was that "our young men on the Rhine . . . were *learning* to be real soldiers," an ongoing process that improved "through strenuous efforts."[24]

Imagine an American soldier in Germany just after the First World War. He's young, white, and victorious. The Central Powers (Germany, Austria-Hungary, the Ottoman Empire [Turkey], and Bulgaria) have been defeated—the German "Hun" is beaten. Our soldier arrives in the Rhineland as part of the American Expeditionary Forces who marched into Germany after the armistice to establish the American occupation zone. It is Christmas Day and he smears burnt cork on his face as he prepares for his performance of blackface minstrelsy: "Dec 25th [1918] Had a bum Dinner, I took part in a black face show given by the Co (8 of us) and tried to occupy my mind, but was thinking of home like 'hell' the show was a success, my name was Mr. Boten."[25]

The American troops were in former enemy territory and would remain for four years, but the thrills of victory were few and far between. The military administration sought to curb troop enthusiasm for retaliation and maintain order. If there would be no party, American troops wanted to go home. For unruly, uncomfortable, and bored American troops, blackface minstrelsy provided one of the more tantalizing forms of entertainment available in the sudden monotony of the occupation zone, and this genre, spawned by the practice of race in the United States, became their substitute for a real African American presence that had been earned through combat. Some white troops performed and countless others watched the shows. Amateur actor soldiers participated in small performative acts of vaudeville minstrelsy up and down the Rhine River, in hotels, beer halls, and confiscated town halls to sellout crowds. They danced, gestured, and grimaced under the gaze of their fellow American soldiers and before that of the exhausted and defeated German populace. One description in the *Stars and Stripes* on March 15, 1919, in a column called "Yank Doings Hereabouts," gave blow-by-blow details of the festivities:

> "See dat Niggar ball de jack"—applause—"Come back yo coon an do dat sum mo'"—more applause—"Hey, seconds on that" shouted the audience as Private Bernard Miller, blackface comedian, danced, jiggled and joked in the Fifty-eighth Infantry Show "Some of This and Some of That" at the Mayen Y.M.C.A. Tuesday evening of this week. The Jazz band which was the *backbone* of the whole show rendered a selection after each of the acts.[26]

By the first week of occupation in December 1919, the Knights of Columbus established sixty-seven clubs in the American occupation zone to help craft a social life for the American fighting man far from home. Swiftly refashioned from confiscated German hotels, clubs, and restaurants, the clubs featured vaudeville shows that showcased talented doughboys, films, musical performances, and readings. The vaudeville shows headlined blackface minstrelsy as a crucial component of their consumptive pleasures. The American military government arranged for the entertainment of American soldiers in Germany as one of an assortment of methods to discipline and control troop behavior. Administrators needed to stem the rampant reports of the doughboys' barbaric behavior toward German men and their indecent actions when around German women. Supporting and promoting blackface minstrelsy along with other features of the variety shows provided a two-pronged solution: they imported a sense of home to the troops, and they relieved the incessant tedium of the occupation zone described in the men's diaries, journals, periodicals, and cartoons.

The last remnants of American troops in the occupied Rhineland packed up and left for home on January 24, 1923. Four years and two months after the armistice ended World War I, American troops refused to buffer the tension between the Allies and the Germans any longer. For the last time, the Eighth Infantry marched to the Coblenz train station and General Allen observed "genuine sorrow depicted on the faces of both allies and Germans."[27] Back in March 1922, *Der Tag* speculated that few would "mourn the passing of the doughboy," only, for example, jilted fiancées or barbershop crews.[28] The editor's words, though scornful, accurately predicted the final scene at headquarters: "Headquarters at Coblenz was like a domestic-relations court, with German women clamoring to marry soldiers before the American departure. Claims for the support of illegitimate children, requests for work and charity, demands for payment of overdue bills—all suddenly mushroomed in number."[29]

"The late-arriving Americans had not suffered the endless ordeal" of the Germans or "the Europeans; the New World and the Old World had, in reality, fought different wars." Into this troubled crucible marched a quarter million doughboys with an "almost carnival spirit."[30] Irvin L. Hunt, colonel in the infantry and officer in charge of civil affairs for the American Forces in Germany, found the situation difficult from the start. In the early days nearly 300,000 American troops were billeted (or quartered) on the 893,345 Rhineland citizens in the American occupation zone; in other words, one soldier for every three civilians. Mistakes were made, Hunt admitted: "Unfortunately, the unexpected close of the war with its occupation of enemy territory, left little time for the study of the problems confronting the military government. The time between the signing of the armistice and the occupation of Germany (less than three weeks) was too short to organize completely a civil administration with formulate policies. General Headquarters was therefore confronted with the necessity of adopting such temporary expedients as would tide over the situation until some permanent organization could be devised."[31]

In 1923 the *Amaroc News* reported that the Germans and the Americans were once again at peace. The short occupation by Americans was over, and any disruptions were now forgotten. Richard Evans made the following remarks in a review of Branowski's *Nazi Empire*:

In the peace settlement that followed defeat in 1918, Germany lost all its overseas colonies, 13 per cent of its territory in Europe (including Alsace-Lorraine to France, and industrial areas in the east to the newly created state of Poland), and almost all its military equipment. Its armed forces were restricted to 100,000 men, and the government had to agree to the payment over subsequent decades of large sums of money in reparations for the economic damage caused by the war. These terms caused general disbelief and then outrage; after all, the war had ended while German troops were still on foreign soil, and military defeat had been far from total. Moreover—a fact often overlooked by historians—British and French troops occupied the Rhineland for most of the 1920s, providing a constant reminder of Germany's subjugation to foreign powers. In 1923, when it fell behind with reparation payments, the French sent an expeditionary force into the industrial region of the Ruhr to seize key resources, causing further resentment.

He continues to wonder if the terms were indicative of a colonization by the Allies: "Certainly, propaganda attacks on the occupation of the Ruhr focused heavily on the racial defilement symbolized by the French use of troops from its African colonies. But by the mid-1920s the violent clashes between revolutionary and counter-revolutionary forces that had brought machine guns and tanks onto the streets of Germany's major cities in the immediate aftermath of the war had subsided and the economy had stabilized."[32] However, some things were not and would not be forgotten. It was not the remarkable experience of occupation that crafted this new brotherhood. The Americans would go back home. The French would face issues still unresolved on the Ruhr, and the Germans would receive personal demonstrations of a daily systematic program of humiliation and brutality that would prove useful in their future power struggles.

Further evidence of the role of World War I in demonstrating a vicious common bond of racism between the dominant Western powers can be seen in a closer glance at France's policies governing her wartime African colonial troops and workforce immediately after the war. Even during the war the larger presence of African troops in France had sparked physical assaults and riots. Like the racial incidents of their respective American counterparts, French social conflagrations sparked by the presence of African troops on French soil also offer insights into the more general history of race, class, and racial violence. In the words of Tyler Stovall, "In important ways, they correspond to analyses of whiteness and intra-class racial conflict proffered by David Roediger and Alexander Saxton, but with some significant twists." Stovall concludes that the French succeeded in constructing a common white identity out of people from divergent European backgrounds, as did the United States in the interwar years. However, instead of American strategies of racial exclusion that integrated disparate Europeans into a racial upper stratum of "whiteness," in France Stovall finds a "consolidation of racial hierarchy through a denial of its existence." In France the construction of whiteness involved an attempt at removing obvious "otherness." Stovall also reports that "after 1918, the French government sent colonial workers home as quickly as possible, judging that France was not ready to become a multi-racial society."[33]

One place where parts of this colonial exodus dwelled for ten years was on the Rhine, in French-occupied Germany. So although at home France managed to construct an artificial silence around racial conflict in the interwar years by holding colonial immigrations at arm's length and encouraging European immigration, in occupied Germany, France unleashed racial conflicts it sought to avoid at home. This is also compelling evidence that the French enthusiastic acceptance of African American troops upon their arrival in France was not a sign of greater racial tolerance on their part. It suggests, rather, that the French were simply more silent and perhaps were more rational partners in the shared racism among the dominant world powers than the Americans and Germans. Their willingness to at least afford African soldiers from their colonies as well as African Americans the dignity of actual combat in exchange for sacrificing their bodies in place of Frenchmen was apparently more pragmatic than principled.

When African American soldiers went to war in during World War I, they brought American racial structures and sensibilities with them, as did the women who supported them. They fought battles against two enemies—one abroad, or "over there," proclaimed in American war aims, and one at home against the racially motivated disparate social conditions. The embracing and inverting of an internal national paradox was nominally captured in the African American "Double V" victory campaign that was publicized more broadly during World War II. However, two observations are of note in this comparison: (1) these dynamics were already in effect during and after World War I and were countered by African American soldiers and African American women who supported them or engaged in the war effort, and (2) the American military sought to both diminish the role that African American soldiers played and contain them within agreed-upon structures of domestic social dominance—by importing American racial strategies into Europe. This chapter then serves as a pre-text to the discourse of American race and foreign policy that sees World War II as a major node of transformation and suggests that the successes, as well as failures, of civil rights policies—most often celebrating the abolishing of segregation within the U.S. Army as a linchpin of alteration of U.S. racial dynamics—may be seen as the limited intervention they were in practice. The practice of race being made part of strategies of domination continues to set the stage of U.S. foreign policy in unspoken and invisible threads that embrace us and our sought-after allies. I have tried to make visible here some of these elusive tendencies and their consequences so that the Great War, the aftermath of that war, and the next to follow, may be understood as one long continuum wherein nations employed race as a weapon. This new global consciousness of race encompassed Germany, and the trajectories and strategies of American race abroad helped reconcile Germany as a civilized nation. Its visible and unseen webs and strands were woven into the social fabric of the United States and extended onto the world stage of Europe, not just into the American colonial spaces. Its threads still entangle us.

Notes

1. See Tyler Stovall, "The Color Line behind the Lines: Racial Violence in France during the Great War," *American Historical Review* 103, no. 3 (1998): 737–69.

2. I. L. Hunt, *American Military Government of Occupied Germany, 1918–1920: Report of the Officer in Charge of Civil Affairs, Third Army, and American Forces in Germany* (Washington D.C.: United States Government Printing Office, 1943), 27.

3. W.E.B. Du Bois, "The Souls of White Folk," *Darkwater: Voices from within the Veil* (New York: Harcourt, Brace, 1920). During the First World War, in his essay "The African Roots of the War" (*Atlantic Monthly* 115 [May 1915]), Du Bois had emerged as a leading critic of imperialism in the very same year that Lenin wrote his classic *Imperialism: The Highest Stage of Capitalism*. By the end of 1919, 66 black men and women had been lynched, while some 250 more died in urban riots in events now known as the "Red Summer" of 1919. David Levering-Lewis wrote in his biography of Du Bois: "[He] construed the failure of American racial democracy to be integral to the evolving European world order. . . . The Great War was not aberration nor insanity, he wrote: 'This is Europe: this seeming Terrible is the real soul of white culture—back of all culture—stripped and visible today.'" David Levering Lewis, *W. E. B. Du Bois, 1919–1963: The Fight for Equality and the American Century* (New York: Henry Holt, 2001), 14.

4. Étienne Balibar, "Racism and Nationalism," in *Race, Nation, Class: Ambiguous Identities* (London: Verso, 1991), 62.

5. Thomas Borstelmann, *The Cold War and the Color Line: American Race Relations in the Global Arena* (Cambridge, Mass.: Harvard University Press, 2001).

6. David W. Blight, "W.E.B. Du Bois and the Struggle for American Historical Memory," *History and Memory in African-American Culture* (New York: Oxford University Press, 1994), 45.

7. Arthur W. Little, *From Harlem to the Rhine: The Story of New York's Colored Volunteers* (New York: J. J. Little and Ives, 1936), 335.

8. Robert W. Mullen, *Blacks in America's Wars* (New York: Anchor Foundation, 1973), 44.

9. Ibid., 47–48.

10. Frank E. Roberts, *The American Foreign Legion: Black Soldiers of the 93rd in World War I* (Annapolis, Md.: U.S. Naval Institute Press, 2004).

11. Ibid., 1.

12. Chad L. Williams, *Torchbearers of Democracy: African American Soldiers in the World War I Era* (Chapel Hill: University of North Carolina Press, 2010), 158.

13. Ibid., 154.

14. "You'll Find Old Dixieland in France" was introduced by Bert Williams in *Ziegfeld Midnight Frolic*, which Will Rogers, Fanny Brice, Lillian Lorraine, and Bert Williams made an all-star show. "The first of a late-night series that Ziegfeld staged in The New Amsterdam's intimate rooftop theater and featured a glass runway that let the chorus girls parade over the audiences' heads—Ziegfeld had them wear tasteful ankle-length linen bloomers." http://www.musicals101.com/ziegshows.htm.

15. "You'll Find Old Dixieland in France," words by Grant Clarke; music by Geo. W. Meyer (New York: Leo Feist, 1918).

16. Maurice O. Wallace, "Framing the Black Soldier: Image, Uplift, and the Duplicity of Pictures," *Pictures and Progress: Early Photography and the Making of African American Identity* (Durham, N.C.: Duke University Press, 2012), 245.

17. Martin Andresen, "Books for the Doughboys," April 4, 2010, Army Military History Institute (MHI) Archive, Army Heritage and Education Center, Carlisle, Pennsylvania.

18. Addie W. Hunton and Kathryn M. Johnson, *Two Colored Women with the American Expeditionary Forces* (New York: G. K. Hall, 1997).

19. Khalil Gibran Muhammad, *The Condemnation of Blackness: Race, Crime, and the Making of Modern Urban America* (Cambridge, Mass.: Harvard University Press, 2010).

20. Eric Lott, *Love and Theft: Blackface Minstrelsy and the American Working Class* (New York: Oxford University Press, 1995), 137.

21. David Levering-Lewis, *W.E.B. Du Bois: A Biography* (New York: Henry Holt, 2009), 376.

22. For extensive discussion of this with graphic propaganda illustrations, see Peter Martin, *Zwischen Charleston und Stechschritt. Schwarze im National sozialismus* [Between the Charleston and the Goosestep: Blacks under Nazism] (Hamburg: Dolling und Galitz Verlag, 2004).

23. Keith Nelson, *Victors Divided: America and the Allies in Germany, 1918–1923* (Berkeley: University of California Press, 1975), 31.

24. Henry T. Allen, *The Rhineland Occupation* (Indianapolis: Bobbs-Merrill, 1927), 72–73.

25. "The Diary of Henry Jetton Tudury: Mississippi's Most Decorated Doughboy of World War I." Written between April 1917 and August 1919, this document was first published in the *Journal of Mississippi History* in 1981. Edited by Charles Sullivan, the text includes research and footnotes by Mr. Sullivan.

26. *Stars and Stripes,* March 15, 1919.

27. Nelson, *Victors Divided*, 251.

28. *Der Tag* was a German newspaper, the second daily edition of the *Lokal-Anzeiger* printed in Berlin, noted for its sensational stories.

29. Nelson, *Victors Divided*, 251.

30. David M. Kennedy, *Over Here: The First World War and American Society* (New York: Oxford University Press, 1980), 366.

31. I. L. Hunt, *American Military Government*, 27.

32. Richard J. Evans, "The Scramble for Europe," in *London Review of Books* 33, no. 3 (2011): 17–19. This is a review of Shelley Baranowski, *Nazi Empire: German Colonialism and Imperialism from Bismarck to Hitler* (Cambridge, U.K.: Cambridge University Press, 2011).

33. Stovall, "Color Line," 737–69.

6

Goodwill Ambassadors

African American Athletes and U.S. Cultural Diplomacy, 1947–1968

DAMION THOMAS

During the early days of the Cold War, international condemnation of U.S. domestic race relations was a major hindrance to American foreign policy objectives. Consequently, the State Department began to send prosperous African Americans on overseas goodwill tours to showcase African Americans as the preeminent citizens of the African diaspora rather than as victims of racism. These tours were designed to undermine anti-Americanism as a foundation for racial and political identity formation throughout the African diaspora. Because sports were, arguably, the most publicly visible American institution to integrate, athletes were prominently featured in the State Department campaigns. Between 1947 and 1968 hundreds of African American athletes, including Rafer Johnson, Jesse Owens, Wilma Rudolph, and Mal Whitfield, were sent abroad. Bill Russell's 1959 trip to Africa embodies the challenges, contradictions, and political nature of the goodwill tours.

The U.S. State Department asked the 6'10" African American professional basketball player Bill Russell to take a goodwill tour of Libya, Liberia, the Ivory

Coast, Sudan, and Ethiopia. Russell was an intriguing choice for a goodwill ambassadorship, because he had a self-acknowledged reputation for being grouchy, opinionated, and ungrateful to the white establishment. Described as one of the "most cantankerous figures ever to have walked across the American sports page," Russell did not try to curry favor with the public, especially if that meant being silent on racial abuses.[1]

Russell's "grouchiness" was sparked immediately upon his arrival in Africa. "The State Department representatives who greeted me were seedy, alcoholic types who started calling me 'boy' before I reached the last step of the exit ramp from the plane, and they spoke of their African hosts with contempt," Russell said. "One after another they seemed to be arrogant louts, almost competitively eager to be racist. I was stunned."[2] Despite his experience with the American representatives, he found the energetic atmosphere, the pervasive air of expectation, and "the fever for independence" invigorating.

"Why are you here?" was the initial question posed during a large press conference at Russell's first stop in Tripoli. The American State Department had warned him to be careful, because communist writers would try to embarrass the United States through his visit. "I am here to play basketball and to show the people of Tripoli something about a sport which I love because I believe they will love it, too," Russell replied. This response revealed a truth that Russell would later admit: he was uninformed about international politics and unaware of the political undercurrents of his trip.[3]

Ostensibly, Russell traveled throughout northwest Africa conducting basketball clinics. He opened his presentations by explaining the sport with the aid of an interpreter. Then he would motion for the kids to stand. Singling out one of the young participants, he would playfully toss the ball in the child's direction. Basic passing and dribbling drills followed. Russell closed the clinics by holding his long arms in a huge circle so that the children could practice shooting baskets. The kids would be laughing, crawling all over him, and bubbling with energy when the clinic finally ended.

Russell was energized by his experiences teaching basketball to the African youth. "I felt renewed by the notion that I could go out under the sky in a foreign land, with nothing but a hundred words and a basketball, and communicate so well with kids that within a half hour I'd see the same looks of joy that I'd felt with my first high leap," he said. "The experience made me feel like a magician."[4] The excitement, joy, and fun that accompanied the play activities did not require the aid of a translator. Russell's experiences testify to the powerful communicative potential of athletics across linguistic and cultural barriers.

Toward the end of his trip, during a question-and-answer period held in a schoolroom in the upcountry section of Liberia, a young black child asked Russell a now familiar question: "Why are you here?" Unlike his earlier response, Russell, noted for his unemotional disposition on the basketball court, became choked with emotion: "I came here because I believe that somewhere in Africa is my ancestral home. I came here because I am drawn here, like any man, drawn to seek the land of his ancestors." With those two brief sentences, he "poured forth a deep, inner feeling" that he had never recognized. The feeling was so strong that it moved him to tears and he ended the question-and-answer session. Russell's comments prompted the Liberian children to rise to their feet in a standing tribute to the passion, sincerity, and fraternal nature of his pronouncement.[5]

Why was Russell sent on a goodwill tour to teach basketball in Africa? The basketball champion initially suggested that his trip was motivated by an altruistic desire he shared with the State Department to help promote the international growth of the American sport. His later explanation that his trip had helped him come to grips with his ancestry was certainly not the purpose of his State Department–sponsored tour. In fact, Russell's co-optation of the tour for his own personal growth and sense of identity had not been the outcome that the government had desired or anticipated. The multifaceted issues that Russell's tour highlights demonstrate the complexities of involving popular culture as a manipulative tool of U.S. foreign policy.

Russell was aware that his tour was sponsored by the government, but there were many athletes who did not know their trips were funded by the government and intended to influence foreign perceptions of U.S. race relations. The State Department was often able to hide its involvement in the tours by partnering with private organizations that had been awarded international jurisdiction over amateur athletics. For example, in the case of basketball and track and field, the two most popular sports in the State Department program, the government agency worked in collaboration with the Amateur Athletic Union (AAU). Typically, when the State Department decided to send a sports team abroad, it developed the team's itinerary but let the sports' governing organization choose the specific players who would be involved. Consequently, many of the touring athletes were unaware of the State Department's sponsorship of their visits or the nonathletic aims of their goodwill tours abroad. However, as the tours became more extensive and controversial in the 1960s, African American athletes began to provide counter-narratives to State Department claims about American exceptionalism—most notably during the 1968 Mexico City Olympic protest. Hence, sports became highly contested sites for competing interpretations of American race relations.

Before the beginning of the Cold War, African Americans had been depicted as symbols of American democracy, but these efforts had been sporadic and uncoordinated, and they lacked significant government involvement. For example,

Jesse Owens's success at the 1936 Nazi Olympic Games and Joe Louis's two fights with the German boxer Max Schmeling had placed African Americans in the international arenas as symbols of the American way of life. During the Cold War, however, U.S. government officials consciously attempted to systematically promote African American athletes as examples of the American willingness to incorporate people of color into the American social system.

The unpunished lynching of African Americans, segregated schooling, and rampant obstruction of black voting rights were increasingly becoming problematic for American efforts to assume a leading role in world affairs after the onset of the Cold War. By the late 1940s reports from diplomatic posts made it clear to the U.S. government that segregation was having a negative impact on its foreign policy. One diplomat in Ceylon (present-day Sri Lanka) wrote that racial segregation in the United States attracted more attention than any other subject. Another report said that local papers in Accra, Ghana, had little interest in international news, with the exception of racial discrimination in the United States. Furthermore, prominent American figures such as Walter White, Richard Nixon, A. Philip Randolph, Paul Robeson, Eleanor Roosevelt, and Secretary of State Dean Rusk publicly stated that the biggest single burden the United States carried in its foreign policy was its domestic policy of racial discrimination. The United States ambassador to the United Nations, Henry Cabot Lodge, accurately described American race relations as its "international Achilles heel," because nations of color saw the treatment of African Americans as reflective of the nation's attitude toward all people of color.[6]

In the late 1940s State Department officials estimated that almost one-half of Soviet propaganda focused on American racial discrimination.[7] By drawing connections between imperialism and the exploitation of people of color and between capitalism and racial discrimination, the Soviet Union made effective use of American segregation as a valuable means to undermine American foreign policy throughout the African diaspora. Only South Africa, an American ally, received greater criticism than the United States for its policies of racial discrimination in the immediate years after World War II. As the United States assumed responsibility for protecting the security and social system of the West during the Cold War, it drew attention to itself and unintentionally to its policies of racial discrimination. When people looked at the United States they saw the achievements of democracy, but they also saw a society deeply divided by its systematic racism—de jure and de facto.[8]

Chester Bowles, the United States ambassador to India, maintained that questions about race were the most frequently asked about American life. "A year, a month or even a week in Asia is enough to convince any perceptive American that the colored peoples of Asia and Africa, who total two-thirds of the world's population, seldom think about the United States without considering the limitations under which our 13 million Negroes are living," Bowles said before an audience at Yale University. The racially based denial of rights gave American claims to world leadership "a distinctly hollow ring." Bowles asked rhetorically, "How can the colored peoples of Asia be sure we are sincere in our interest in them if we do not respect the equality of our colored people at home?" On another occasion the ambassador acknowledged that it was impossible to exaggerate the impact that achieving racial harmony in America would have upon America's foreign interests. Similarly, Dean Rusk wrote to Walter White of the NAACP that the "greatest burden we Americans have to bear in working out satisfactory relations with the peoples of Asia is our minority problems in the United States."[9]

Incidents like the lynching of Robert Mallard were the basis of criticisms leveled against U.S. race relations. As Carol Anderson noted, on November 20, 1948, black businessman Robert Mallard, his wife, and three other family members were driving toward his thirty-two-acre farm in Toombs County, Georgia. Cruising in their new automobile, they were ambushed by three other cars filled with unmasked white men wearing white robes. Mallard was killed when a shot fired from one of the cars struck him in his chest. Police officers later interrupted Mallard's funeral and arrested his grieving wife during the ceremony, charging her with his murder as an act of intimidation and expression of local white political power. Nine hours later the charges were dropped and she was released into the custody of her attorney.[10]

Mrs. Mallard provided the name of two men whom she recognized as participants in the ambush: William L. Howell and Roderick Clifton. Both men were arrested and charged with the murder of Robert Mallard. As the case became the subject of national inquiry, Georgia's governor, Herman Talmadge, derided the case as part of a "campaign to destroy states' rights . . . through the civil rights campaign." Talmadge's invocation of states' rights as an issue is significant because Mallard was murdered for voting in the November 1948 election, in which President Truman was elected based upon his appeal to the black vote. Just four months before the lynching of Mallard, President Truman had issued two executive orders—one desegregating the military and the other outlawing discrimination in the federal government.[11] Both orders were seen as a threat to the "Southern way of life." Therefore, many Southerners remained determined to stifle the economic and political advancement that Robert Mallard's successful farm and civic engagement represented.

At the trial of the two defendants, T. Ross Sharpe, the defense attorney, called two jurors as character witnesses. Under Georgia law, anyone in a courtroom, except a trial judge, could be called as a character witness. Both jurors testified on behalf of the defendants by asserting that the testimony of Mrs. Mallard, a schoolteacher, should not be believed, based upon her "bad reputation." Immediately after their testimony, they returned to their seats in the jurors box. After deliberating for twenty-six minutes, the jury (including the two character witnesses) returned with a verdict of not guilty. Frustrated by Southern justice, NAACP legal counsel Thurgood Marshall said the trial illustrated "the incapacity of local authorities to deal with the crime of lynching." He called the arrest, indictment, and trial of the men "perfunctory motions" for the sole purpose of preventing federal intervention.[12] This case provides an illustration of the corruption of the Southern justice system, where white men who were known to be guilty of murdering African Americans went unpunished. High-profile incidents focused international attention on the racial abuse that African Americans faced even as the United States tried to position itself as the leader of the free world and principal protector of the rights of mankind worldwide.

Similar instances of "justice" had captured the attention of the President's Committee on Civil Rights, which had been commissioned in 1946 by President Truman. The committee argued that rather than focusing on the Soviets as prime sources for the critique of the nation's racial problem, the United States needed to concentrate on bridging the gap between its inclusive rhetoric and divided reality. The committee's 1947 report, "To Secure These Rights," reflected President Truman's support for civil rights reform. The committee recommended that if the United States could "establish the fact that our darker skinned citizens are truly first class citizens, it will create a reservoir of sympathy for us among all the dark skinned peoples of the world." Acting secretary of state Dean Acheson's letter to the chairman of the Fair Employment Practices Commission (FEPC) captured the mounting frustration many government officials felt regarding the growing influence of American segregation on America's moral leadership. Acheson exasperatedly noted, "Frequently we find it next to impossible to formulate a satisfactory answer to our critics in other countries."[13]

Dean Rusk, an assistant secretary of state, received two letters from the President's Committee on Civil Rights concerning the impact of race relations on U.S. foreign policy. More specifically, the committee wanted to know: "Do you feel that the formulation and conduct of a sound and desirable foreign policy is handicapped by our bad domestic record in the civil rights area? If the answer is in any sense in the affirmative, does this mean that American security is in fact endangered by this condition?" Rusk responded, "There is no question . . . the moral influence of the United States is weakened to the extent that the civil rights proclaimed by our Constitution are not fully observed in practice." "Our failure," Rusk continued, "to maintain the highest standards of performance in this field creates embarrassment out of proportion to the actual instances of violation." Rusk was willing to acknowledge that "on a small scale" African Americans were affected by racial discrimination, but his judgment that foreign press coverage of racial oppression was more important than the prevalence of racial discrimination in the United States was crucial. Although Rusk's suggestion was contrary to the recommendations of the President's Committee, his strategy became the primary response to dealing with international condemnation of American racism during the Truman and Eisenhower administrations. Because Southern segregationist congressmen were unwilling to support civil rights legislation, President Truman used Rusk's analysis to justify focusing on altering international perceptions of the nation's race relations rather than removing the legal impediments to African American advancement.[14]

President Truman and his immediate successor, President Eisenhower, defined the protests of African Americans as a threat to the nation's security. Hence, as the Cold War intensified, the U.S. government began a campaign of silencing dissenting black voices. W.E.B. Du Bois and Paul Robeson, both harsh critics of American racism, had their passports revoked because of their ability to attract large international audiences. Silencing Du Bois, Robeson, and other dissenting voices was crucial to the State Department's attempt to manipulate foreign perceptions of race relations in the United States.[15] Consequently, rather than providing immediate, substantive changes to the social landscape, the U.S. government moved to redefine and recontextualize the slow and unsteady advancement of African Americans into the American mainstream as a narrative of progress and as an example of American democracy.

After working to marginalize prominent African Americans who were critical of American race relations, the State Department recruited prosperous African Americans who projected middle-class American values to participate in goodwill tours abroad. With this goal in mind, African American athletes, along with jazz musicians and other artists, were sent abroad as cultural ambassadors and "rebuttal witnesses."[16] By overemphasizing the extent to which social mobility was achievable for African Americans, the State Department sought to influence diasporic political alignments during the Cold War. The U.S. government tried to show that American policies were supportive of the liberation and rise of all people of color worldwide, and the touring athletes were depicted as symbols of America's commitment. Hence, sports were at the forefront of American propaganda efforts.

Henry Luce, one of the most important media figures of the twentieth century and a principal shaper of the post–World War II world, advocated for a more concerted and directed effort to utilize the appeal of popular culture as a political medium in his über influential text *The American Century*. One of the most poignant of Luce's observations was his recognition of the leading role that American popular culture would play in the "American Century." "Once we cease to distract ourselves with lifeless arguments about isolationism," Luce charged, "we shall be amazed to discover that there is already an immense American internationalism. American jazz, Hollywood movies, American slang, American machines and patented products, are in fact the only things that every community in the world, from Zanzibar to Hamburg, recognizes in common." Heretofore, Luce had maintained that the internationalism of American popular culture was "blind, unintentional, and trivial."[17] One of the most overlooked arguments that his article pushed was the notion that America needed to develop a systematic approach to exporting the unique aspects of American culture. *The American Century* suggested that the United States needed to turn to seemingly insignificant aspects of American society, such as sports, as effective means to answer questions about American values and social customs.

President Eisenhower's Committee on Information Activities Abroad, otherwise known as the Sprague Committee, affirmed Luce's notion that popular culture was a valuable means to export the "American way of life." The committee's report asked, "Why are we so confident that what we stand for is in line with the aspirations of other peoples?" The committee concluded that the interests of the United States were consistent with the aspirations of peoples in Europe, Africa, Asia, South America, and the Middle East because human nature, regardless of cultural, national, and social background, shared the same inherent desires. Although that perspective is difficult to prove, by defining American conceptions of freedom, justice, individuality, property ownership, and religion as universal, the Sprague Committee reinforced the notion that the United States had a responsibility to remake the world in its image, or at least defend the world against Soviet disregard for "fundamental human desires."[18] Notwithstanding this "American-centric" notion, the pervasiveness of racial discrimination was one of the most scrutinized aspects of American society, and for America to assume a leadership position it had to convince the world that its racial problems were being solved. Consequently, the success of African American athletes was marshaled as a means to answer international charges.

The Sprague Committee clearly expressed the purpose of goodwill tours involving African Americans: "to *define* and *influence* the African Diaspora."[19] The tours were a crucial aspect of the State Department's three-pronged approach to transforming international understandings of American racial dynamics. The effort included (1) subversion of the rhetoric and organizational affiliations established in the prewar period that linked the African American struggle for equal rights with African and Asian struggles against colonialism; (2) reconfiguration and reinterpretation of the battle to end American racial segregation within the contours of the American democratic tradition of progress rather than as a facet of the global anticolonial movement; and (3) portrayal of the "advancement" of African Americans as evidence of American commitment to creating a world where race was not a basis for oppression.

There were a variety of reasons that sport was prominently featured in the complex State Department efforts. After Jackie Robinson integrated baseball, the swiftness with which sports integrated far outdistanced all other American institutions, thus giving sports a privileged space in the discussion of U.S. race relations. In addition, foreign audiences were less likely to see sport tours as politically motivated. Consequently, the mistaken yet widespread notion that sports was nonideological minimized athletics' vulnerability to the charge of cultural imperialism that plagued other American propaganda efforts. The Cold War contest between the United States and the Soviet Union elevated the significance of sports in the international arena, because it was one of the few places where the two nations competed head-to-head after the Soviet Union reentered the Olympic Games in 1952. Finally, sports appealed to children, teenagers, and other "high-value" audiences whom officials hoped to reach before they developed hostile, anti-American attitudes.

Given the rising international significance of U.S. race relations in the post–World War II period, when Jackie Robinson integrated baseball he was taking part in shaping the political and social destiny of this country. For an African American man to play in the national pastime had ramifications that extended far beyond the playing field. It is not too strong to assert that Jackie Robinson became a symbol of the Cold War; in particular, he symbolized the accessibility of the "American Dream" to African Americans. As the symbol of Cold War integration, his success was advanced to support the notion that aligning with the United States as the "leader of the free world" held forth a realistic change that people everywhere would be able to live the American Dream.

When Robinson integrated Major League Baseball in 1947, the National Football League (NFL) had just reintegrated the year before, and the National Basketball Association (NBA) integrated three years later. However, by 1968 one-fourth of the professional baseball league, one-third of the NFL, and one-half of the players in the NBA would be African American. Given the growth of the popularity of all of the leagues in the postwar period stemming from television, an improved travel infrastructure, and postwar prosperity, this development was astonishing. The rapidity of the advancement of the black athlete served as a reference point for those who were calling for widespread integration. For a generation of African Americans the exploits of Robinson, Joe Louis, and others confirmed their belief that if they were provided a fair chance, African Americans would show that they were capable of performing at the highest levels in all professions.

Initially, most African Americans were supportive of the tours because integration of the athletic arena was thought to be a foreshadowing of widespread integration. However, the symbol of the black athlete became contested terrain during the mid-1960s. The articulation of African American athletic success as a positive, progressive racial force became contestable because the success of black athletes did not translate into widespread access to better housing, education, or other high-prestige employment.

One of the unintended consequences of the State Department goodwill tours was that they helped politicize athletes and former athletes such as Tommie Smith, John Carlos, and Harry Edwards. Edwards, the organizer of the Olympic Project for Human Rights, which helped produce the lasting symbols of the athletic revolution—the raised fists of John Carlos and Tommie Smith at the 1968 Mexico City Olympics—became determined to produce a counter-narrative to the State Department's story of progress.[20] Rather than celebrating the suggestion that sports were at the forefront of racial advance, the athletes increasingly came to assert that sports were tied to a racist, oppressive system.

As one of the most publicly visible spaces to integrate in the first half of the twentieth century, sports held a privileged space in national and international discussions of U.S. race relations. As a means to capitalize on the geopolitical significance on the integration of sports during the early days of the Cold War, the U.S. government began to sponsor trips abroad by prominent African American athletes in a propaganda campaign to influence emerging nations throughout the African diaspora. These tours proved to be highly controversial and helped to politicize a generation of African American athletes.

Notes

1. Leigh Montville, "Bill Russell," *Sports Illustrated*, September 19, 1994, 124.

2. Bill Russell, *Second Wind* (New York: Basic Books, 1976), 99.

3. Ibid., 100.

4. Ibid.

5. Bill Russell, *Go Up for Glory* (New York: Berkley Medallion Books, 1966), 152–54.

6. Paul Gordon Lauren, *Power and Prejudice: The Politics and Diplomacy of Racial Discrimination* (Boulder, Col.: Westview Press, 1988), 190, 192–93, 228; Thomas Borstelmann, *Apartheid's Reluctant Uncle* (New York: Oxford University Press, 1993), 142.

7. Michael Krenn, *Black Diplomacy: African Americans and the State Department, 1945–1969* (London: M. E. Sharpe, 1999), 76; Walter L. Hixson, *Parting the Curtain: Propaganda, Culture, and the Cold War, 1945–1961* (New York: St. Martin's Press, 1997), 121; David Southern, *Gunnar Myrdal and Black-White Relations: The Use and Abuse of "An American Dilemma," 1944–1969* (Baton Rouge: Louisiana State University Press, 1987), 102.

8. Lauren, *Power and Prejudice,* 187–88; George Shepherd Jr., ed., *Racial Influences on American Foreign Policy* (New York: Basic Books, 1970), 4.

9. Lauren, *Power and Prejudice,* 188; Mary Dudziak, *Cold War Civil Rights: Race and the Image of American Democracy* (Princeton, N.J.: Princeton University Press, 2000), 77, 80; Krenn, *Black Diplomacy,* 30–31, 33.

10. "Negro Slaying Spurs Inquiry in Georgia," *New York Times,* November 25, 1948; "Widow Held in Killing: Arrested at Funeral of Negro Victim in Georgia," *New York Times,* November 28, 1948; "Slain Negro's Widow Released in Georgia," *New York Times,* November 29, 1948; Carol Anderson, *Eyes Off the Prize: The United Nations and the African American Struggle for Human Rights, 1944–1955* (New York: Cambridge University Press, 2004), 125.

11. Anderson, *Eyes Off the Prize,* 125.

12. Ibid., 190.

13. Krenn, *Black Diplomacy,* 30–31, 33; Dudziak, *Cold War Civil Rights,* 80.

14. Letter from Mr. Rusk to the Secretary of State, National Archives (NA), RG 59, 800/432.213.

15. Penny Von Eschen, *Race against Empire: Black Americans and Anti-Colonialism, 1937–1957* (Ithaca, N.Y.: Cornell University Press, 1997), 126.

16. Nikhil Pal Singh, *Black Is a Country: Race and the Unfinished Struggle for Democracy* (Cambridge, Mass.: Harvard University Press, 2004), 178.

17. Henry R. Luce, *The American Century* (New York: Farrar & Rinehart, 1941), 33–34; Robert E. Herzstein, *Henry R. Luce: A Political Portrait of the Man Who Created the American Century* (New York: Macmillan Books, 1994), 180.

18. "USIA Basic Guidance Paper," October 22, 1957, File on Agency History, USIAA.

19. "The President's Committee on Information Activities Abroad: Africa, PCIAA no. 31," box 21, folder PCIAA # 31, U.S. President's Committee on Information Activities Abroad (Sprague Committee), Dwight D. Eisenhower Presidential Library (DDEL); emphasis in original.

20. For a detailed examination of the athletic revolution, see Jack Scott, *The Athletic Revolution* (New York: Free Press, 1971).

7

The Paradox of Jazz Diplomacy

Race and Culture in the Cold War

LISA DAVENPORT

In January 1965, Jazz Night at the Blue Bird Youth Café in Moscow was in full swing. Soviet club managers closely monitored the club's clientele, and audiences were carefully selected by Soviet cultural authorities. Those attending included U.S. cultural attaché Ernest G. Weiner, who had visited Jazz Night with a select group of people at the invitation of a Soviet friend. Weiner characterized the café as though it had a mystical aura. He commented that it was ensconced "on a narrow and dimly lit street" and gave "practically no outward indication of its existence." It was especially alluring at night, when "the small white globe light over the entranceway [did] not even illuminate a perfunctory 'Kafe' sign nearby on the wall of the building."[1]

Inside, however, Western influence abounded. A young Russian trumpeter played with an "upturned bell *a la* Gillespie." Such developments attested to the enduring impact of American jazz on Soviet culture and society. Jazz imbued the Soviet bloc with unique and bold American values, and in the 1960s several American officials reported on the ubiquitous presence of jazz in many Soviet bloc cities.[2] Ultimately, the proliferation of jazz in the Soviet Union and throughout the world helped determine the course of the Cold War cultural rivalry between the superpowers while it reshaped the American image worldwide. As the United States propelled jazz into new international arenas, jazz diplomacy created a bold Cold War paradox: the cultural expression of one of the nation's most oppressed minorities came to symbolize the cultural superiority of American democracy.

As the idea of race, always central to the American character, arose as a controversial dimension of Cold War diplomacy, it remained difficult for the State Department's Bureau of Educational and Cultural Affairs (CU) to contain international criticism of U.S. race relations and cultural affairs that raged in the 1950s and became acute in the 1960s against the backdrop of domestic racial conflicts and the Vietnam War. This resulted from what W.E.B. Du Bois, a premier black activist and intellectual, identified as "the problem of the twentieth century"—the "color line."[3] The dual injustices of race and Vietnam amplified the paradox of jazz diplomacy on the world stage and compelled a profound reassessment of Cold War cultural policies. Under the scrutiny of the *informationalists*—U.S. officials who viewed culture simply as an instrument of *realpolitik* and who often prevailed in devising jazz policy—jazz diplomacy no longer seemed viable. In the mid-1960s the CU consequently suspended jazz tours. It did not reinstate them until the resurgence of internationalism in the CU and the expansion of black cultural production led to a reevaluation of jazz in a transnational context. Thus, although internationalist ideals in part gave impetus to cultural diplomacy, the causes of art, jazz, and internationalism did not merge in cultural policy until the late 1960s, when the Soviet Union increasingly showed signs of its impending disunity. Thus the years 1954 to 1968 represent a critical arc in the cultural rivalry between the superpowers. Even as jazz, an analog of American freedom and racial equality, spoke to America's cultural modernity, the American image grew increasingly enigmatic amid the Cold War confrontations between communism and democracy that engulfed the world. Never before had American policy makers faced this political paradox, one they could not ignore: race relations reflected a contradiction in American democracy that undermined the nation's ability to implement the policy of cultural containment both inside and outside the world of people of color.

Jazz and "Cultural Containment"

Containing the criticism of America that emanated from the jarring, trenchant propaganda that the Soviet Union disseminated throughout the world became central to American cultural efforts. Although Soviet elites held complex views of the United States, ranging from cultural reverence, envy, curiosity, and admiration to boldfaced ideological mistrust, the fear and anxiety created by U.S. actions against Japan at the end of World War II, along with the onset of tensions that gave rise to the Cold War, gave impetus to strident anti-Americanism in Soviet foreign policy. Soviet imperial ambitions distinctly shaped these international efforts. The Soviet Union characterized Americans as racist segregationists and criticized American culture as decadent, amoral, materialist, and individualistic.[4] Not surprisingly, as the United States wrestled to redefine its racial and cultural identity, frequent racial incidents that caused considerable embarrassment for the country altered official views toward *kulturpolitik*. America's Cold War cultural rhetoric consequently changed as the course of the Cold War shifted in its focus, scope, and intensity. Black nationalism worldwide led American policy makers to view new black nations with caution and sometimes fear.[5] As jazz musicians traveled abroad, the U.S. government actively curtailed and censured the activities of some black intellectuals they regarded as firebrands in the domestic and international arena, including W.E.B. Du Bois, Paul Robeson, and Josephine Baker.

Such American cultural tours first became possible in 1954, a watershed year in U.S. domestic and foreign affairs. With *Brown v. Board of Education* the United States ended its legally sanctioned system of racial segregation, the culmination of legal efforts to end segregation since the end of Reconstruction in 1877. *Brown* symbolized the flourishing of liberal ideas with regard to race. In July 1954, President Dwight D. Eisenhower, seeing it as a Cold War imperative, called for the creation of a worldwide cultural exchange program for the performing arts to improve the world's perception of American cultural and political life. Under Eisenhower's Cultural Presentations Program (CPP), hundreds of performing artists traveled the globe as representatives of the U.S. government. In the midst of cultural tours that included high culture, science, technology, athletic groups, and many other American cultural products, jazz held a unique place in American cultural policy.[6]

As Nicholas Cull has deftly shown in *The Cold War and the United States Information Agency*, cultural diplomacy became part of an expansive American effort to invest the "P" factor—the "psychological dimension of power"—to wage the Cold War.[7] Cull explains that public diplomacy—"an international actor's attempt to conduct its foreign policy by engaging with foreign publics"—involved five "core practices: listening, advocacy, cultural diplomacy, exchange diplomacy, and international broadcasting."[8] Following Cull, this chapter underscores the centrality of Western cultural forces in diminishing the credibility and appeal of Soviet communism in the Eastern Bloc through the use of public diplomacy. Like Walter Hixson's *Parting the Curtain*, I present a cultural approach to diplomacy. In addition, like Penny von Eschen's *Satchmo Blows Up the World*, I portray jazz as a pivotal Cold War trope and emphasize that jazz diplomacy reflects the United States' symbolic acknowledgment that the dual problems of race and culture had to be addressed in a global context.[9]

But unlike von Eschen, my research suggests that, ultimately, the problem of culture and jazz diplomacy in American foreign policy had to be addressed apart from worldwide economic and military exigencies that had arisen during this era. Even in the midst of critical Cold War disputes, jazz diplomacy existed in a realm that often transcended economic and strategic priorities. Jazz often became the subject of heated debates about aesthetic agency and cultural property. Moreover, the goal of containing communism remained paramount in shaping the course of jazz diplomacy and prevailed over America's policy of redefining relations with emerging new nations in Africa, Asia, and Latin America. The United States addressed the issues of race and jazz in a global context only to align its cultural policies with its anticommunist agenda—to win the Cold War, counter Soviet cultural propaganda, and defeat communism. Jazz diplomacy thus remained steeped in both America's cultural realism and its cultural idealism. It became a unique and enigmatic instrument of ideological and intellectual warfare.

Moreover, as the United States grappled to devise policies to keep neutral countries from "going communist," Cold War competition necessitated conveying sympathy, not disdain, for the very same values the United States often subverted at home: healthy race relations and the sanctity of civil liberties. Likewise, America had to buttress its racial and cultural image to maintain credibility among the declining colonial powers of Britain, France, Spain, Portugal, Belgium, and the Netherlands. Toward this end, U.S. policy makers began to appropriate black cultural products, most notably jazz, to foster the idea that America had a robust and resilient culture despite prevalent racial conflicts. U.S. officials argued that American democracy made such creativity possible and that jazz, a uniquely American art form, was a critical reflection of America's cultural exuberance. In building upon the cultural dynamics of the Cold War struggle, and by employing jazz to exemplify U.S. race relations as a positive feature of American life, American Cold Warriors redefined the global policy of cultural containment. Jazz became another instrument in the effort to "contain" criticism about America's cultural and racial identity. It symbolized integration and the country's emergence from colony to nationhood as the paradigm of race and culture shifted during the Cold War: blacks once seen as "separate but equal" began to signify modernist ideals. Theoretically, racial equality and integration became emblematic of American democracy.

As Ingrid Monson points out, this dynamic reflected the arch of modernity in Western thought that embraced "transcendence, universality, freedom, autonomy, subjectivity, and progress." "Modernity" broadly refers to "the expansive sense of Western thought since the Enlightenment." In the realm of civil rights this meant "political democracy, equality before the law, and individual freedom."

Du Bois dramatically redefined the modern idea of race in a global context during the postwar years. In 1948, he illuminated his idea of race when he declared, "I came then to advocate, not pride of biological race, but pride in a cultural group, integrated and expanded by cultural ideals."[10] At the same time, aesthetic modernism incorporated a set of "ideas about form and content, abstraction, individuality, iconoclasm, rebellion, the autonomy of art, authenticity, progress, and genius."[11]

Although modernist ideals abounded in theory, in practice these ideals had not yet been realized for African Americans. Not surprisingly, Du Bois and other black intellectuals denounced Western imperialism, and numerous black artists and musicians supported their cause. In this vein, the "worldview" of Americans and their conception of "self" and of society remained critical for American officials in their efforts to reconstruct the image of America's cultural and racial life. Anthropologist Clifford Geertz characterized a nation's and a people's ethos as "the tone, character, and quality of . . . life, its moral and aesthetic style and mood . . . the underlying attitude toward themselves and their world that life reflects. Their world view is their picture of the way things in sheer reality actually are, their concept of nature, of self, of society. It contains their most comprehensive ideas of order. . . . The world is made emotionally acceptable by being presented as an image of an actual state of affairs of which such a way of life is an authentic expression."[12]

Jazz was often presented abroad as an "authentic expression" of American life. This effort to use culture to portray the country's changing Cold War ethos represented a form of cultural internationalism—one of the most pivotal elements of the Cold War cultural struggle.[13] Cultural internationalism occurred when "individuals and groups of people from different lands . . . sought to develop an alternative community of nations and peoples on the basis of their cultural interchanges. . . . Their efforts have significantly altered the world community and immeasurably enriched our understanding of international affairs. [Cultural internationalism is] the inspiration behind these endeavors and the sum of their achievements."[14] In this international context, official person-to-person contacts between nations strikingly redefined the American ethos.

Jazz in the Cold War

As Monson has shown, the "story of jazz" in the 1950s and 1960s—the "golden age of jazz"—became a story of cultural experimentation and unprecedented aesthetic innovation, set against the backdrop of political and social limits that redefined the country's cultural milieu. Jazz music took on a "set of symbolic meanings" that defined the jazz genre well into the twenty-first century.[15] A potent symbol of resistance, jazz music "in many ways" became the "sonic alter ego" of the American struggle for racial equality.[16] As American values shifted, many jazz performers saw their music as a means to bring about "social change" and assert "cultural self-determination."[17] They were a minority resisting a dominant power through cultural means. Jazz's polyrhythms, syncopation, collective improvisation, and melodic lines often emerged in opposition to what musicologist Gunther Schuller calls the "democratization of rhythmic values."[18] Race relations became axiomatic accentuating of a moral tension: jazz challenged its practitioners either to affirm their heritage by struggling against racial oppression or to seek acceptance into white society. Such jazz theorists as Amiri Baraka saw that the political implications of jazz were unavoidable. The musicians themselves asked: Did they hold a place in the postwar world that set them apart? Did the civil rights movement promise them a more secure place in American society?[19]

This tension in part gave rise to the clearer assertion of a unique black aesthetic in jazz, sometimes resulting in racial unity and at other times disunity. It also epitomized the moral dilemma that Du Bois put forth in 1903 in *The Souls of Black Folk*:

> The Negro is a sort of seventh son, born with a veil, and gifted with second-sight in this American world, a world which yields him no true self-consciousness, but only lets him see himself through the revelation of the other world. It is a peculiar sensation, this double-consciousness. . . . One ever feels his twoness—an American, a Negro; two souls, two thoughts, two unreconciled strivings; two warring ideals in one dark body. . . .
>
> He simply wishes to make it possible for a man to be both a Negro and an American . . . without having the doors of Opportunity closed roughly in his face. . . . This, then, is the end of his striving: to be a co-worker in the kingdom of culture.[20]

Amid this cultural depth and complexity, the more vocal assertion of jazz modernism, and the expansion of the jazz intelligentsia, shifts in ideology continued to occur in the jazz community, and some musicians spearheaded a new form of jazz in the 1960s—free jazz. Some free jazz musicians played with the principles of cultural nationalism in mind; others embraced revolutionary nationalism. In short, revolutionary nationalists followed the tenets of Marxism, while cultural nationalists rejected Marxism and "favored African socialism." Both emphasized autonomy and black cultural identity.[21] Unlike many mainstream artists, free jazz men often defined their own national culture through national struggle, echoing yet not completely mimicking Africans taking up arms against colonial rule. Rather than advocate the idea of color-blind race relations in jazz, free jazz musicians and supporters of the music asserted a renewed black consciousness in which the idea of universality centered on black musical values. Some embraced Leopold Senghor's concept of *negritude*: a black culture separate from that of the national culture. The musicians used their instruments as arms to fight creative monotony, conformity, and oppression. They capitalized on the music's "revolutionary potential."[22]

Free jazz performers were often maligned in the press for their outspokenness.[23] Excluded from performing in the clubs, they created an underground movement, performing instead in alluring cafés. Like the native intellectuals in Frantz Fanon's *The Wretched of the Earth,* free jazz musicians, "since they could not stand wonderstruck before the history of today's barbarity, decide to back further and to delve deeper down. . . . The claims of the native intellectual are not a luxury but a necessity in any coherent program. The native intellectual who takes up arms to defend his nation's legitimacy and who wanted to bring proofs to bear out that legitimacy, who is willing to strip himself naked to study the history of his body, is obliged to dissect the heart of his people."[24]

Although the world of ideas acquired new meaning in the jazz world, American policy makers still viewed jazz through the prism of containment and the Cold War—as a trope that reflected the cultural "affluence" of American society and the uniqueness of American democracy. Jazz tours paradoxically aimed to depict racial equality, integration, American exceptionalism, and even the idea of republicanism, both as cultural aspirations and realities on the world stage. These tensions between containment and the color line increasingly undercut the viability of jazz diplomacy. As tours ensued, elitism and ethnocentrism remained common among American cold warriors in the CU and abroad. Two kinds of elitism emerged. First, officials frequently expressed elitist attitudes toward race. As pianist Quincy Jones, who toured with Dizzy Gillespie in 1956, recounts, on Dizzy's tour, in such countries as Greece, it was the officials who patronizingly warned the "Greek women to steer clear" of the black guys and who often indulged in partying and revelry. Additionally, although the CU characterized jazz as a component of America's superior cultural heritage, it did not embrace the black freedom struggles at home or abroad that helped shape that heritage. Consequently, it ardently shunned free jazz because the music embodied the ideologies of revolutionary and black cultural nationalism. Moreover, as European empires crumbled, cultural tours that increased U.S. contacts with people of color often reinforced policy makers' paternalistic notions of black peoples as primitive and backward.[25]

Officials also articulated elitist attitudes toward culture. Some put forth the view that American culture had grown more sophisticated than the cultures of Europe and expressed beliefs in cultural hierarchies—high and low culture. For the CU, only mainstream jazz, not avant-garde or free jazz, represented American high culture. Other forms of jazz reflected lowbrow music.[26] In international circles, however, many regarded free jazz as a component of high culture and believed it represented a unique Western art form. For them it was not just a type of entertainment of which the "sole purpose" was to elicit an "intrinsic perceptual interest" or have a "fleeting" influence on "aesthetic sensibilities." Free jazz as art "require[d] . . . active involvement," was "highly charged with content, and profoundly influence[d]" one's sense of self "and the world for years to come."[27] American cultural officials, especially informationalists, often downplayed the significance of these cultural nuances.

Not surprisingly, showcasing mainstream jazz and black performing artists to highlight blacks' improving status in American life and to rectify perceptions of American race relations appeared illusory to many peoples and nations.[28] In 1961 esteemed African American writer James Baldwin offered an eloquent expression of such a paradox in *Nobody Knows My Name*. He wrote, "The American Negro can no longer, nor will he ever again, be controlled by white Americans' image of him. This fact has everything to do with the rise of Africa in world affairs. . . . Any effort, from here on out, to keep the Negro in his 'place' can only have the most extreme and unlucky repercussions."[29]

It was in 1957, after the successful tours of such bandleaders as Dizzy Gillespie, Benny Goodman, and Wilbur De Paris, that the paradox of race became even more glaring in the international arena. The school desegregation crisis in Little Rock, Arkansas, set off a chain of events at home and abroad that dramatically altered the course of jazz diplomacy: from 1957 to 1960 jazz policy makers became reluctant to sponsor black jazz musicians in cultural tours and questioned the efficacy of using black jazz in cultural policy. In CU's view, the use of black jazz musicians might heighten attention on America's racial problems. Contrarily, conservative, mainstream white jazz bands would offset controversies about race and help avoid a common Soviet exposé associated with jazz and Little Rock: "regime propaganda linking jazz" to the subjugation of blacks in the United States.[30] The activities of expatriates and free jazz performers added to the perceived chaos the United States sought to quell. In this vein, Little Rock signified a critical turning point in America's rhetorical approach to Cold War cultural relations. It was not until the independence of French West Africa in 1960 that the CU again sponsored a majority of all-black and racially integrated groups in its jazz tours.

The Little Rock crisis played out when Arkansas governor Orval Faubus defied a federal court order and refused to integrate Central High School. President Dwight D. Eisenhower sent federal troops, as well as the National Guard, to the town to try to protect the black students who were integrating the school. Violence and rioting ensued as the federal troops escorted a group of nine black children into the school. The "Little Rock Nine" came to symbolize America's paradoxical racial image in the Cold War era: they underscored that the leader of the free world was committed to democracy only in theory rather than in actual practice.[31] In the words of Thomas C. Holt, Little Rock exemplified how blacks worldwide remained "anchored in a past time, but always looking to a future time."[32] To add to the fervor, in October 1957, the Soviet Union launched *Sputnik,* the world's first satellite. Symbolically, this represented a Russian triumph and an American defeat in the race for space.

As Little Rock and *Sputnik* reshaped the global context of cultural containment, the Soviets intensified anti-American propaganda campaigns and emerged as the most vocal critic of the incident in Arkansas. Eisenhower became deeply concerned that Little Rock imperiled "national security," especially because America's adversaries worldwide celebrated the country's embarrassment.[33] Historian Cary Fraser argues that what happened in Little Rock led the United States to shift its policies and practices with "colored nations." As the United States sought to counter its image as a "bastion of white supremacy," it saturated the world with black cultural products, launching a steadfast effort to contain the international censure arising from the event.[34]

The most explosive controversy surrounding Little Rock arose when Louis Armstrong decisively canceled an impending State Department tour to the Soviet Union. In a provocative article, a reporter declared that the lessening of international tensions boded well for an Armstrong tour to the Soviet Union, but the Little Rock crisis had changed that. Little Rock impelled Armstrong to divulge one of the most fervent expressions of America's racial paradox during the Cold War. On September 19 the *New York Times* reported that, in Grand Forks, North Dakota, "Louis Armstrong, Barring Soviet Tour, Denounces Eisenhower and Gov. Faubus." Armstrong asserted that "the way they treat my people in the South, the government can go to hell." Moreover, he reportedly remarked, "It's getting so bad a colored man hasn't got any country." Armstrong, "a voice long quiet in world affairs," had "unloaded a verbal blast echoed virtually around the world." He even called President Eisenhower "two-faced" and claimed that Eisenhower was an "uneducated plow boy" who "let Faubus 'run the country.'"[35]

Armstrong subsequently remarked to the *Pittsburgh Courier*:

> I wouldn't take back a thing I've said. I've had a beautiful life over 40 years in music, but I feel the downtrodden situation the same as any other Negro. My parents and family suffered through all of that old South. . . . My people . . . are not looking for anything . . . we just want a square shake. But when I see on television and read about a crowd spitting on and cursing at a little colored girl . . . I think I have a right to get sore and say something about it."[36]

American officials inordinately worried about the propaganda value that the "Reds" might derive from Armstrong's "verbal blast." One reporter commented that "Satchmo's Words Rocked [the] State Dept." and caused a "political earthquake."[37] Similarly, an official denounced Armstrong's "insult to beloved President Eisenhower" and adamantly discouraged State Department funding. Another professed that "as an American" he protested "most vigorously anyone who has made such a statement as 'the government can go to hell' being sponsored by any branch of our government."[38]

The public reaction to Armstrong's "blast" grew equally controversial. A headline in the *Gazette and Daily* pointed out that "Negro Entertainers Back Up Armstrong's Action in Cancelling Trip." Yet, while some of Armstrong's friends supported him, others, including the popular entertainer Sammy Davis Jr., vehemently criticized his provocative candor.[39] In a letter to the State Department, one person called Armstrong a "sacred cow" and declared that he objected to his tour "not because I think his music is drivel, which it is, but I certainly can't see how" a musician who makes such a remark about the government "can be any sort of an effective salesman for it." The *Miami Herald* likewise reported that Armstrong's remarks "destroyed his 'good will' usefulness behind the Iron Curtain."[40]

Notably, those who defended Armstrong included American jazz critic Ralph Gleason. Gleason firmly denounced Armstrong's critics and praised his ability to stand up and talk back to the president. He simultaneously expressed the opinion that the verbal dispute reflected the resilience of American democracy; he believed that Armstrong experienced no significant reprisals after making his cacophonous comments. In Gleason's view, Armstrong had taken jazz, the "legacy of the Negro race, and had given it to the world."[41]

Significantly, after Eisenhower sent federal troops to Little Rock to resolve the crisis there, Armstrong had a change of heart.[42] In a telegram to President Eisenhower, Armstrong exposed his politically savvy approach to race and culture and revealed that he remained an astute observer of social affairs. He proclaimed: "Da[d]dy if and when you decide to take those little Negro children personally into Central High School along with your marvelous troops please take me along. O God it would be such a great pleasure I assure you. My regard to brother [Attorney General Herb] Brownell and may God bless you President. You have a good heart."[43]

Armstrong later told *Variety* that he extolled jazz's international appeal and its potential to "lessen world tensions," especially in the context of U.S.–Soviet relations. He professed that "everywhere I have gone in the world, I have been well received and understood." Armstrong then insisted that he supported the idea of touring the Soviet Union, proclaiming that when "you sit down to play jazz, to blow with Satchmo, there is no enmity. One man rule has no influence in such a background."[44]

As controversies surrounding Little Rock ensued, U.S. officials sought to effectively implement cultural containment without relinquishing broader Cold War interests. They deeply feared potential alliances of powerful African and Asian states with the Soviet Union. Seeking to reach prominent sectors of these societies, especially in such politically important countries as Ghana and Vietnam, officials debated the propaganda value of sponsoring a variety of black cultural figures.[45] The secretary of state received a pressing request from an official in the Middle East in September 1957. It suggested that in such regions as India and Africa, the United States immediately should counter the effects of Little Rock by printing an Associated Press wire photo in newspapers that depicted "Vice President Nixon presenting the winner's trophy to Miss Althea Gibson, the first Negress ever to win the National Women's Tennis Championship."[46]

Most notably, the CU sponsored world-renowned opera singer Marian Anderson on a tour to Asia in 1957 as Cold War tensions escalated further. In North Vietnam, under the leadership of Ho Chi Minh, communist nationalists had begun their quest for control of the North and the South. After the North Vietnamese communists defeated the French at Dien Bien Phu in 1954, the Eisenhower administration increasingly sent military advisers and economic aid to South Vietnam. With U.S. support, Ngo Dinh Diem became the leader of South Vietnam and ruled until he was assassinated in 1963.[47] These events foreshadowed the political and social conflicts in Vietnam that perilously eclipsed other Cold War rivalries in the 1960s.

Because Anderson performed an art form derived from Europe, she showcased the exuberance of American culture and helped redress the American dilemma without the racial stigmas and implications of jazz. Anderson toured such cities as Seoul, Korea, where the reporting officer characterized her visit as "the most important cultural exchange event of the year." When she responded to questions about American race relations, according to an official report, the "colored lady who sang a song at the inauguration of the President of the United States" expressed her deep hope that the U.S. race problem would be "cured."[48]

Anderson met with continued success in such cities as Saigon, according to Thomas D. Bowie, the counselor for political affairs at the Saigon embassy.[49] Anderson's broadcast on Radio Saigon's Voice of Vietnam became the "first exception to the rule that no American singer of any sort should be heard on that channel."[50] She also visited a refugee camp and gave a concert at a motion picture house (Majestic Theatre) where audiences were mostly European and American. Equally important, Anderson met with President Diem. Afterward, Bowie claimed that the "benefits from Miss Anderson's tour . . . went far beyond merely the cultural performances in the theatre; the Anderson personality and the charm of the entire party were felt wherever they appeared, whether it was at a diplomatic reception or at a refugee camp, and they presented their side of America in the best imaginable way."[51]

After Anderson's tour, a movie about her travels, *The Lady from Philadelphia*, was made for Edward R. Murrow's *See It Now* program, which appeared on CBS television. Many applauded the film and Anderson's popularity soared.[52] The *Saturday Review* emphatically proclaimed that Anderson, as depicted in the movie, vividly epitomized American ideals in the context of anticommunism. She conveyed the idea that "forme[r] slaves to white masters from the West" were now their "own masters free to choose between the Communists and us." The movie professed that slavery and a "poverty of spiritual values" would result if newly independent countries chose communism over American industry and culture. Anderson epitomized the promise of the nation through her stunning "sense of song" and her impassioned artistry. She symbolized the potential of Western civilization to triumph over Soviet foes. Her tour was a "propaganda triumph."[53]

Despite this historic tour, the paradox of race still resonated loudly on the world stage, especially in Africa. Wilson C. Flake, ambassador to Ghana, put forth the view that the American policy of sending blacks to perform in cultural presentations might have backfired. He discouraged sending black artists to the region, arguing that "mediocre" black performers could do a disservice to the program, and contending

> Ghanaians . . . like to see Americans who really have something to offer, regardless of ethnic origin. In fact, there is an ever-present danger that the Ghanaians may think that we tend to discriminate against them in a sense by sending a number of persons from one ethnic group out of all proportion to the population ratio in the United States. Even some thoughtful American Negroes who have visited here have expressed to me some concern about the emphasis on racial factors when we are choosing Americans to come here for cultural presentations. Some of them have felt, and I most certainly agree, that we are doing the American Negro himself a disservice when we send mediocre Negroes here for cultural presentations.[54]

Likewise, in April 1958 Cushman C. Reynolds, public affairs officer (PAO) to Khartoum, declared:

> It is a well known fact here that the United States has a racial problem as does the Sudan. The lamentable incidents at Little Rock certainly did much to focus world attention on this problem and resurrect widespread condemnation of the

treatment of the Negro in the United States. It is well to show other people in every way possible that we are at least trying by legislation, if not by other means, to remedy the evils of racial discrimination. But it would seem that by over stressing our earnest endeavors to proclaim that we have goodwill to all men, we may be drawing too much attention to the fact and thus defeating our purpose. . . . We are not fooling anyone here in Khartoum by so far selecting only Negro artists to come to the Sudan.[55]

Thus Reynolds, like Flake, claimed that "in fact, it would seem to stress to the people here that they are of a different color, and will undoubtedly bring forth some rather caustic remarks from Sudanese friends." Reynolds urged that the United States send white performers to Africa in order to present "balance" in the cultural program and to represent the United States more "correctly."[56]

These sentiments also resulted in part from the need to offset the impact of black expatriates abroad as the paradoxical complexity of the cultural forces shaping containment expanded in many venues. In Latin America, Josephine Baker had openly criticized the race problem in the early 1950s, and the State Department convinced governments in the region to ban her performances.[57] At home, the passports of expatriates like W.E.B. Du Bois and Paul Robeson were revoked in the early 1950s.[58] Du Bois was indicted and fined when he refused to sign a State Department document denying that he was a communist.[59] Such incidents further ignited his belief in the virtues of Soviet socialism. After his passport was reinstated in 1958, he visited the Soviet Union, and in a letter to the foreign editor of the *Literary Gazette,* he extolled the courage of the USSR ("a miracle") to withstand the moral attack from the West.[60]

Policy makers likewise believed that Robeson's impact in Eastern Europe and the Soviet Union appeared ominous, especially after the heated dispute over the military occupation and political division of Berlin. Robeson traveled to Berlin and Moscow in 1960, having become a devout supporter of communist regimes.[61] He expressed admiration for Khrushchev, and in Moscow, Llewellyn E. Thompson, U.S. ambassador to Moscow, reported on Robeson's efforts to promote Soviet-black cooperation through spirituals and jazz. Robeson was praised by such Soviet newspapers as the *Literary Gazette* and *Trud* and expressed support for the Soviet zone in Berlin at the third annual Press Festival of Art.[62] To add to the fervor, he had allegedly claimed that black Americans would not take up arms against the Soviet Union and, when commenting on Little Rock, stated that "he would have asked 'thousands of Negroes from all over the U.S. to go there armed' and he was sure nothing would have happened."[63]

Not surprisingly, American racial attitudes and the activities of black expatriates reinforced perceptions abroad of America's cultural paradoxes. Officials from Malaysia and Singapore who visited the United States expressed their belief in the "stereotype of the average American as an ignoramus." Apparently, an American official concluded, Malaysians assumed that they knew "more about the Americans than they kn[e]w about themselves."[64]

These factors shaped the context that led policy makers to continually emphasize the need to present white groups for jazz tours. W. K. Bunce, counselor for public affairs in New Delhi, recommended Gerry Mulligan, a white performer, for a tour. An official in Rio requested such jazz groups as Woody Herman's band, while the embassy in Czechoslovakia pointed to the popularity of Dave Brubeck.[65] In Poland, Edward A. Symans, attaché in Warsaw, believed that, for propaganda and cultural purposes, a white jazz group "would rekindle waning sentiments and strongly reinforce relationships still alive."[66] Ultimately, even after American embassies throughout Africa—from Senegal to the Congo—made numerous requests for jazz, especially for Louis Armstrong, the CU chose Dave Brubeck to represent the country on the next jazz tour.[67] Brubeck's group was all white, except for the African American bass player, Eugene Wright. Not surprisingly, some black jazz musicians sharply opposed the CU's choice.[68] A deep rift in jazz policy had clearly emerged.

Brubeck traveled abroad for the CU in 1958, his music embodying the white mainstream values of Cold War America that had come to define the parameters of commercial jazz in the 1950s. Significantly, his group traveled to Poland, South Asia, and the Middle East, but did not tour Africa. This policy came about in part because the Eisenhower administration continued to identify relations with Europe as a priority over those with Africa and sought to buttress cultural containment in the Soviet sphere. Brubeck's music engendered passion in this region and helped break down Cold War cultural barriers in neutral nations. The U.S. Information Service (USIS) presented Brubeck's jazz as the artistry of the "elite" high culture, the "finest modern music" in the United States.[69] Amid the fervor of Little Rock, jazz policy keenly reflected Du Bois's proposition that "all art is propaganda and ever must be, despite the wailing of the purists."[70]

Although Brubeck helped advance the policy of cultural containment in turbulent Cold War regions, he endured tremendous hardship upon returning home. He scheduled a series of performances at a group of Southern universities that subsequently canceled his concert dates because Brubeck's bass player was black. The colleges had devised rules that stipulated that interracial bands could not perform on their campuses. Yet Brubeck had repudiated the "lily white" clause in his contract by refusing to replace Wright with a white musician.[71] He lost a reported forty thousand dollars as a result of the cancellation. Brubeck himself expressed his dismay at the incident, calling it "unconstitutional" and "ridiculous," and saying, "All we want is that authorities accept us as we are, and allow us—and other integrated groups—to play our music without intimidation or pressure."[72] His alto saxophone player, Paul Desmond, agreed, and Wright lamented, "It's a shame we can go travel all over the world and not have problems and come home and have such a 'silly problem.'"[73]

Not long after, white jazz trombonist Jack Teagarden toured for the United States in 1959 and created a "splash" abroad in former British possessions as well as in other volatile parts of Asia.[74] The world had seen the increasing division of Asia into communist and noncommunist blocs in the 1950s, most notably in Korea, Taiwan, and Vietnam. Moreover, the offshore island crisis and Chinese nationalist leader Chiang Kai Shek's continued demands for control of China exacerbated U.S.–Asian relations. Fearing cultural dominoes in Asia, many cultural policy makers sought to reach a wide spectrum of communities, from indigenous and folk groups to the Vietnamese elite.[75] From Hue to Saigon, American officials assessed how the Vietnamese might respond to American cultural products. An American official believed that, while Burl Ives and Harry Belafonte might achieve astounding success, an artist like Elvis Presley, because of his excessive effervescence, might "spell the end of the post's cultural effort."[76] In Hue, an official asserted that "since the end of the Communist strife," the culture remained conservative and isolated but "receptive to Western music." He did not believe that the more unfamiliar 1920s-style jazz would become "completely acceptable . . . for another two or three years." He also remarked that it would "be a long time before the music of the Brubeck style could be successfully presented here."[77]

Nonetheless, Robert C. Schnitzer, the general manager of the American National Theater Academy (ANTA), pointed to Teagarden's astounding success. Schnitzer noted that in such places as Karachi, Ceylon, Bombay, the Philippines, Malaya, Hong Kong, South Korea, and Okinawa, Teagarden charmed and delighted audiences. Howard Elting Jr., counselor of embassy in Saigon, believed jazz would widely appeal to educated Vietnamese. Although he acknowledged that the older generation exhibited a "condescending tolerance of jazz," he extolled Teagarden's music by avowing that his band might be "well on the way towards universalizing jazz in Asia." He highlighted jazz's overall popularity in the region when he declared that, if jazz "spreads more widely [to] the lands of the Indochina Peninsula, nobody over there will believe that jazz [came] up the Mississippi from New Orleans. They will think it came up the Mekong."[78] Herbie Nichols's band, a white group, also performed abroad on an official tour in Asia and the Middle East and exhibited great artistic appeal.

It was in mid-1960, with the burgeoning of social protest, the intensification of the Cold War rivalry in Europe, and the independence of French West Africa, that CU began to reappropriate black jazz. The activities of Martin Luther King Jr. and his Southern Christian Leadership Conference (SCLC), along with the

Student Nonviolent Coordinating Committee (SNCC), founded in April 1960, had a pivotal impact on racial affairs. Vociferous student demonstrations increasingly occurred nationwide. In May 1961 Freedom Riders, who became emblems of nonviolent protest, intensified the movement to bring fairer treatment to blacks in bus terminals and train stations in the South. Yet, when some activists were beaten by whites in Birmingham, Alabama, the incident provoked fervent international calumny, and people of color throughout the world looked upon the event with marked disdain.[79] This racial conundrum deepened when King was jailed in Birmingham. Sen. John F. Kennedy called King's wife, Coretta Scott King, to express his dismay at the incident and to help free King from jail. The United States Information Agency (USIA) surmised that such developments keenly influenced international reactions to cultural overtures from the West.[80] They sparked ardent skepticism toward cultural policy and the American race question, skepticism that found expression in the works of such celebrated African American artists as poet Langston Hughes. In devising jazz diplomacy, American policy makers responded by increasingly endorsing the notion of "jazzocracy"—a democratic country unified racially and politically through the arts and jazz—to implement the policy of cultural containment.[81]

As the repressive era of the 1950s gave way to an age of cultural ferment in the 1960s, jazz musicians faced a critical aesthetic dilemma; they increasingly embarked upon a search for "heroes, symbols, [and] myths."[82] Yet, jazz simultaneously lost its American and international audiences to rock and roll and the music became more eclectic. In attempting to find their niche in this new Cold War culture, African American artists continued to express an affinity for the international black cause as blacks at home and abroad fought what George Fredrickson has called "an analogous form of racial oppression." Eventually, in the words of Elliott Skinner, these struggles resulted in "political emancipation . . . from European racial hegemony."[83]

In the wake of these transnational dynamics, the CU recognized the need to reclaim black jazz in cultural programs. The CU appropriated black jazz not only in an effort to convey the core liberal values of social justice, egalitarianism, and democracy, but also to create sympathy for the U.S. position in the world. Simultaneously, it worked to assist newly independent nations in their evolution toward a multiracial democracy and "groped" for a way to "enhance multi-racial cooperation."[84] Not surprisingly, however, the CU, still viewing jazz through the prism of containment, rebuffed the music that arose out of the free jazz movement, fearing it because it advocated protest and rebellion against existing social and political structures. As in the 1950s, when Eisenhower did not seek to further "stir up unrest" in Africa or other regions of the world, with the rise of black nationalism policy makers feared that revolutionary forms of jazz music might inspire rather than quell the drive for rebellion against the West that was already brewing on the international stage.[85]

The CU's choice of mainstream jazz in this new context seemingly reflected its belief that mainstream musicians embodied the values of cultural containment in that the notion of freedom they embraced was different from that of the jazz rebels. Mainstream artists "wanted to claim the banner of freedom, but, in order to appeal to a broad spectrum of people across racial and political boundaries . . . they also wanted to distance themselves from the term's association with individual license and whimsical choice."[86] The idea of freedom came to mean not simply the idea of free enterprise and ultimately "private choice," but also the freedom to move the music into a larger "social setting" in an attempt to correspond to the country's larger "needs" and broader goals. Freedom meant seeking collaboration and social participation while receiving affirmation as individual participants in the political and social structures of the day. Ultimately, freedom came to mean participation in a republican democracy.[87] Echoing the 1950s, the policy to globalize the jazz mainstream often met with brusque criticism and instigated restlessness in the jazz establishment.

As the United States recognized the need to expand cultural containment and capitalize on the cultural and political fervor brewing abroad, the CU chose Louis Armstrong for a tour to Africa.[88] It was as much this changing Cold War atmosphere as Armstrong's tremendous appeal that led to his unparalleled and exuberant welcome by African peoples. By the end of 1960 Armstrong, who disdained communism, had become the most controversial jazz artist to tour abroad for the United States. The CU initiated the tour with "a massive promotional campaign" for Pepsi Cola, showcasing Armstrong on rousing posters: "in Armstrong's hand, instead of the familiar horn, was a glistening bottle of Pepsi Cola."[89] As the tour ensued, enthusiasm for "Ambassador Satch" reverberated throughout the continent. When Armstrong discussed his powerful appeal as a cultural ambassador, he did not reflect on the political climate, remarking to a reporter that "the reason I don't bother with politics is the words is so big that by the time they break them down to my size the joke is over. . . . I'm just a trumpet player."[90]

After Armstrong's pivotal tour, the *Journal American* referred to "Ambassador Satch" as a "Good-Will Asset" who "captivated" Africans "at a time when Kremlin agents were whipping up African feelings against" America.[91] An official said that, in light of the fact that many "new nations imported their concepts of American culture from Europe," jazz diplomacy established a strong American cultural presence in new nations as well as a "shared devotion to cultural values that transcend[ed] political differences."[92]

Yet, jazz diplomacy did not dispel the paradox of race and American anticommunism that increasingly imperiled the American image. After the riots in Little Rock, American policy makers continued to express ethnocentric views toward jazz and new nations. Although a proponent of jazz, Lawrence J. Hall, Morocco's public affairs officer, for example, observed that such artists as Herbie Mann had made jazz popular for "its rhythmic qualities rather than . . . its melodic or harmonic qualities." Hall believed that Moroccans did not understand jazz, because it diverged from Middle Eastern music. Additionally, Hall remarked that "progressive jazz," with its "complex harmonics," might not have much appeal. He even considered Moroccans "much more at ease when shouting and clapping hands to the beat of a jazz drummer." Likewise, several American officials perceived people in some African nations as backward or as "outsiders" and feared their fervent nationalism in the same way they feared the activities of African American expatriates.[93]

By the end of the year, the world recognized that Eisenhower's policies on race and integration had not significantly improved the status of blacks at home or abroad. John F. Kennedy had been elected president in a close race and turned his attention to Cold War exigencies in Europe and Asia. Kennedy, however, expressed greater support than Eisenhower for the cause of black justice at home and abroad and gained black advocacy in the United States by championing the African cause. Unavoidably, in efforts to revitalize the image of the country, jazz diplomacy significantly highlighted American weaknesses. Jazz diplomacy engendered both pride and pessimism in audiences at home and abroad as conservative ideas of jazz reached new parts of the globe.

Such sentiments endured even after Cozy Cole's Jazz Revue, a black 1920s-style New Orleans jazz band, traveled throughout Africa on an official tour in 1962. Cole toured from October 1962 until early 1963 in the wake of the Cuban missile crisis. He promoted an image of American prosperity and cultural abundance. During his concerts, the immense appeal of jazz among African youths became clear. Even French youths in Marrakech, "quite out of character for the French," were "screaming like demented banshees" when he performed. They "tried to hoist a battered Cozy Cole to their shoulders and parade him around the stage."[94] *Variety* portrayed Cole's tour as an impressive feat, calling it "top cultural diplomacy." Cole's astounding tour became one of the most successful U.S. cultural presentations in Africa in the 1960s.[95]

Despite Cole's triumph, although many new nations seemed impressed by how the U.S. government had "gone to bat for the Negro," they recognized that a crisis of American mores endured.[96] How could black art embody the soul of American culture and the essence of American civilization when black Americans were an ill-treated people? This paradox became even more glaring after noted civil rights events like the civil rights march in Birmingham, Alabama, in 1963, where police used water guns, police dogs, and fire hoses to disperse peaceful protesters. Kennedy ordered federal marshals to the city to quell the violence, and the Soviet Union capitalized on this incident with sweltering anti-American propaganda. Moreover, on May 21 the governor of Alabama, George Wallace, attempted to prevent the integration of the summer session of the University of Alabama. Such officials as Mark B. Lewis, public affairs officer to Ghana, pointed out that, overall, the events at Birmingham had significantly harmed the American image and resulted in "lost ground." He called the consequences of the episode "serious." In Lewis's view, although cultural presentations often "enhance[d]" the American image and such incidents as what happened with James Meredith in Oxford resulted in an exalted view of President Kennedy "even in the leftist press," the paradox of race in America had manifested itself on the world stage too frequently.[97]

Such incidents led many world leaders to reassess their support for American policies. On September 15, 1963, when four young black girls were killed after white supremacists bombed the Sixteenth Street Baptist Church in Birmingham, this brutal event profoundly reinforced the image of the United States as a cultural wasteland. As President Kennedy expressed his "outrage," the Soviet Union energetically lambasted the incident.[98] The paradox of race poignantly reverberated again when Duke Ellington brought the message of "jazzocracy" to the Middle East on an official tour in 1963. Ellington met with resounding praise worldwide. He convincingly portrayed the idea of American cultural exceptionalism to foreign peoples, a remarkable feat in a fretful Cold War world. The *Foreign Service Journal* declared many years later that Ellington had triumphed during a pivotal moment in the Cold War.[99] However, during Ellington's travels, on November 22 President Kennedy was assassinated and the remainder of the tour had to be canceled.

Against the backdrop of unyielding domestic unrest in the early 1960s, the American image waned to such an extent that cultural policy makers saw the need to drastically redirect cultural containment policies. As early as January 1963, *Variety* had claimed that the State Department had ordered a moratorium on all cultural tours, while in February *Down Beat* reported that the government planned to dismantle the cultural program.[100] By the middle of the year, the CU underwent vast changes and the cultural Cold War nearly came to a halt. This occurred for several reasons. First, the CU had sent surveys to embassies around the world to reexamine cultural efforts and numerous embassies generated critical accounts of cultural efforts.[101] Second, the CU fired the American National Theater Academy, which had administered the program since its inception, and react vated the Advisory Committee on the Arts (ACA). Though established in 1954, the ACA had remained inert until 1963.

Third, and equally important, some members of the CU's music panel, which had become increasingly divided between *kulturalists* and *informationalists,* attacked the competence of PAOs in Africa, contending that they did not understand the role of jazz or black artists in cultural affairs and that their elitism undermined cultural efforts.[102] In March 1963 even the director of the Cultural Presentations Program revealed his unawareness of Africa when he exclaimed, "Africa is Africa, whether it is North, Central, or South."[103] On another occasion, he retorted that Africans knew only "the beat, rhythm, and missionary hymns" and called Armstrong's jazz meaningless to Africans. A member of the musical panel criticized what he saw as the panel's blatant ethnocentrism, declaring that it approached Africa "as if it were some dark continent."[104]

Fourth, officials believed that U.S.–Soviet competition for the allegiance of African leaders called for a shift in jazz diplomacy because, by the end of 1963, more than thirty African countries had become independent.[105] American officials surmised that jazz diplomacy could no longer engender the support of educated leaders and intellectuals. Not only had the communists—the Soviet Union and China—immersed Africa with stupendous cultural products, but also Europe often sent various performing arts troupes to the African continent: Germany sponsored a chamber music group, and England sent a Shakespearean company. It seemed that much of Africa remained steeped in the more "sophisticated" cultures of France, Belgium, Spain, and the Netherlands. Thus, to successfully achieve American aims, the CU advocated sending examples of American "high culture" to Africa, including an orchestra or a chamber group.[106] Lastly, the paradox of jazz diplomacy had become so deleterious to the American image that the CU deemed it had "saturated" Africa with jazz; it did not want to further reinforce this paradox by endorsing the notion that jazz was all the United States had to offer.[107] These developments consequently led the CU to suspend all jazz tours. This decision precipitated the most explosive controversy the American cultural bureaucracy had seen since the inception of Eisenhower's CPP. By the end of 1963 cultural internationalists challenged Cold War cultural ideologues to reframe cultural containment policy.

While the passage of the Civil Rights Act of 1964 and the Voting Rights Act of 1965 markedly enhanced the declining image of the United States, in the words of George Fredrickson, they ultimately "failed" to redress black Americans' problems. The consequent "aftermath" of the "ghetto insurrections of 1965–1968" "encouraged a bitter and rebellious mood in the black urban communities of the North and West."[108] Thus the Soviet Union continued its "digs" at American democracy and further exploited renowned civil rights events in extensive propaganda campaigns. In 1965 an urban uprising in Watts, California, shocked the world. Thousands of blacks had looted the city, and the National Guard was summoned to quell the violence. In March 1965, during a protest march in Selma, Alabama, whites physically assaulted scores of black and white protesters, and police even killed a black man who demonstrated for civil rights. On this "Bloody Sunday" state troopers simultaneously blocked the marchers, beating them with nightsticks and diffusing them with tear gas when they refused to disperse.[109] Despite USIA efforts, many Soviet people still believed that Americans treated African American citizens "no better than . . . caged animal[s]."[110] African students pointed out how Africans in the United States were "forced out of restaurants and hotels and beaten up."[111]

President Lyndon B. Johnson felt a formidable tension during these years; he believed that "as President and as a man, I would use every ounce of strength I possessed to gain justice for the black American." And he observed that, although "the barriers of freedom began tumbling down," "the long history of Negro-white relations had entered a new and more bewildering stage."[112] The rueful events in Selma led President Johnson to make noble attempts to counter worldwide criticism of the country. He addressed the U.S. Congress in a provocative speech, "The American Promise," recalling in his memoirs that he "wanted to talk from [his] own heart, from [his] own experience." In the address, he invoked the legacy of Abraham Lincoln and proclaimed that the United States had an obligation to fulfill the promise of Lincoln's Emancipation Proclamation. He asserted that "equality depends not on force of arms or tear gas but upon the force of moral[ity]." He further insisted that "rarely are we met with a challenge, not to our growth or abundance, our welfare or our security, but rather to the values and the purposes and the meaning of our beloved nation. The issue of equal rights for American Negroes is such an issue. [If] the U.S. does not attend to this . . . we will have failed as a people and as a nation.[113]

Louis Armstrong similarly denounced the racial injustice in Selma when visiting Copenhagen and Prague. In Copenhagen he told a reporter that he "became physically ill after watching a television news program showing Selma Police action against civil rights marchers in the Alabama city." He guilelessly played up the irony of the event when he proclaimed, "They would beat me . . . if I marched."[114]

Policy makers further reassessed jazz diplomacy as U.S. involvement in Vietnam escalated. By 1964, with jazz on hold, President Johnson pledged to continue Kennedy's legacy and vowed to defeat communism in Asia.[115] Criticism of U.S. involvement in Vietnam especially surfaced in August 1964 after the Gulf of Tonkin incident when Johnson alleged that the North Vietnamese attacked U.S.

ships in the gulf and enunciated the Gulf of Tonkin Resolution. The resolution, which the U.S. Congress passed, approved U.S. military action in the absence of a declaration of war. While praised by some at home, it met with worldwide condemnation and underscored the image of American aggression and militaristic anticommunism.[116] Johnson became especially conflicted after he ordered that troops be deployed in Vietnam in mid-1965 and initiated an extensive bombing campaign, "Operation Rolling Thunder," in the North.[117]

U.S. military escalation in Vietnam changed world opinion of the United States to such an extent that American involvement in the war eventually dwarfed the impact of racial events on the American image. In the mid-1960s, the paradox of Vietnam replaced the paradox of race on the world stage, and Vietnam became the linchpin by which the world measured American credibility as a democracy.[118] Free jazz pioneer Archie Schepp saw a disturbing link between violence toward blacks in the United States and the bombing of the North Vietnamese. He noted that in both instances, violence emerged against peoples of color engaged in ardent freedom struggles.

> I am for the moment a helpless witness to the bloody massacres of my people on streets that run from Hayneville through Harlem. . . . But I am more than the images you superimpose on me, the despair that you inflict. I am the persistent insistence of the human heart to be free. I wish to regain that cherished dignity that was always mine. My esthetic answer to your lies about me is a simple one: you can no longer defer my dream. I'm gonna sing it. Dance it. Scream it. And if need be, I'll steal it from this very earth. . . . Our vindication will be black, as Fidel is black, as Ho Chi Minh is black.[119]

Schepp became a prominent example of an artist who saw music as a way to confront what he saw as oppressive social, political, and artistic structures as he affirmed his belief in his music as a vehicle for social change. "The racial dimension of the Vietnam war" thus caused grave concern among black artists, some of whom embraced Marxist principles to ease the political and intellectual burden of democracy.[120]

In the midst of Vietnam, the global context of cultural containment became increasingly multifaceted with the rise of Little Richard, Elvis Presley, Bob Dylan, the Beatles, Abbey Lincoln, and the "Motown Sound" of Stevie Wonder, Smokey Robinson, and the Supremes, among others. American popular music moved into new venues and new forms of African American culture grew popular around the world. Although public taste for bebop, hard bop, and cool jazz declined, and jazz lost its audiences to rock and roll, many reminisced about Billie Holiday's "Strange Fruit" and the popular Café Society of the 1950s.[121] The jazz ethos persisted in many regions of the world—from Sweden to Japan, from Moscow to Canada, from Bulgaria to Thailand. Echoing the sentiment of internationalism, Leopold Senghor, poet and president of Senegal, hailed negritude and Ellington in a homage to his music:

> Oh! the dull beat of the rain on the leaves!
> Just play me your "Solitude," Duke till I cry myself to sleep![122]

In this new context, while depicting the "brutally honest" facets of American cultural life, the dual injustices of race and Vietnam led cultural policy makers to focus more keenly on portraying how the United States attempted to "change things."[123] In Ghana, after the overthrow of Kwame Nkrumah in 1966, the CU encouraged "meaningful communication" with the youths abroad while exposing them to certain ideas about peace and democracy; it underscored "practical" ideals guided by an open, fair, and just notion of human rights in which race relations appeared to improve day after day more quickly than in the past.[124] Not surprisingly, the topic of the Vietnam War often arose in international discussions abroad. In London, African and European students inquired about "Vietnam, Watts, [and] Kennedy."[125]

Aware of the intersection of Vietnam and the vibrant transnational expansion of black culture, the CU reevaluated the efficacy of jazz diplomacy. In a policy statement, it defended the power of jazz and black cultural products in promoting American Cold War aims, and also acknowledged the importance of internationalism; it declared that "in Sub-Saharan Africa, the performing arts are in a very early stage of development. A new culture is emerging, blending the old African culture with modern influences. American performers, particularly Negroes and American films, have been an important element in this modern influence."[126] The CU pointed to the power of jazz in another pivotal policy statement when it noted that "American jazz is a unique contribution of this country to the world's cultural scene. It is a form of art universally known and appreciated. It is eminently designed to meet the human urge for and love of rhythm. It is in a sense the truest form of individually improvised music that merges into a joint presentation of artists that have the gifts of skill, musical talent, rhythm and the feeling for team work."[127]

The CU simultaneously expressed the belief that the globalization of jazz ultimately signified an important link between race, jazz, and cultural containment. It claimed "we were aware of the fact that an integrated group of performers could go a long way to put the race question in the United States into proper perspective. Two entertainment acts, the Shirleys and the Riches, were selected not only because of their artistic standing but also because they projected the image of the outgoing friendly Americans and of a fine American family. . . . The Vice President of the Republic of Niger told our Ambassador that the Cozy Cole group was the most effective weapon against the di-tribes [sic] of radio Moscow with obvious reference to the race problem."[128]

Recognizing the surge in internationalism that had gained momentum in 1963 along with the need to expand cultural containment, the CU felt impelled to reintroduce jazz in cultural policy. It attempted to reestablish jazz as a symbol of American prosperity, surmising that "jazzocracy" might serve as the best way to bolster the American image in the new context of race and Vietnam. Nonetheless, the CU's choice of bands for the next jazz tours indicated that, despite its awareness of the importance of black cultural production in the mid-1960s, the CU was still playing it safe. In 1966 it chose Woody Herman, a white leader of a New Orleans–style jazz orchestra, for the next jazz tour to Africa and a black New Orleans–style group, led by Earl Hines, to travel to the Soviet Union.

By 1966 the CU's watchful embrace of the evolving jazz ethos reflected its acknowledgment that, to fight the Cold War, the United States had to reclaim jazz as its own intellectual property and no longer as a lowbrow cultural product. As the CU recognized jazz as part of a worldwide artistic and intellectual phenomenon that prevailed over language barriers, American Cold Warriors attempted to demonstrate the intellectual maturity of the United States while conveying respect for new and emerging nations and peoples in the Soviet sphere. By the mid-1960s the pivotal impact of jazz internationalism had impelled the CU to embark on a new era of Cold War cultural expansion.

It was not until the era of détente in the 1970s that a wider range of jazz bands represented the United States abroad in this new context of internationalism. Yet, after the Soviet invasion of Afghanistan in 1979 and the subsequent U.S. Olympic boycott in 1980, a rift in cultural affairs unavoidably arose, and in the 1980s U.S. exchanges came to a halt. The increasingly aggressive anti-Americanism in the twenty-first century, impelled by the horrific events of September 11, 2001, set off a new array of international tensions that gave rise to an even keener need to reaffirm and defend American values abroad and increase mutual understanding. The need to project an image of racial amity and redress the paradoxes of American life intensified, and in 2005 the State Department reintroduced jazz diplomacy in foreign affairs, creating a new exchange program called The Rhythm Road: American Music Abroad, administered by the world-renowned Jazz at Lincoln Center, based in New York. With the election of Barack Obama, the complexity of race at home and abroad became more nuanced as jazz diplomacy reemerged as an inimitable policy weapon. America's unique contribution to world cultures helped the United States reaffirm the efficacy of black culture to redefine the American ethos in the ever volatile arena of international affairs.

Notes

1. Ernest G. Wiener, Counselor for Cultural Affairs, Embassy Moscow to Department of State, Airgam #A-819, "Jazz Night at the Blue Bird Café," January 18, 1965, 3, University of Arkansas Libraries, Special Collections Division, Fulbright Papers, Manuscript Collection (MC) 468, Bureau of Educational and Cultural Affairs (CU), group 2, "Cultural Presentations Program," series 1, "General and Historical Files," boxes 47–52 (hereafter cited as CU, series 1; when all documents are from the same file, the file is listed at the end of the note). For more on jazz in Russia, see Michael May, "Swinging under Stalin: Russian Jazz during the Cold War and Beyond," in *Here, There, and Everywhere: The Foreign Politics of American Popular Culture,* ed. Reinhold Wagnleitner and Elaine Tyler May (Hanover, N.H.: University Press of New England, 2000), 179–91; Reinhold Wagnleitner, "The Empire of Fun, or Talkin' Soviet Blues: The Sound of Freedom and U.S. Cultural Hegemony in Europe," *Diplomatic History* 23 (Summer 1999): 499–524; S. Frederick Starr, *Red and Hot: The Fate of Jazz in the Soviet Union* (New York: Oxford University Press, 1983).

2. For more on cultural relations during the Cold War, see Michael Krenn, *Fall-Out Shelters for the Human Spirit: American Art and the Cold War* (Chapel Hill: University of North Carolina Press, 2005); Wagnleitner and May, *Here, There, and Everywhere*; David Caute, *The Dancer Defects: The Struggle for Cultural Supremacy during the Cold War* (Oxford: Oxford University Press, 2005); Robert A. Haddow, *Pavilions of Plenty: Exhibiting American Culture Abroad in the 1950s* (Washington, D.C.: Smithsonian Institution Press, 1997); Walter Hixson, *The Myth of American Diplomacy: Identity and U.S. Foreign Policy* (New Haven, Conn.: Yale University Press, 2008).

3. W.E.B. Du Bois, *The Souls of Black Folk,* ed. Brent Hayes Edward (New York: Oxford, 2007), 1; Allison Blakely, "European Dimensions of the African Diaspora: The Definition of Black Racial Identity," in *Crossing Boundaries: Comparative History of Black People in Diaspora,* ed. Darlene Clark Hine and Jacqueline McLeod (Bloomington: Indiana University Press, 1999), 91.

4. Akira Iriye, "The Americanized Century," *Reviews in American History* (March 1983): 124–28.

5. Mary L. Dudziak, *Cold War Civil Rights: Race and the Image of American Democracy* (Princeton, N.J.: Princeton University Press, 2000), 249–54. For other cultural perspectives, see Emily Rosenberg, *Spreading the American Dream: American Economic and Cultural Expansion, 1890–1945* (New York: Hill and Wang, 1982), 7; and Frank Ninkovich, *The Diplomacy of Ideas: U.S. Foreign Policy and Cultural Relations, 1938–1950* (Cambridge, U.K.: Cambridge University Press, 1981), 125–27.

6. A pivotal work on the *Brown* decision is Richard Kluger, *Simple Justice: The History of* Brown v. Board of Education *and Black America's Struggle for Equality* (New York: Vintage Books, 1977), 749. See also Mary L. Dudziak, "Josephine Baker, Racial Protest, and the Cold War," *Journal of American History* 81, no. 2 (1994): 543–70.

7. Nicholas J. Cull, *The Cold War and the United States Information Agency: American Propaganda and Public Diplomacy, 1945–1989* (Cambridge, U.K.: Cambridge University Press, 2008), 81.

8. Ibid., xiv–xvi.

9. Penny M. von Eschen, *Satchmo Blows Up the World: Jazz Ambassadors Play the Cold War* (Cambridge, Mass.: Harvard University Press, 2004), 1–57, 92–120, 185–222; Walter L. Hixson, *Parting the Curtain: Propaganda, Culture, and the Cold War, 1945–1961* (New York: St. Martin's, 1997).

10. Quoted in Henry Louis Gates Jr., "W.E.B. Du Bois and the Talented Tenth," in Henry Louis Gates Jr. and Cornel West, *The Future of the Race* (New York: Alfred A. Knopf, 1996), 131; see also 123–25, 132. Gates is referring to Du Bois's speech in 1948, "The Talented Tenth Memorial Address," in ibid., 159–77. Du Bois spoke to the concept of race in many of his writings. See, for example, W.E.B. Du Bois, "The Negro Problems," in David Levering Lewis, *Du Bois: A Reader* (New York: Henry Holt, 1995), 48–53. See also Gates, "W.E.B. Du Bois and the Talented Tenth," 132; David Levering Lewis, *W.E.B. Du Bois: The Fight for Equality and the American Century, 1919–1963* (New York: Henry Holt, 2000), 37–152; and Cull, *Cold War*, 1–21.

11. For Monson, see *Freedom Sounds: Civil Rights Call Out to Jazz and Africa* (New York: Oxford University Press, 2007). She offers a definitive and compelling account of jazz activism and aesthetic agency during the Cold War years as well as the cultural and racial paradoxes that this activism created. A definitive examination of soft power is Joseph S. Nye Jr., *Soft Power: The Means to Success in World Politics* (New York: Public Affairs, 2004). For perspectives on race and the Cold War, see Brenda Gayle Plummer, *Rising Wind: Black Americans and U.S. Foreign Affairs, 1935–1960* (Chapel Hill: University of North Carolina Press, 1997); Brenda Gayle Plummer, ed., *Window on Freedom* (Chapel Hill: University of North Carolina Press, 2003); Paul Gordon Lauren, *Power and Prejudice: The Politics and Diplomacy of Racial Discrimination* (1988; reprt., Boulder, Col.: Westview Press, 1996); Penny M. von Eschen, *Race against Empire: Black Americans and Anti-Colonialism, 1937–1957* (Ithaca, N.Y.: Cornell University Press, 1997); Thomas Borstelmann, *The Cold War and the Color Line: American Race Relations in the Global Arena* (Cambridge, Mass.: Harvard University Press, 2001); and Michael Krenn, *The Color of Empire: Race and American Foreign Relations* (Washington, D.C.: Potomac Books, 2006).

12. Clifford Geertz, *The Interpretation of Cultures* (New York: Basic Books, 1973), 127. For changing ideas of race between the wars, see Elazar Barkan, *The Retreat of Scientific Racism: Changing Concepts of Race in Britain and the United States between the World Wars* (Cambridge, U.K.: Cambridge University Press, 1992).

13. Akira Iriye, *Cultural Internationalism and World Order* (Baltimore: Johns Hopkins University Press, 1977), 3. Iriye offers a definition of culture as the "structures of meaning," which constitute "memory, ideology, emotions, life styles, scholarly, and artistic works, and other symbols" (3). Geertz has defined culture as the "webs of significance" in which man is "suspended" and which "he himself has spun." This includes the "meanings . . . construing social expression on their surface enigmatical." Geertz, *Interpretation of Cultures*, 5.

14. Iriye, *Cultural Internationalism*, 130, 147, 160–68.

15. Monson, *Freedom Sounds*, 4–12; Morroe Berger, "Jazz: Resistance to the Diffusion of a Culture Pattern," *Journal of Negro History* 32 (1947): 461–94. See also Scott Saul, *Freedom*

Is, Freedom Ain't: Jazz and the Making of the Sixties (Cambridge, Mass.: Harvard University Press, 2003); Ron M. Radano, *New Musical Figurations: Anthony Braxton's Cultural Critique* (Chicago: University of Chicago Press, 1993), 13–14, 17; and Iain Anderson, *This Is Our Music: Free Jazz, the Sixties, and American Culture* (Philadelphia: University of Pennsylvania Press, 2007).

16. Saul, *Freedom Is, Freedom Ain't*, 2.

17. Eric Porter, "It's About That Time," in *Miles Davis and American Culture*, ed. Gerald Early (St. Louis: Missouri Historical Society Press, 2001), 139.

18. Gunther Schuller, *Early Jazz: Its Roots and Musical Development* (New York: Oxford University Press, 1968), 8. For a critical perspective on culture and resistance, see Edward Said, *Culture and Imperialism* (New York: Vintage Books, 1993).

19. Saul, *Freedom Is, Freedom Ain't*, 4–5. For an eloquent account of the civil rights movement, see David J. Garrow, *Bearing the Cross: Martin Luther King, Jr., and the Southern Christian Leadership Conference* (New York: Vintage Books, 1986).

20. Du Bois, *Souls of Black Folk*, 8–9. For the emergence of the Black Arts Movement in the mid-1960s, see Eric Porter, *What Is This Thing Called Jazz?: African American Musicians as Artists, Critics, and Activists* (Berkeley: University of California Press, 2002), 191–239.

21. Saul, *Freedom Is, Freedom Ain't*, 2–5.

22. Monson, *Freedom Sounds*, 12, 171, 259–61.

23. Radano, *New Musical Figurations*, 68, 82–83; Porter, *What Is This Thing Called Jazz?*, 191.

24. Frantz Fanon, *The Wretched of the Earth* (New York: Grove Press, 1963), 211. See also Porter, *What Is This Thing Called Jazz?*, 203. For an illuminating discussion of the many aspects of the jazz paradox, see Porter, *What Is This Thing Called Jazz?*, 1–53. For a view of racial redefinition, see Clayborne Carson, *In Struggle: SNCC and the Black Awakening of the 1960s* (Cambridge, Mass.: Harvard University Press, 1994), 1. The United States did not send jazz to Allied countries in Western Europe, where jazz already had considerable patronage and was well known and where artists could easily travel on their own.

25. Foreign Service Dispatch (FSD) 105, "Educational and Cultural Exchange, Kampala, Annual Report for Fiscal Year (FY) 1961," November 3, 1961, box (b) 2, folder (f) Kampala, annual report (ar), Lot Files RG-306, United States Information Agency, Country Project Files, 1951–1964, "Africa," National Archives And Records Administration (NARA); hereafter cited as USIA/Africa). For Jones's view, see, Quincy Jones, *Q: The Autobiography of Quincy Jones* (New York: Doubleday, 2001), 112–14.

26. Early, *Miles Davis and American Culture*, ix, 5. For a discussion of this theoretical dichotomy, see Herbert J. Ganz, *Popular Culture and High Culture: An Analysis and Evaluation of Taste* (New York: Basic Books, 1975).

27. Black music as art is explored in Olly Wilson, "Black Music as an Art Form," *Black Music Research Journal* 3 (1983): 1–22.

28. Lisa E. Davenport, *Jazz Diplomacy: Promoting America in the Cold War Era* (Jackson: University Press of Mississippi, 2009), 238, 284–86.

29. James Baldwin, *Nobody Knows My Name* (New York: Dial Press, 1961), 79–81.

30. Warsaw, Department of State Incoming Telegram (DOS Incom.) 1435, April 12,

1957, box (b) 88, NARA, Records of the Department of State, College Park, Md., Record Group (RG)-59, Decimal File 032, 1955–1959 (hereafter cited as DF 032, 1955–1959).

31. Cary Fraser, "Crossing the Color Line: The Eisenhower Administration and the Dilemma of Race for United States Foreign Policy," *Diplomatic History* 24 (Spring 2000): 233–34.

32. Thomas C. Holt, "Slavery and Freedom in the Atlantic World: Reflections on the Diasporan Framework," in Hine and McLeod, *Crossing Boundaries*, 37. See also Dudziak, *Cold War Civil Rights*, 151.

33. Fraser, "Crossing the Color Line," 233–34.

34. Ibid., 147.

35. "State Dept. Pipes Up with 'Satchmo, for the Soviets,'" *Variety*, July 31, 1957, 1, 7; "Ike Swipe May Cost Satchmo Edsel Spec; Others 'Penalized,'" *Variety*, September 25, 1957, 1; "Louis Armstrong, Barring Soviet Tour, Denounces Eisenhower and Gov. Faubus," *New York Times*, September 19, 1957, f Louis Armstrong, 1955–1958, Rutgers University, Institute of Jazz Studies, Newark, New Jersey. See also "Satch Speaks Twice," *Down Beat*, October 31, 1957, 10.

36. *Pittsburgh Courier*, September 28, 1957, in Thomas Brothers, ed. *Louis Armstrong, In His Own Words: Selected Writings* (New York: Oxford University Press, 1999), 193–94.

37. "Louis Armstrong, Barring Soviet Tour"; "Satch Speaks Twice."

38. Congressman George Grant, HOR, Committee on Agriculture, to Dulles, September 24, 1957; and Hoghland to Grant, n.d., b 93, f Louis Armstrong, DF 032, 1955–1959.

39. *Gazette and Daily*, September 1957, attach. to: Hoghland to Lester Hill, Committee on Labor and Public Welfare, U.S. Senate, October 11, 1957, b 93, f Louis Armstrong, DF 032, 1955–1959. See also Gerald Early, *This Is Where I Came In: Black America in the 1960s* (Lincoln: University of Nebraska Press, 2003), 48; Laurence Bergreen, *Louis Armstrong: An Extravagant Life* (New York: Broadway Books, 1997), 437–74.

40. Richard Zieglar to Sirs, September 22, 1957, b 89, DF 032, 1955–1959; *Miami Herald*, October 9, 1957, attach. to John F. Meagher, Chief, Public Services Division, to Zieglar, October 30, 1957, b 89, DF 032, 1955–1959.

41. Ralph Gleason, "Perspectives," *Down Beat*, February 6, 1958, 33.

42. "Eisenhower's Action Lauded by Satchmo," *New York Times*, September 26, 1957, f Louis Armstrong, 1955–1958, Rutgers University Institute of Jazz Studies.

43. *Pittsburgh Courier*, September 28, 1957, in Brothers, *Louis Armstrong*, 194.

44. "Ambassador Satch Sounds Off: Jazzman Wants Wider Exchange of Artists to Lessen World Tensions," *Variety*, January 29, 1958, 1.

45. See, for example, Department of State Instruction (DOS Instr.) A-021, "President's Program Musical Group," September 5, 1958, b 90, f Louis Armstrong, DF 032, 1955–1959. For more on Africa, see J. B. Webster and A. A. Boahen, *The Revolutionary Years: West Africa since 1800* (Essex, England: Longman Group, 1980), 375–83.

46. Dan Hendrickson to J. F. Dulles, September 9, 1957, attach. Associated Press (AP) Wire photo. See also Dulles to Embassy Ceylon, Colombo, DOS Instr. A-56, November 15, 1957, b 89, DF 032, 1955–1959.

47. Walter LaFeber, *The American Age: U.S. Foreign Policy at Home and Abroad*, vol. 2, 2nd ed. (New York: W. W. Norton, 1994), 552.

48. Richard M. McCarthy, Country Public Affairs Office (PAO), Bangkok, IES, FSD-534, "Evidence of Effectiveness, President's Fund: Marian Anderson," January 20, 1958, b 93, f Marian Anderson, DF 032, 1955–1959.

49. Ibid.; see also Representative Charles O. Porter to Dulles, January 2, 1958; [attach. to] Andrew H. Berding, Assistant Secretary, to Porter, January 9, 1958, b 93, f Marian Anderson, DF 032, 1955–1959.

50. Thomas D. Bowie, Counselor of Embassy for Political Affairs, Saigon, to Department of State (DOS), FSD-14, "Educational Exchange: Marian Anderson Visit," November 18, 1957, 4–5, b 93, DF 032, 1955–1959.

51. Ibid.

52. Robert Lewis Shayon, "The Lady from Philadelphia," *Saturday Review*, January 18, 1958, 57.

53. Ibid.

54. Wilson C. Flake, Ambassador, Ghana, to DOS, DOS Incom., 1958, b 1, f Country Programs (CP) Accra, b 201, USIA/Africa.

55. Cushman C. Reynolds, PAO, Khartoum, to DOS, "Tour of the Florida A&M University Players," April 10, 1958, b 102, f Florida A&M University Players, DF 032, 1955–1959.

56. Ibid.

57. Dudziak, "Josephine Baker"; Dudziak, *Cold War Civil Rights*, 62–63, 67–77. See also Dulles to Embassy, Paris, DOS Instr. A-201, "Josephine Baker," November 4, 1958, b 94, f Josephine Baker, DF 032, 1955–1959.

58. Borstelmann, *Cold War and the Color Line*, 85; Dudziak, *Cold War Civil Rights*, 62–63.

59. Lewis, *W.E.B. Du Bois*, 309–12; W.E.B. Du Bois, "The Souls of White Folk," in Lewis, *W.E.B. Du Bois*, 464.

60. W.E.B. Du Bois to the Foreign Editor of the *Literary Gazette*, September 26, 1957, in Herbert Aptheker, ed., *The Correspondence of W.E.B. Du Bois*, vol. 3, 1944–1963 (Amherst: University of Massachusetts Press, 1978), 412–14. Du Bois did not believe that socialism could work in the United States, a capitalist society, and "disdained" the American Communist Party.

61. Martin Bauml Duberman, *Paul Robeson* (New York: Alfred A. Knopf, 1989), 381–464. Allison Blakely provides an astute critique of Robeson's activities in the Soviet Union in *Russia and the Negro: Blacks in Russian History and Thought* (Washington, D.C.: Howard University Press, 1986), 147–55. See also Lightner, Berlin, to DOS, "Robeson for Berlin Cultural Festival," 1960; and Dillon, Acting [Assistant Secretary], to Wellington, Department of State Outgoing Telegram (DOS Out.), "Robeson's Statements and Actions Abroad," 1960, 1–2, b 40, f Paul Robeson, 1–2260, NARA, Records of the Department of State, Record Group-59, Decimal File 032, Foreign Policy File, 1960–1963; hereafter cited as DF 032, 1960–1963.

62. [Ambassador] Llewellyn E. Thompson, Moscow, to DOS, DOS Incom. G-825, "Paul Robeson in Moscow," April 28, 1961, 1–2, attach. Translated newspaper articles from *Trud* and the *Literary Gazette*.

63. Howard Trivers, Chief, Eastern European Affairs, to DOS, FSD-782, June 23,

1960; James P. Parker, American Consul, Auckland, FSD-11, "Paul Robeson Gives Three Concerts in Auckland," November 7, 1960, 1–2, b 40, f Paul Robeson, 1–2260, DF 032, 1960–1963; and Lightner, "Robeson for Berlin Cultural Festival."

64. FSD-15, James A. Elliot, PAO, Singapore, to United States Information Agency (USIA), December 1, 1958, 2, b 90, DF 032, 1955–1959.

65. W. K. Bunce, Counselor for Public Affairs, New Delhi, to DOS, FSD-963, February 28, 1958, b 89, DF 032, 1955–1959; Briggs, Rio, to SOS, DOS Incom. 1187, March 18, 1958; and Johnson, Prague, to Secretary of State (SOS), #279, b 89, DF 032, 1955–1959.

66. Warsaw, DOS Incom. 1435, April 12, 1957. See also J. Magdanz and Herter, DOS Out. 778 to Warsaw, April 10, 1957, and March 26, 1957, b 88, DF 032, 1955–1959.

67. See, for example, DOS Instr. A-021, "President's Program Musical Group," September 5, 1958, b 90, f Louis Armstrong, DF 032, 1955–1959.

68. Porter, *What Is This Thing Called Jazz?*, 119–24.

69. Frank J. Lewand, Cultural Attaché, Warsaw, to DOS, FSD-355, "Report on Dave Brubeck Jazz Quartet Concerts in Poland," March 24, 1958; Edward A. Symans, Press Attaché, Warsaw, to DOS, FSD-399, April 17, 1958, b 97, f Dave Brubeck, DF 032, 1955–1959; and W. K. Bunce, Consul for Public Affairs, Bombay, New Delhi, FSD-1512, "Combined Report on Brubeck in India," 3, June 6, 1958, 1, b 97, f Dave Brubeck, DF 032, 1955–1959.

70. W.E.B. Du Bois, "Criteria of Negro Art," in Lewis, *W.E.B. Du Bois*, 514.

71. "U. of Ga. Nixes Brubeck (Bassist a Negro) but OK at Atlanta Race Spot," *Variety*, March 4, 1959, 49. For more on this story, see "Brubeck's 'No Play Sans Negro Bassist,' Cues Shoutout at Dixie U.; Buck Ram, in U.K. Hits U.S. 'Bigotry,'" *Variety*, January 20, 1960, 63; Ralph Gleason, "An Appeal from Dave Brubeck," *Down Beat*, February 18, 1960, 12–13.

72. "U. of Ga. Nixes Brubeck."

73. Gleason, "Appeal from Dave Brubeck," 12–13.

74. George Hoefer, "The Change in Big T: From Footloose Jazzman to Musical Statesman," *Down Beat*, November 26, 1959, 18–21.

75. Ibid., 18.

76. Ibid., 19. For Phnom Pehn, see Edmund H. Kellogg, Chargé d'affaires, ad interim, Phnom Pehn, to DOS, FSD-367, "Problems of Cultural Presentations in Cambodia," April 6, 1959, 7, b 91, DF 032, 1955–1959. Previously such American artists as the Westminster Singers and Benny Goodman had performed there with mixed results. Thomas D. Bowie, Saigon Counselor of Embassy for Political Affairs, to DOS, FSD-373, "Proposed Tours of American Folk Singer," April 19, 1958, b 91, DF 032, 1955–1959.

77. Walter M. Oden, Vice Consul, Hue, to DOS, FSD-8, "Conditions Affecting Cultural Presentations," March 16, 1959, b 91, DF 032, 1955–1959.

78. Howard Elting Jr., Counselor of Embassy, Saigon, to DOS, FSD-385, "CP: The Program in Vietnam during the Winter of 1958–1959 and Program Recs.," May 25, 1959, b 91, DF 032, 1955–1959.

79. Garrow, *Bearing the Cross*, 127–72. See also Dudziak, *Cold War Civil Rights*, 153–54, 157–61.

80. Dudziak, *Cold War Civil Rights*, 153–54, 157–61.

81. Arnold Rampersad, ed., with assoc. ed. David Roessel, *The Collected Poems of Langston Hughes* (New York: Vintage Books, 1994), 562, 572. The term "jazzocracy" appears in Robert G. O'Meally, ed., *The Jazz Cadence of American Culture* (New York: Columbia University Press, 1998), 117–22.

82. Martha Boyles, "Miles Davis and the Double Audience," in Early, *Miles Davis and American Culture,* 158.

83. George Fredrickson, "Reform and Revolution in American and South African Freedom Struggles," in Hine and McLeod, *Crossing Boundaries,* 72; and Skinner, "Hegemonic Paradigms," in ibid., 65.

84. Dillon, DOS Instr. CA-1851, "CP, President's Special International Program: Cultural Presentations," August 24, 1960, 1–4, b 24, f 8–160, DF 032, 1960–1963; Joseph Palmer 2nd, American Consul General, Salisbury, FSD-616, "President's Program: Visit of Herbie Mann Jazz Group," April 8, 1960, b 36, f Korin Maazal, 6–462; Dorros, FSD-490; and Palmer, Salisbury, to SOS, August 12, 1960, G-24, f David Apter, 3–1760, DF 032, 1960–1963. For African developments, see Webster and Boahen, *Revolutionary Years,* 282. For a discussion of domestic core values in the United States, see Conrad Arensberg and Arthur Niehoff, *Introducing Social Change: A Manual for Community Development,* 2nd ed. (New York: Aldine Atherton, 1971), 226–31.

85. For the conservatism of the Eisenhower administration, see, for example, *Foreign Relations of the United States* (*FRUS*), vol. 14, *Africa, 1958–1960* (Washington, D.C.: U.S. GPO, 1992), #332, "Memorandum of Conversation," October 27, 1959, 699.

86. Saul, *Freedom Is, Freedom Ain't,* 12, 13, 16–18.

87. Ibid.

88. *FRUS,* vol. 19, *Africa, 1958–1960,* #30, "Report of the Conference of Principal Diplomatic and Consular Officers of North and West Africa, Tangier, May 30-June 2, 1960," 136–41, esp. 140.

89. "Pepsi Calls Satchmo African Safari Big Booster for Sales," *Advertising Age,* October 31, 1960, f Louis Armstrong, 1960–1961, Rutgers University Institute of Jazz Studies; "Satchmo to Hit Spots in Africa for Pepsi-Cola; State Dept. Rep. in Congo," *Variety,* September 21, 1960, 1. For an example of Armstrong's view on Communism, see reel #126, service #50, cassette, Louis Armstrong Archive, Rosenthal Library, Queens College. "Satchmo Is Real Cool about S. Africa Ban," *New York Post,* October 12, 1960, f Louis Armstrong, 1960–1961, Rutgers University Institute of Jazz Studies; Palmer, "President's Program: Visit of Herbie Mann Jazz Group"; Dorros, FSD-490; Palmer, Salisbury, to SOS, August 12, 1960, [DF 032, 1960–1963].

90. *New York Times Magazine,* untitled article, f Louis Armstrong, 1960–1961, Rutgers University Institute of Jazz Studies.

91. "Good-Will Asset," *Journal American,* December 27, 1960, f Louis Armstrong, 1960–1961, Rutgers University Institute of Jazz Studies.

92. ["Report on Cultural Exchange, 1960"], Records of the Bureau of Educational and Cultural Affairs of the Department of State (CU), Special Collections Division, University of Arkansas Library, Fayetteville, Arkansas, series 1; hereafter cited as CU, series.

93. Laurence J. Hall, Country PAO, Rabat (Casablanca, Marrakech, Rabat, Fes), FSD-

465, "Cultural Presentations: President's Program: Herbie Mann Jazz Group," April 20, 1960. Comments also appear in Laurence J. Hall, FSD-3, "Performance of Holiday on Ice in Casablanca," June 22, 1960, b 36, f Korin Maazal, 6–462, DF 032, 1960–1963.

94. Davenport, *Jazz Diplomacy*, 293–94.

95. "Cozy Cole's African Tour Drumming up 'Top Cultural Diplomacy' for U.S.," *Variety*, November 28, 1962, 2. See also Bangui to SOS, DOS Incom., November 28, 1962; and Melone, Bangui, to SOS, DOS Incom. 75, November 30, 1962, b 27, f 11–162, DF 032, 1960–1963. For a seminal example of Kennedy's views on race, see John F. Kennedy, "Special Message to the Congress on Civil Rights, 28 February 1963," in John Hope Franklin and Alfred A. Moss Jr., *From Slavery to Freedom: A History of Afro-Americans*, 7th ed. (New York: McGraw Hill, 1993), 623.

96. Dudziak, *Cold War Civil Rights*, 165.

97. Mark B. Lewis, PAO, United States Information Service (USIS) Accra, Message #91, "Birmingham," May 22, 1963, 1, b 1, f Country Background (CB) Accra, USIA/Africa. For JFK's response, see John F. Kennedy, "Radio and Television Report to the American People on Civil Rights," June 11, 1963, *Public Papers of the Presidents of the United States Containing the Public Messages, Speeches, and Statements of the President: John F. Kennedy*, January 1-November 22, 1963 (Washington, D.C.: USGPO, 1964), 469; for the entire speech, see 468–71. In 1962 James Meredith made history as the first African American to be admitted to the University of Mississippi; he enrolled at the Oxford campus in the midst of heated controversy.

98. For Kennedy's response, see John F. Kennedy, "Statement by the President on the Sunday Bombing in Birmingham," September 16, 1963, *Public Papers of the Presidents: Kennedy*, January 1-November 22, 1963, 681. Lewis, *W.E.B. Du Bois*, 570–71. See also Dudziak, *Cold War Civil Rights*, 198–99, 170–71.

99. "'Musicians' Musician' to Tour Near East, South Asia," Regional Feature, IPS, Near East Branch, 1–7, USIA Information Agency Library, Washington, D.C.; and Jewell Fenzi and Carl L. Nelson, "The Duke in Baghdad," *Foreign Service Journal* (August 1991): 24–26, f Duke Ellington (2), USIA Library. For press comments from the Middle East regarding Ellington's tour, see f Duke Ellington (2), USIA Library. For a portrait of Ellington, see Harvey G. Cohen, *Duke Ellington's America* (Chicago: University of Chicago Press, 2010).

100. "State Department Alters Program Affecting Jazz," *Down Beat*, February 14, 1963, 15; "Bump ANTA from Overseas Touring; State Dept. Will Have Own Panels," *Variety*, January 2, 1963, 47.

101. Embassy Tunis to Department of State (DOS), Operations Memorandum, "Educational and Cultural Exchange: Special Examination of the Department's Cultural Presentations Program," November 15, 1962, 1–2; Embassy Lagos, to DOS, Department of State Airgam A-434, "Educational and Cultural Exchange: Special Examination of the Department's Cultural Presentations Program," January 17, 1963, 1, CU, series 1.

102. Minutes of U.S. Department of State, Bureau of Educational and Cultural Affairs, Office of Cultural Presentations, Music Panel Meeting, April 24, 1963, 2–7, CU, series 5.

103. Minutes of Music Advisory Panel Meeting, International Cultural Exchange Service of ANTA (American National Theater Academy), March 26, 1963, 4, CU, series 5.

104. Minutes of U.S. Department of State, Bureau of Educational and Cultural Affairs, Office of Cultural Presentations, Music Panel Meeting, July 24, 1963, 8, CU, series 5.

105. Joseph E. Harris, *Africans and Their History,* rev. ed. (New York: Penguin Books, 1987), 171–75, 178, 248–53.

106. Minutes of U.S. Department of State, Music Panel Meeting, April 24, 1963, 3; Minutes of U.S. Department of State, Music Panel Meeting, July 24, 1963, 7–9, 12–13, CU, series 5.

107. Embassy Tunis to DOS, "Educational and Cultural Exchange"; Embassy Lagos to DOS, "Educational and Cultural Exchange." This reevaluation came in a paper by Roy E. Larson and Glenn G. Wolfe, "U.S. Cultural Presentations—A World of Promise," Report of the Subcommittee of the U.S. Advisory Commission on International Educational and Cultural Affairs, Department of State, Bureau of Educational and Cultural Affairs, in *Cultural Presentations USA: Cultural Presentations Program of the U.S. Department of State, July 1, 1963-June 30, 1964, A Report to the Congress and the Public by the Advisory Committee on the Arts,* 77–99, USIA Historical Collection, Washington, D.C.

108. Fredrickson, "Reform and Revolution," 80.

109. Garrow, *Bearing the Cross,* 399.

110. Blakely, *Russia and the Negro,* 116. See also Dudziak, *Cold War Civil Rights,* 210–11. Some African reactions in 1964 are discussed in *FRUS,* vol. 24, *Africa, 1964–1968,* #187, "Memorandum from the Director of the United States Information Agency, (Rowan) to President Johnson," July 17, 1964 (Washington, D.C.: USGPO, 1999), 283–84.

111. Carl T. Rowan, USIA Memo for Hon. George Ball, Under Secretary of State, "Attitudes of North African Students in France: A Preliminary Report," USIS Research and Reference Service, December 10, 1964, Africa-A, NARA, Records of the Department of State, Record Group-59, Central Files 1964–1966, Culture and Information, Educational and Cultural Exchange, b 387, f EDX 32 CPP, 1164 (hereafter cited as CF-EDX, 1964–1966; when all documents are from the same file, the file is listed at the end of the note).

112. Lyndon B. Johnson, *The Vantage Point: Perspectives of the Presidency, 1963–1969* (New York: Holt, Rinehart and Winston, 1971), 157, 164, 167; and Garrow, *Bearing the Cross,* 242–44, 354–55. Shortly thereafter King also wrote *Why We Can't Wait* (New York: New American Library, 1964), the work that espoused his philosophy of nonviolence.

113. Johnson, *Vantage Point,* 164; and Lyndon B. Johnson, "Remarks of the President to a Joint Session of Congress: The American Promise" (Special Message to the Congress), March 15, 1965, in *Lyndon B. Johnson, Public Papers of the President, 1965,* vol. 1, January 1, 1965, to May 31, 1965 (Washington, D.C.: USGPO, 1966), 281–82, 284. For the text of the entire speech, see 281–87.

114. "Armstrong Speaks Out on Racial Injustice," *Down Beat,* April 22, 1965, 14, 15. Armstrong was on a private trip to Europe.

115. Nancy Bernkopf Tucker, "Lyndon Johnson: A Final Reckoning," in *Lyndon Johnson Confronts the World: American Foreign Policy, 1963–1968,* ed. Warren I. Cohen and Nancy Bernkopf Tucker (Cambridge, U.K.: Cambridge University Press, 1994), 311–20.

116. George Herring, *America's Longest War: The United States and Vietnam, 1950–1975,*

3rd ed. (New York: McGraw Hill, 1996), 133–37; Johnson, *Vantage Point*, 95; and Dudziak, *Cold War Civil Rights*, 208.

117. Herring, *America's Longest War*, 120–201.

118. #208, "Memorandum from President's Deputy Special Assistant for National Security Affairs (Komer) to President Johnson," March 10, 1966, *FRUS, Africa, 1964–1968*, 322–23. See also Dudziak, *Cold War Civil Rights*, 223.

119. Archie Schepp, "An Artist Speaks Bluntly," *Down Beat*, December 16, 1965, 11.

120. Carson, *In Struggle*, 273; Porter, *What Is This Thing Called Jazz?*, 305, 318, 203, 207. See also Ted Gioia, *The History of Jazz* (New York: Oxford University Press, 1997), 354; Fredrickson, "Reform and Revolution," 80–81. An engaging account of American actions in Vietnam is Herring, *America's Longest War*, 133–37. Porter, *John Coltrane*, 231–49, 260–61. For more on the links between music and protest, see Margaret Reid, *Black Protest Poetry: Polemics from the Harlem Renaissance and the Sixties* (New York: Peter Lang, 2001); Suzanne Smith, *Dancing in the Streets: Motown and the Cultural Politics of Detroit* (Cambridge, Mass.: Harvard University Press, 1999). For a discussion of these diasporic links, see Monson, *Freedom Sounds*, 264–65. See also Miles Davis with Quincy Troupe, *Miles: The Autobiography* (New York: Simon and Schuster, 1989), 271.

121. Davis and Troupe, *Miles*, 272. David Margolick recounts the allure of 1950s jazz in *Strange Fruit: Billie Holiday, Café Society, and an Early Cry for Civil Rights* (London: Running Press, 2000).

122. Leopold Sedar Senghor, "Blues," in *The Jazz Poetry Anthology*, ed. Sascha Feinstein and Yusef Komunyakaa (Bloomington: Indiana University Press, 1991), 192, 337–38.

123. Foley to DOS, Department of State Airgram (DOS A)-77, August 25, 1966, b 396, f Educational and Cultural Exchange (ECE) Ghana, 1164, NARA, Records of the Department of State, Record Group-59, Central Files, 1964–1966; hereafter cited as CF-EDX, 1964–1966.

124. DOS, A-140, October 30, 1966, b 396, f ECE Ghana, 1164, CF-EDX, 1964–1966.

125. William B. King, Counselor for Political Affairs, London, to DOS, A-2369, April 1, 1966, 1, enclosure, 1, b 404, f Educational Exchange (EDX), (ECE) United Kingdom 1164, CF-EDX, 1964–1966.

126. Department of State, Bureau of Educational and Cultural Affairs, "Paper for the Advisory Committee on the Arts on the Fiscal Year 1964, Cultural Presentations Program Planning for Africa," n.d., 1–2, CU, series 1.

127. Department of State, Bureau of Educational and Cultural Affairs, "Jazz in the Cultural Presentations Program," n.d., 1–2, CU, series 1; Davenport, "Jazz and the Cold War," 290.

128. Department of State, CU, "Jazz in the Cultural Presentations Program," 1–2; Parsons, Stockholm, to DOS, DOS Incom., "Last Night Heard Oscar Brown, Jr. at Biggest Stockholm Night Club," May 2, 1964, b 402, f EDX, Educational and Cultural Exchange, Sweden 1164, CF-EDX, 1964–1966.

PART III

The Advent of the Age of Obama

African Americans and the Making of American Foreign Policy

8

African American Representatives in the United Nations

From Ralph Bunche to Susan Rice

LORENZO MORRIS

In a matter of days Americans saw the previously inconspicuous ambassador Susan Rice catapulted from the intricate corridors of United Nations negotiations to the national media spotlight, articulating the consciousness and competence of the U.S. foreign policy establishment on the heels of an international crisis. Her inescapable televised image would penetrate the campaign politics of that September 2012 and linger in the recollections and recriminations of Capitol Hill combatants for many months to come. Although the substance of her statement and her claims about a terrorist attack on American embassy staff in Libya led to incendiary debate and enormous controversy about partisan distortions, it was probably her visibility itself, in the context of a foreign policy dispute far removed from the U.N. format, that would be particularly striking. From the fall election debates of 2012 to the following summer's congressional hearings on the Benghazi attack, her personality, as much as her politics, would be targeted by critics, but rarely analyzed except on matters of competence, or so the critics claimed. Her defenders, however, would reproach these criticisms as biased by partisanship, ideology, and occasionally by race. This kind of criticism, with its mix of race and ideology, connects her to her predecessors in ways this chapter explores.

Assumptions and Expectations

The ideal American ambassador is "the invisible man or woman," who conforms to the policy directives of the White House while refining them, adjusting them, and occasionally correcting misconceptions but consistently minimizing personal visibility. Where visible the ambassador should be seen as the spokesperson in a specific issue area or agency while any role in policy formulation should be invisible to the public. For African American U.N. ambassadors in the past, however, this has proven to be a near impossibility. At most these ambassadors could only hope to escape the defining pressures of race relations by sinking into the kind of active inertia bemoaned by Ralph Ellison in *The Invisible Man*. In this case that means minimizing personal initiative and denying or rejecting other initiatives that may involve race in order to avoid the unwarranted assumption of a racial factor. In avoiding such initiatives ambassadors are most likely to be seen as insignificant and effective when they are seen in the media at all. That would be fine for approximating the ideal of ideological and political neutrality for ambassadors if it were not for the persistent assumptions and global expectations that have historically surrounded African Americans in the United Nations.

This chapter seeks to identify those assumptions and expectations and to determine whether they significantly affect or have affected African Americans in senior positions in the United Nations in the execution, interpretation, or evaluation of their responsibilities. The examination focuses on the role of the ambassador, but the research begins with a focus on Ralph Bunche, whose role as a "first" and whose breadth of responsibilities in the U.N.'s foundation help to define the parameters in which race is likely to pass between insignificance and prominence. Building on continuing issues exposed by Bunche's experience, the experiences of the three African American U.S. ambassadors to the U.N.—Andrew Young, Donald McHenry, and Susan Rice—can each be examined on the basis of similar issues. Unfortunately, although the information that exists about the public and political relations of other African Americans in the U.N. is significant, there is not enough of it to allow for similar assessments. Accordingly, the relatively short seven-month tenure of Ambassador Edward Perkins (1992–1993) is difficult to include.

The United Nations is composed of blocks of disunited nations separated by histories of cultural, political, and economic inequality and held together in blocks by common histories, overlapping cultures, and shared economic interests. The whole is held together by a shared political and military necessity that is linked to the history of unequal political and military forces that continues to divide them. In the post–World War II years since its founding, the place of U.S. diplomacy has been relatively consistent. U.S. relations with and among the U.N. member nations, as well as their occasionally disruptive extra-national constituents, have changed significantly while the influence of race in modifying diplomatic exchanges has ebbed and flowed. From its initial colonial and Eurocentric emergence to the post-1950s flood of newly independent states, international alliances were unmade and remade generating recurrent pressures on the U.N. for recognition, resources, and occasionally military involvement. In the post–Cold War climate, unstable religious group accommodations and changing economic and military alliances have pushed race from the forefront of international conflict while linking it to other components of instability.

Racial Factors: National and International Pressures

Given the fundamentally representative functions of ambassadors, coupled with the policy articulation functions of diplomats generally, the emergence of race as a factor in the interactions of any U.N. diplomat is problematic. When any individual takes a prominent place in public, media, or policy discussions, it is rare for the individual's race to draw particular attention, and yet it is just as rare for the individual's race to go unnoticed in public situations. The current concern is to determine the extent to which such notice may reach a level of political significance versus indifference. In a historically race-sensitive context, like that of U.S. national politics or in the foreign policy context of European or African relations, race-conscious behavior has the potential to impose pressures that influence or deform decision making. While it may well be politically appealing, the untested assumption that race is inconsequential flows more readily from national ideological prerogatives than from careful analysis.

Historically these pressures have been of four types:

A. Internal pressure within the foreign policy or political base:
  (1) Positive pressures (recently more common) and
  (2) Negative pressures (uncommon in recent years);
B. External pressure from domestic political opponents or foreign allies:
  (1) Positive pressures with high (progressive) expectations and
  (2) Negative pressure linked to international lobbying.

Internal pressures (A) consist of domestic demands or influence coming from inside the representative's support base, normally the black community, based on the representative's prior interests or commitments, or they may come from the

State Department's own hierarchy or informal political structures. They could be either positive (A1) or negative (A2), but in modern conditions they are very unlikely to be negative. A negative pressure would involve an expectation of race-related failure, making it very unlikely that the individual ever would have been selected for a position as representative in the first place. Positive pressures, on the other hand, would imply that the ambassador's race relations would help to transcend existing cultural or racial prejudices in relations among states or cultural groups—much as apparent ethnic or cultural links of ambassadors in the past have sometimes been thought to increase access to foreign political leaders or facilitate communications across formal barriers.

External political pressures (B) may emanate from political opponents of the current administration or from foreign allies and are focused on the assumed influence of race-related attitudes originating either with the representative or from political reactions to the racial issues and racial identity itself. These pressures, involving assumptions and expectations, are external to the State Department and other American foreign policy authorities as well as the normal course of American diplomacy.

The positive external pressures (B1) most often come from the foreign "progressive" sources or from leaders in the African diaspora who are expecting a progressive, race-conscious influence on U.S. policy. They are positive only in the sense that there is an assumption or expectation that the interpretation of U.S. policy would be more favorably disposed toward the interests of the developing world or special subnational groups than previously. The negative external pressures (B2) result from the opposite assumptions or expectations. Such pressures are most likely to come from those outside the African diaspora, but they may also come from within it, particularly when the individual representative is burdened with a history of hostile relations in international circles that are separate from the United Nations.

This is an informal typology of racial factors in American foreign affairs representation, and it is not intended to provide a basic empirical determination of the race-conscious behavior in international settings. Specifically, the initial determination that any behavior or decision making involves race starts from the assessments of the foreign policy actors themselves. This reserved approach to race specificity responds to a common suspicion that racial labeling is arbitrary or normative. The former head of the U.S. Census Bureau, Professor Kenneth Prewitt, raises this point in criticizing the political context in which racial definitions have been historically applied and refined as census data have evolved. Adapting a popular metaphor that "when you have a hammer . . . [everything looks like a nail]," he warns that the labeling itself can redirect public attention.[1] Instead, these observations begin with the public sector articulation of racial issues—in particular, events or occasions that have included significant public discussion of race as a factor or symbol in political behavior.

The Bunche Model

At a time when racial identity was a salient factor in most domestic exchanges, including any public events involving nonwhite Americans, it was readily assumed that race could have a perceptible influence on discussions, and occasionally on outcomes, regardless of how irrelevant race itself might have been to the issues at hand. At the same time, particularly in the 1940s, 1950s, and 1960s, international issues were rarely seen as significantly racial even where national groups were divided by race. Colonialism and instability, for example, might well have represented the issue focus of what was a substantially racially motivated disagreement between states, but the issues actually debated in international organizations virtually never went beyond the state-level composition of the issues.

However solid Bunche's individual credentials and experiences may have been—and they were impeccable—he apparently could not have reached the Nobel Prize–winning position he earned without an exceptional confluence of circumstances both sad and serendipitous. As a political science professor and researcher on international relations, his selection from among wartime consultants to join the U.S. staff at the San Francisco conference establishing the United Nations created small waves in the State Department only in response to the uniqueness of its departure from the racial norm. Still, it was an impressive indication of racial openness, but at that point there was not an investment of public authority comparable to that of ambassadorial appointment.

In the extended historical wake of the last postwar American attempt to form an inclusive multinational organization, the choice of American participants may have seemed less auspicious than the eventual importance of the United Nations would suggest. The failure of President Woodrow Wilson to garner senatorial support for the League of Nations after World War I seems to have cast a shadow over the U.N. planning meetings in post–World War II San Francisco. There were still memories of the earlier recalcitrant Congress that could not have been stirred out of its ideologically grounded isolationism by careful planning, however effective, for any organizational unity of nations. As a consequence, the experimental character of including a black representative in the meetings should have easily paled in significance behind the larger experimental character of the unpredictable organizational effort.

To some extent the choice of Bunche was indirectly linked to a "positive" racial assumption stemming both from Bunche's earlier selection for a wartime consulting role and from his proposed initial responsibility in the U.N.

Secretariat. In 1941 the U.S. Coordinator of Information, later called the Office of Strategic Services (OSS), asked the Harvard University history department to recommend an "African specialist." The department responded by citing a professor who referred to Bunche as the only "'Negro graduate student' he has known at Harvard who [was] able to compete for fellowship on equal terms with the better white students."[2] That position was a bridge, though uncertain, to his selection for his initial U.N. role as acting director of the Trusteeship Division, dealing with current and former colonies. The OSS perhaps heeded the advice Bunche had given in 1942 when he cautioned that "the elite African especially is even more sensitive on racial matters than is the American Negro."[3]

In the intervening years his experience as an adviser in the Washington-based State Department may have served as much to propel him toward the U.N. as to include him as American representative. He complained that the segregated environment of Washington, into which the State Department comfortably fell, left him no reason to expect that he would rise to the kind of position of responsibility that the initial U.N. appointment entailed.[4] Still, he was posted on loan from the State Department to the U.N., which indirectly made him a U.S. representative. More precisely, the appointment exposed the early positive and negative racial assumptions related to U.N. representation. Rather than a preference or professional choice, only the work on U.N. involvement with colonial relations was initially open to Bunche. His success in developing the trusteeship program, and particularly in formulating an unarmed role for U.N. peacekeepers, opened his path to broader responsibility. In seeking to intercede in unstable colonial situations with U.N. pressure and occasionally with U.N. troops, Bunche demonstrated an agreeable and accommodating personality, one that was tolerant of diverse and even hostile political attitudes. As a consequence, the initial Africa-oriented pressures on his options exposed his potential for and value in the tense Middle Eastern negotiations.

Perhaps the first point at which an agreeable personality was essential was in working for the head of the U.N. negotiating team, Count Folke Bernadotte of Sweden, whose aristocratic trappings seemed excessive to many, including Bunche. Although they worked together closely, both the Israeli and the Arab negotiating parties were apparently distrustful of Bernadotte. Bunche, on the other hand, was assumed to be more objective, in part because he was not Swedish or European, a neutrality apparently reinforced by the fact that he was African American. Although ambiguous, that is arguably an external positive aspect of racial pressure to the extent that it was viewed as outside of, or removed from, informal Euro-American intrigues.

By the same token, such relationships would also imply negative racial pressures on other occasions. Ironically, one such occasion emerges many years later according to Bunche's own account of his awkward discussions with Congolese leaders during the chaotic and violent period of Belgium's decolonization.[5] Patrice Lumumba, in the heat of his revolutionary struggle, apparently placed little confidence in Bunche's warnings about the limits of U.N. support potential. At the same time, according to the extant U.N. representative from the Congo, Thomas Kane, "the Belgians saw Bunche 'as just another colored man. His position was very delicate in that he could never take any position or express any view about the relations the white colonizers and the black colonized without being misinterpreted and suspected by either or both.'"[6]

In essence the shadow of race hangs, however delicately, over the struggles and accomplishments of Bunche's work in the U.N. The significance of that influence can be usefully tested by considering the extent to which race has shadowed the work of subsequent African Americans carrying out representative functions in the U.N. The first and most prominent issue for Bunche, the Israeli-Palestinian conflict, suggests positive and negative racial assumptions. The second major issue—Congolese instability—though persistent, does not have the U.N. significance of the first. The U.N.'s initial concern, and Bunche's personal one for decolonization, falls into the category of human rights, which constitutes a second issue area of continuing concern to the U.N.

Decolonization's significance for multilevel state conflict as well as conflict prevention exhibits two issue areas of continuous concern for the U.N. In fact, Bunche's multistate agreements for the trusteeship programs that he introduced were also the U.N.'s introduction to the building of effective alliances among states with competing economic and territorial interests. This third area is historically tied to the fourth continuing issue area, that of "conflict prevention." In the end, and at the apex of Bunche's career, that issue may have been the most controversial and yet the least encumbered by racial factors. In his 1950 Nobel Peace Prize address, when Bunche warned that those who call for "preventive war" will inevitably be responsible for inciting war, he brought into focus an issue that has typically marked U.S. disagreements with U.N. members in the developing world through the last "coalition of the willing" in Iraq.[7]

Of four continuing issue areas—the Israeli-Palestinian conflict, human rights and failed states, multistate agreements, and conflict prevention—only conflict prevention appears to have been uninfluenced by race during Bunche's career. Any racial influence, however, cannot be confirmed without additional evidence. A way to explore the evidence and to determine the potential and limits of racial factors is to examine these four issue areas as they intersect with the careers of subsequent African American representatives in the U.N.

Ambassador Andrew Young

Issue Area: Israeli-Palestinian Conflict

If the presence of race as a factor in Bunche's experiences was ever speculative or ambiguous, it was far from ambiguous in the experiences of the first official African American U.S. representative to the United Nations, Ambassador Andrew Young.

President Jimmy Carter's appointment of Ambassador Young in 1976 was greeted with the kind of clamor and reaction that groundbreaking events can be expected to generate. There was celebration in liberal circles, reservation in moderate circles, and noisy disapproval in conservative ones. In the course of Young's three-year tenure, the hostility of his initial, politically motivated conservative critics proved contagious across the political spectrum—a contagion eased by his own race-conscious faux pas. Given the early skepticism about Young and his exclusively domestic, civil rights–based political background, his willingness to invoke race on occasion may well have stirred the diplomatic cauldron.

As a consequence the case of "negative race pressure" is generally best illustrated by Young's tenure at the U.N. and events in several issue areas. Particularly striking is his unfortunate reference in 1979 to the circumstances of dissident Jews detained in the Soviet Union when they were seeking to migrate to Israel.[8] He apparently sought to demonstrate an openness to broader negotiations with the Soviets on the issue of Jewish dissidents by admitting to past American transgressions in the case of civil rights and antiwar protesters, but he grossly miscalculated the reaction at home. He was seen as disparaging the hardships of prospective Israeli immigrants in the Soviet Union. His role and reliability in dealing with Israeli-Palestinian issues, among others, were immediately brought into question in the U.S. Congress and in the media.

In an interview with French newspaper *Le Matin,* Young casually referred to imprisoned American political activists by saying, "We still have hundreds of people that I would categorize as political prisoners in our prisons."[9] In response, Representative Larry McDonald (R-GA) called for Young's impeachment, but the motion was defeated. McDonald had already accused Young of "subordinat[ing] American interests to those of the Third World."[10] While still in Congress, Representative Dan Quayle (R-IN) argued that Ambassador Young should resign in order to "spare the nation further embarrassment."[11]

This largely verbal exchange would soon be aggravated by a tangible diplomatic misstep in the same issue area from which Young's ambassadorship would not recover. Young met briefly and informally with a Palestinian Liberation Organization (PLO) observer at the U.N. in the apartment of a Kuwaiti U.N. representative. Angry reaction to that presumed violation of U.S. policy of non-negotiation with the PLO compelled his resignation. While the instance itself was not race-specific, the reactions were racially focused. Civil rights groups, including the NAACP, rushed to his defense.[12] The U.S. State Department, monitoring African reaction, concluded that the ouster "jeopardized" diplomatic relations.[13]

Issue Area: Human Rights and Failed States

Of course, Young had done enough to provoke his conservative antagonists in Congress from the moment of his nomination by suggesting that his political experience in race relations would positively influence his approach to international relations. Particularly, when he indicated that some of our European allies were "racists," the statements were seen as unwarranted by and inappropriate for the U.N. context. For example, in 1977 he referred to the British in a televised statement as "chicken" on racial matters, both domestic and African, in Rhodesia (Zimbabwe) and South Africa, and he called the Swedish "terrible racists."[14]

Although they were unacceptable blunders for his colleagues, and they probably had an adverse impact, these incidents are linked to what may be called positive racial assumptions. First, in selecting Young, Congress and President Carter seemed to expect a bonus for international relations based on human rights and race. According to a Gallup poll, Ambassador Young was second only to Rev. Jesse Jackson as the most admired African American at the time.[15] During his confirmation hearings the senators concentrated on African affairs, even though they were rarely mentioned on most such occasions. The senators' newfound concern with Africa no doubt reflected what they feared or assumed was Young's positive disposition toward African democratization without regard to old alliances.

Young was, after all, the only U.N. representative who had ever organized "a demonstration against US foreign policy and a demonstration at the UN at that."[16] While none of their suspicions justified any assumption that he would do more for Africa than any other American diplomat, the positive value of the racial perspective he hoped to bring to international diplomacy is indicated by his critiques of the previous administration. In a 1977 *Playboy* interview he "accused the Russians, Henry Kissinger, Richard Nixon, and Gerald Ford of racism."[17]

When it came to Africa and its multistate agreements, racial identification seems to have given Ambassador Young a kind of confidence to speak about Africa's goals and values that would have been provocative coming from his predecessor Ambassador Daniel Moynihan. Given Moynihan's previous publicity in speaking about African Americans and social welfare policy, that image is noteworthy. Young implied that the best interests of Africa resided in imitating the West. He added, "I frankly approach Africa in terms of U.S. self-interest."[18] Although his predecessors may have agreed, the sensitivity of the topic would have prevented them from saying so. Young, on the other hand, seems to have been asserting the privilege of racially positive perspective to justify assuming a more unreserved approach.

In fact, such an approach would be consistent with the conditions surrounding his nomination by President-elect Jimmy Carter. Young was traveling with other members of the Congressional Black Caucus in Lesotho when a reporter first relayed rumors of the possible appointment. His side trip to visit a political prisoner in Africa reinforced his concern for human rights. When he returned to the United States, Carter invited him to report on the Lesotho experience and offered him the U.N. position. At that time he noted it was important that Young "had been 'associated with Martin Luther King [and that] would help people take human rights seriously from the United States.'"[19] Apparently they both saw international human rights as an elaboration of King's civil rights focus.

Issue Area: Multistate Agreements

However positively Ambassador Young may have viewed his place in the African diaspora as grounds for improving the American image in the U.N., his international interlocutors were much less receptive. The British were clearly dismayed by his attempts to focus on their historic links to Rhodesia and apartheid South Africa. Given his consistently American-oriented approach to Africa and negative international reaction around these southern African issues, which had already provoked global consternation, European reactions to Young went beyond simple diplomatic sensitivities to more racial ones.

Still, there was a clear substantive point to Young's approach to Africa that was also expressed in the lead roles on Africa policy that President Carter accorded Vice President Walter Mondale. On the heels of increasing American protests, especially on college campuses, against southern Africa oppression, Ambassador Young pushed President Carter to action. Carter's decision "to maintain sanctions against Southern Rhodesia in the summer of 1979 was one of the high points of Young's service in the U.N."[20] The fact that this decision was a broad act of foreign policy, perhaps circumventing the authority of Secretary of State Cyrus Vance, is evidence of a special primacy accorded Young's perspective on Africa.

Issue Area: Conflict Prevention

While still in the confirmation process, Andrew Young sought to heighten American awareness of violent conflict in Africa as well as the potential for its spread. The Angolan civil war was seen as an immediate concern for American foreign policy. Not long after his confirmation, Ambassador Young ventured into territory that was unfamiliar among American diplomats by publicly affirming the potential value of Cuban military intervention as critical in minimizing African conflict. In a response during a televised Dan Rather interview he denied that Cuban troops would aggravate a "protracted guerilla war" in Angola, adding, "In fact, there's a sense in which the Cubans bring a certain stability and order."[21]

He subsequently "clarified" and moderated his response, but it still represented a substantial digression from the norm. Although African Americans have generally supported comparatively left-leaning foreign policy, this idea normally would not have had racial overtones if it were not for his strong association with Trans-Africa and its leader, Randall Robinson. Among other things, TransAfrica had been an organizer of the recent trip to Lesotho. Robinson subsequently argued extensively for more open relations with Cuba and traveled there to meet with Cuban leaders.[22] While Young probably would not have agreed with Robinson's later comments on Cuba, the fact that the TransAfrica leadership and other civil rights leaders were pushing for a more open approach to Cuba and Africa, which Young had suggested, indicates a positive race-related influence. By the same token, the likely reactive pressure from the State Department on Young to dissociate from this group indicates a "negative" influence of race-related politics. In the end these latter pressures won out and Young had to be replaced.

Ambassador Donald McHenry

Almost as if to mitigate racial sensitivities, Ambassador Young's replacement was one of the few African Americans with senior status in the State Department, Ambassador Donald McHenry. As a career diplomat McHenry could be expected to be much more circumspect on racially sensitive issues, and in this regard he met the most exacting expectations. At the same time, he was expected to embody the presumed positive benefits of race relations that had been expected of Young. As the *Washington Post* rather bluntly put it: "President Carter today nominated Donald F. McHenry, a black career diplomat, as the new U S. ambassador to the United Nations, praising him as a 'professional' who can continue the Third World relations forged by his predecessor, Andrew Young."[23]

Issue Area: Israeli-Palestinian Conflict

Still, the international reception he received in relationship to Israeli-Palestinian questions was not without negative expectations that at least in their expression reflected racial overtones as reported by *Newsweek*: "Israeli officials are privately unhappy about Donald McHenry, the U.S. ambassador to the U.N. and the man who cast the anti-Israel vote that Jimmy Carter later renounced. Israeli sources say McHenry made a poor impression on Menachem Begin and other leaders on a recent visit. Some describe McHenry as 'arrogant' in his meeting with Begin."[24] Of course, the baggage Ambassador McHenry carried from having served as Young's deputy should not be overlooked. The issues before the two ambassadors at the U.N. were largely unchanged along with policies of the Carter administration, although the perspectives and language of their diplomacy diverged considerably.

In addition, Ambassador McHenry may have benefited from a tightened adaptation of the State Department hierarchy that reduced the focus on his individual choices. For example, when he voted in favor of a March 1980 resolution "condemning Israeli settlements on the West Bank and Gaza Strip," harsh reaction should have been expected.[25] President Carter's disavowal of the decision two days later may have exposed McHenry to broad personal criticism. Secretary of State Vance, however, took responsibility and deflected substantial criticism.[26] Aside from the early association of McHenry with Young that had negative racial overtones, at least in the media, and this latter incident, McHenry fared relatively well. His role on these Israeli-Palestinian questions was a careful balance of political and race-neutral interaction in the United Nations. A background of experience for all the players apparently matters.

Issue Area: Human Rights and Failed States

Whereas Young came to the U.N. with a great deal of sympathy for Africa and its development, McHenry, it may be argued, came with a lot of empathy for Africa and a personal understanding of constraints on its development. Before he took the seat of "permanent representative" to the U.N., as a diplomat in the State Department he had developed a strong interest in the conflicts of southern Africa and particularly in Namibia. While South Africa's human rights violations were increasingly drawing international attention, Namibia's instability in the midst of its continuing colonial subjugation was ripe for U.N. intervention in the spirit of democratization. Yet, on the level of personal style the contrast between McHenry and Young could scarcely have been more striking. McHenry continued the articulation of American human rights interests that President Carter had originally encouraged through Young. Through McHenry, however, he sought and received the kind of "professional" detachment that one would expect of a career diplomat but particularly one who would "continue the Third World relations" developed by his predecessor.[27] As a consequence, the role Washington envisioned for McHenry was probably somewhere between one that was free of racial influence and one that held a positive influence of race on some of these U.N. issues. In any event, McHenry's reserved though effective diplomacy indicates that his personal image and behavior on human rights issues distinguished him more from Young than from other American U.N. ambassadors.

Issue Area: Multistate Agreements

Perhaps more characteristic of his special exposure to southern Africa in his State Department background than of any sensitivity to the African diaspora, McHenry sought to impose a strong U.N. on the region. In 1966 he had worked on a Namibia case before the International Court of Justice that involved South Africa, Southern Rhodesia, Angola, and Mozambique. Showing an unusual attentiveness to multinational perspectives, he developed a policy paper at that time on the Liberian and Ethiopian case against southern Africa and its oversight of Namibia.[28] Apparently, McHenry saw very early the advantages of multistate consensus building and involvement in the resolution of national and bilateral instability.

Issue Area: Conflict Prevention

Still, questions of Namibian independence and U.N. relations with its militant independence organization, South West Africa People's Organization (SWAPO), rapidly led to friction over the U.S. leadership in the U.N. Security Council. As U.N.-supervised elections in Namibia approached in 1980, apartheid South Africa became very critical of the U.S. role as represented by McHenry. After repeated South African allegations against the U.N. for bias toward SWAPO, the black independence movement, Ambassador McHenry responded. According to David B. Ottaway of the *Washington Post*: "Regarding the South African charge of UN partiality toward SWAPO, McHenry said the Security Council, which would be in charge of the elections, had never endorsed the guerilla group as the sole representatives."[29]

McHenry's leadership on the Namibian question was easily attributed to his extended experience, as noted above, rather than to any personal preference or political consciousness linked to African American international pressures. Unless the parameters of race-related influences are stretched to include any strong interest in Africa, then McHenry's behavior should be seen as race-neutral. The international response, however, was laden with racially significant assumptions, as suggested by the South African accusation. The suspicion of an undercover endorsement was most likely based on assumptions about the personality or personalities of the leading country representatives, since previous U.N. policies had been largely disengaged, if not indifferent.

Ambassador Susan Rice

Susan Rice is the first African American ambassador to the U.N. to be born in the period of desegregation and to mature in a period when racial barriers to mobility would finally dissolve at door of the White House. Ambassador Rice was also the first to emerge from a partisan political background and yet have acquired substantial foreign policy experience. Her road to the U.N. had been smoothed by her role on the Obama presidential campaign staff, and her ability to contribute foreign policy advice to the campaign had been refined when she was the assistant secretary of state for Africa under President Clinton. As such, she was well prepared to become a team player at the U.N. She would play a role made easier by the fact that she is the only U.N. ambassador to be part of her country's foreign policy cabinet.[30] Whatever inescapable attention to race-sensitive national and international issues may have emerged, any reflection on American leadership in the U.N. would just as likely have fallen on the White House as on her. In this context she is as close to the "deracialized" representative as the ideal toward which sixty-plus years of U.N. history inclines the American presence.

Still, there are continuing signs that the ideal of representation, if in sight, may not be as free from political flaws as earlier American diplomats seemed to hope. The irony of expecting to "deracialize" a political environment charged with race-related ideological differences occasionally surfaces at critical times. The expectations or pressures come from the logical assumption that African American and African political actors will continue to make decisions based on their previous political roles. First, from internationalist and liberal Americans, there was criticism of her initiatives, or lack thereof, in East Africa as assistant secretary of state in the Clinton administration in dealing with Sudan and Rwanda. In the latter case the assumption in media commentary seems to be that she should have done more to promote Washington intervention in Rwanda. In the case of Sudan, as one blogger among others complained after her confirmation to the U.N.: "Susan Rice . . . has overplayed her hands in setting up Omar al-Bashir for war crimes so that western corporations can seize control of Sudan's natural resources."[31] While the policy criticism could and should apply equally to Clinton representatives in the area, the sense of disappointment with application of White House policy is striking. Additional criticisms with representatives in the African Union seemed to have a similar though less strident tone.

On the domestic side, black politics and foreign policy analyst Professor Ronald Walters perhaps made the starkest case for negative expectations when in retrospect he criticized John Kerry's presidential campaign in *Newsweek* for not having any black senior staffers. It was clear nevertheless that Rice was a senior staff member of Kerry's campaign.[32] Yet, as former George W. Bush administration U.N. spokesman Richard Grenell argues in the *Huffington Post,* others saw her as primarily very reserved, too reserved for Grenell's tastes. He comments that she is "an absentee ambassador who is 'widely inattentive' to matters before the UN and a 'weak negotiator.'"[33]

In some sense such a reserved posture brings Rice closer to the ambassadorial ideal than her predecessors, but the idea of detached negotiator calls to mind the constraints of the invisible man character who could not clearly commit to any political position because ambiguous racial attitudes of others left him unsure about how and where he could fit in. Still, the criticism of her negotiation prowess may well be premature, and the criticism of her "inattentiveness" seems to rest on the more marginal concerns of the U.N. representative, such as her failure to play a major role in the U.S. relief effort in Haiti from U.N. headquarters. In fact, her extended absences from New York at the time in order to deal with her ailing parents are easily verified. By contrast, others, such as her communications deputy, Mark Kornblau, praise her for pushing through tough sanctions on North Korea.[34]

Where Ambassador Rice's personal contributions to U.S. influence in the U.N. should be most visible, they may escape media attention because of her exceptional integration into the presidential cabinet. More than in the cases of her predecessors, her presence on the U.N. floor has probably been managed and mellowed by Washington-based decision making that actively ties her to former secretary of state Hillary Clinton and to President Obama. The link to Obama may well make her appear to be less responsive to civil rights organizations and Pan-African lobbies' demands, because the demands on the president have often assumed shared political preference that was not present in the White House.

Similarly, the human rights community's disappointment with Secretary of State Colin Powell over a U.N. initiative on racial injustice was reflected in criticism of Obama more than that of the secretary or the U.N. representative. Powell's failure to push the Bush administration beyond its refusal to fully participate in the 2001 U.N. High Commissioner's World Conference against Racism held in South Africa was rehashed in the media by similar groups criticizing the Obama administration's failure to encourage such a conference.[35]

Unlike General Powell and his politically nurtured civilian boss, George W. Bush, President Obama and Ambassador Rice share experiences beyond race that make the hints of personal touches more difficult to detect. Among other things, they were both active Democratic Party mobilizers, graduated from elite universities, took office in their forties, and had prior links to Africa. Curiously, they were both outstanding basketball players in their exclusive prep schools. Obviously, then, they share personal links to diverse black communities, but their links to the typical black political communities are strikingly marginal. Their roots in the Democratic Party, among other mainstream groups, appear far stronger than their attachments to civil and human rights associations like TransAfrica, with which Andrew Young was affiliated.

However vast the changes in the social and political environment surrounding the American role in the U.N. may have been since its beginning, there remains a substantial continuity in the kind of political issues confronting the American representatives. Judging from State Department–oriented websites, Ambassador Rice has dealt primarily with six major issues since assuming the position in 2009. At least four of these fit into the issue areas discussed here: (1) the crisis in Israel over the Turkish-based flotilla, (2) the U.N. sanctions resolution on North Korea, (3) human rights and government responsibility in Sudan, and (4) international responses to Iranian nuclear development.[36] The other two issues—instability in Somalia and development and climate change–related support for Africa—are historically traceable as well but less clearly so. Ironically, these latter issues are perhaps least visible in terms of U.N. progress but most visible in Rice's background of career experience.

Issue Area: Israeli-Palestinian Conflict

For Ambassador Rice's African American predecessors the passage through U.N. debates on the Middle East was particularly foreboding. For two representatives, Young and McHenry, it was an impasse in which they were forced to confront critical political and personal challenges. For McHenry it was an immediate challenge to which his response seems to have appeased his critics. For Young it was a persistent challenge. In contrast, for Bunche it was the focus of his internationally acclaimed achievement. For Ambassador Rice, however, it is too soon to draw a broad conclusion, but some patterns are already apparent.

If there is an African American model that Ambassador Rice might emulate on the Middle East issue, it would probably be Ambassador McHenry, except that her profile is much lower than his was in this case, bordering on invisibility. As with McHenry, however, she successfully faced an early media-sensitive policy dilemma shortly after assuming office. Following an Israeli decision to board and arrest human rights activists supporting Palestinians on a Turkish flotilla approaching Israel, Turkey demanded U.N. condemnation of Israel. Given the bloodshed involved, that debate commanded international attention in early summer 2010. Still, the articulation of the United States in the U.N. was largely left to Rice's deputy, Alejandro Wolff, who negotiated with Turkey in the U.N. Security Council while Rice advised the president.[37]

Still, in contrast to all the predecessors, this case demonstrates a level of progress away from the racial sensitivity indicated before. There were no expectations, negative or positive, for Rice. Her performance elicited only disappointment on the political left, in the Arab world, the developing world, and, of course, in

Turkey, where there were strong hopes for a change of U.S. foreign policy and not just its U.N.-based articulation. By the same token, she clearly reflected Washington's position in a way that was neither more provocative nor reserved than White House predispositions on the Middle East generally.

Issue Area: Human Rights and Failed States

Susan Rice may have given up her primary focus on East African instability when the Clinton administration left the White House, but when she returned to public office along with Secretary of State Clinton, East Africa would continue to demand her attention. As noted above, Sudanese leader Omar al-Bashir had not submitted to international justice nor had he faded from international attention. Charged with war crimes before the International Criminal Court, al-Bashir has been a continuing target of Ambassador Rice. While she clearly reflects White House policy, her history on this question gives her a head start for influence with American allies and a negative image among countries, particularly in the Arab League and African Union. The disagreement apparently focuses more on the appropriateness, or lack thereof, of international intervention rather than support for the Sudanese leader's behavior.

Here, in the criticism of Ambassador Rice, there are indications of race-related expectations going from positive to negative. Under President Clinton the choice of the relatively inexperienced and young Susan Rice as assistant secretary for Africa did not fit the typical profile, except, of course, it is the position at its rank most commonly held by African Americans. The selections of some African Americans for State Department leadership, such as the 2009 choice of Johnnie Carson for assistant secretary for Africa, have evoked immediate public and international approval on the basis of their well-established careers. For African Americans and Africans responding to Clinton's choice of Rice, race became more salient in the absence of an established track record. In addition, American missteps on other questions of humanitarian crises in Africa helped to breed a sense of disappointment as the reverse side of unjustified expectations. The crisis in Somalia added only a sense of disapproval among some in the international community that an eight-year interval would not dissipate.

On the other hand, when Rice assumed her latest post, she sought to bring new emphasis to American humanitarian commitment by focusing on the Millennium Development Goals as one of her four priorities mentioned in her confirmation hearing. Noting that "President-elect Obama has called for us to invest in our common humanity," she referred to global threats of "poverty, disease, environmental degradation, rampant criminality, extremism and violence."[38] It was a strong statement but one that stuck to the dimensions of a team player.

Issue Area: Multistate Agreements

For some American diplomats, particularly her deputy, Mark Kornblau, Ambassador Rice has shown outstanding skill and persistence in bringing the international community together in placing restraints on states the American government sees as most threatening. In particular, she is viewed as playing an effective role in pushing through a U.N. resolution calling for sanctions on North Korea as well as contributing to the isolation of Iran.[39] In both cases, however, the strength of White House policy does not leave much room for the individual attribution of initiative to the U.S. representative in the United Nations.

When Ambassador Rice took a more public unreserved role in foreign policy articulation, the domestic political reaction seems to have been more personal than normal for U.N. diplomats. In particular, her statements on the violence surrounding the U.S. diplomats in Benghazi, Libya, provoked extreme personal criticism on Capitol Hill while raising the specter of race. When members of Congress called Ambassador Rice "incompetent" following her television appearance, Congressman Jim Clyburn (D-SC) responded, "You know these are code words." He explained, "These kinds of terms that those of us—especially those of us who were grown and raised in the South—we've been hearing these little words and phrases all of our lives and we get insulted by them."[40]

On questions involving multistate action, the accomplishments of the U.N. in the past two years are sufficiently ambiguous that affirmation of individual accomplishments is difficult. For example, African Union representatives have sought U.N. action through the General Assembly on environmental programs and climate change. Commenting on these demands, Richard Downie of the Center for Strategic and International Studies observes, "Africa has the misfortune of being the continent least responsible for global warming but the one most likely to suffer its negative consequences."[41] On this question there is evidence of heightened expectations for Ambassador Rice, but, given her relatively extensive exposure to Africa policy issues, the absence of such expectations might also be significant. Nevertheless, rather than the initiative of Rice, the inertia of the U.N. might well constitute the best meter by which any such action should be measured.

In 2011 the political constraints on American efforts to build multistate agreements was illustrated through the Obama administration's decision to veto a U.N. Security Council resolution denouncing the extension of Israeli settlements as an impediment to peace negotiations. The announcement of a veto, clearly a presidential decision, briefly put Ambassador Rice in the center of media attention. She was cited as being sympathetic to the concerns of the other fourteen member states, as she has been to U.N. member concerns generally. That distinguishes her and the Obama administration from the Bush administration in 2006, the last time the U.S. veto was exercised, also on an Israeli issue. Deferentially, she explained that the veto should not be interpreted to mean "we support settlement activity. . . . Continued settlement activity violates Israel's international commitments, devastates trust between the parties and threatens the prospects for peace."[42] With this statement she fits into the Obama administration policy much as U.N. Representative John Bolton fit into that of George W. Bush in 2006—with one notable difference. Bolton took a leading and visible role in articulating the Bush administration's skeptical, if not hostile, perspective on the U.N. In contrast, Rice is indistinguishable in her formulation of policy, neither progressive nor conservative. In this regard she may truly approach the ideal suggested above of the politically invisible ambassador. Still, multistate agreements and negotiations that avoid awkward vetoes may require individual initiative independent of the president or secretary of state.

Issue Area: Conflict Prevention

Two of the four priorities Ambassador Rice affirmed in her confirmation testimony involve conflict prevention. First, she said she would work to "improve UN peace," keeping operations that she linked to Darfur and restraints on Sudanese government practices. Second, referring to nuclear regulation in North Korea and Iran, she testified that she would concentrate on "preventing the spread . . . of nuclear weapons" in those two countries. For Rice, the Sudanese issue is tied to her relatively personal political experience under President Clinton, while the Iranian and North Korean nuclear issues were relatively new and yet far more central to international media attention.

Over the years, however, Darfur had garnered substantial African and African American attention. As noted above, the African Union had disagreed with the American effort Rice led to bring the Sudanese leader before the International Criminal Court for human rights violations. This disagreement may have led to fairly negative assumptions among African leaders about her emerging role in the U.N. On the other hand, any expectations or pressures should have been counterbalanced by the heavier American pressure for sanctions intended to prevent militia or government aggression in that Sudanese region. In particular, liberal American and African American groups, including TransAfrica, were prominent in pushing for U.S. and U.N. intervention programs. The similarity of diverse American interest-group concerns with those of the national government in peacekeeping has meant the special interests of African American groups are not clearly special.

Accordingly, the U.S. representative in the U.N. can once again fade into the racially undifferentiated American background. It is a far cry from the days when Andrew Young held the American U.N. chair, but, ironically, when it comes to Africa, it is not that far from the position taken by Ralph Bunche in seeking to keep the peace in the Congo, Sudan's neighborhood. When Bunche warned against individual state claims of "preventive war" in his Nobel Prize address in 1950, he was referring substantially to the Korean War. Now, more than sixty years later, the U.N. is committed to supplanting any attempts by individual nations to militarily prevent other countries from initiating aggressive action. Consequently, Ambassador Rice's affirmation of that U.N. role looks a lot less like an individual contribution and more like standard American liberal policy. Special interests, beyond those of defense-related associations, do not stand out, and African American interests on these issues are largely invisible. The parameters of Rice's individual initiative are therefore set by the Obama administration, to which she intricately belongs, in ways that are uncharacteristic of any previous African American representative in the United Nations.

Conclusion

"Ultimately," Susan Rice concludes in a Brookings Institution publication, "building effective states in the developing world . . . must become a significant component of U.S. national security policy."[43] Ironically, this rather scholarly reflection on U.S. foreign policy might well have suited the first African American in the U.N. except for the primacy given to American global interests. Ralph Bunche began his U.N. career by encouraging peacekeeping intervention from Western countries in Africa and the Middle East while promoting national independence in the developing world. Although he doubtlessly saw that change as being in the best interests of the United States and the Western world, the policy focus was on development. For Ambassador Young, who followed two decades later, the policy focus of his comments on Africa was closest to development as a means of encouraging and strengthening alliances. Young's advocacy for the developing world overshadowed other Americans for its intensity and openness, but it was seemingly shared by his immediate successor, Ambassador McHenry. McHenry, though less vocal, was forceful in his insistence on the elimination of many lingering colonial constraints on African political development. Yet, it is only with the emergence of Susan Rice that that part of the world is seen primarily through the lens of American interests.

That is an unusual perspective for African American policy analysts, who have generally responded to audiences influenced by African supportive lobbies and human rights groups. It is particularly noteworthy because she took this position before becoming ambassador, in contrast to the more "pro-development" stances of others while in the United Nations. In her continuing leadership in the U.N., Rice has remained consistent with the central emphasis of her earlier position. In some important ways that consistency represents real progress for African American roles in the U.N. When Ralph Bunche arrived at U.N. headquarters, no one knew quite what to expect except his solid professionalism—an expectation based on his background in the State Department, although national and international evidence of unrefined racism was inescapable. When Young arrived, positive and negative expectations relating to African American civil rights activity and African interests were on full public display. With the arrival of McHenry, the public focus, though colored by race-related expectations, largely returned to his professionalism but initially took the form of deracializing remediation of his predecessor. Finally, with the arrival of Rice, international sensitivities to her political past of working on Africa may remain, but on the national level her representation of the United States seems to bring the long sought invisibility of race to the African American international presence. Of course, the problem with such invisibility in American political history, using the images of Ralph Ellison, is that it tends to generalize to other aspects of political activity.

Perhaps the Benghazi incident was an isolated one, tied to speculation about her nomination for secretary of state, exposing Rice to harsher criticism aimed partly at the president. Perhaps it was also a reflection of the peculiar vulnerability of all outspoken diplomats, particularly African American ones. The minute Rice stepped outside the narrower enclaves of U.N. policy debates, political comments turned personal. Since many of her personal characteristics seemed open to commentary, it should be less surprising that racial comments penetrated. The cost of race-neutral foreign policy representation at this level, it could be argued, may be personal invisibility. That invisibility, however, may carry with it the cost of greater vulnerability to personal criticism in times of foreign policy crisis. Still, it may now be possible for African Americans to expect to hold and leave office in the U.N. and leave behind only a footprint of professionalism in diplomacy rather than an imprint of their individual and ideological political impact.

Notes

1. Kenneth Prewitt, "When You Have a Hammer . . . The Misuse of Statistical Races," *Du Bois Review: Social Science Research on Race* 9, no. 2 (2012): 281.

2. Brian Urquhart, *Ralph Bunche: An American Life* (New York: W. W. Norton, 1993), 101–2.

3. Ibid., 103.

4. Ibid., 133–34.

5. Charles P. Henry, *Ralph Bunche: Model Negro or American Other?* (New York: New York University Press, 1999).

6. Urquhart, *Ralph Bunche,* 312. See Thomas Kanza, *The Rise and Fall of Patrice Lu-mumba: Conflict in the Congo* (Boston: G. K. Hall, 1979).

7. Ralph J. Bunche, "Some Reflections on Peace in Our Time," Nobel Lecture, Oslo, Norway, December 11, 1950; Charles P. Henry, ed., *Ralph Bunche: Selected Speeches and Writings* (Ann Arbor: University of Michigan Press, 1995).

8. Andrew DeRoche, *Andrew Young: Civil Rights Ambassador* (Lanham, Md.: Rowman and Littlefield, 2003), 102–3.

9. Ibid., 102.

10. Bartlett C. Jones, *Flawed Triumphs: Andy Young at the United Nations* (Lanham, Md.: University Press of America, 1996), 6.

11. DeRoche, *Andrew Young,* 103.

12. Jones, *Flawed Triumphs,* 130.

13. Ibid., 150.

14. Ibid., 130.

15. Ibid., preface, 5.

16. James Haskins, *Andrew Young: A Man with a Mission* (New York: William Morrow, 1979), 11.

17. Jones, *Flawed Triumphs,* 111.

18. Ibid., 59.

19. DeRoche, *Andrew Young,* 74–75.

20. Ibid., 110.

21. Ibid., 76–77.

22. Randall Robinson, *The Debt: What America Owes to Blacks* (New York: Dutton, 2000), 151–54.

23. Martin Schram and James L. Rowe, "Young Deputy Named to Succeed Him," *Washington Post,* September 1, 1979, A1.

24. Bill Roeder, "Donald McHenry Irks the Israelis," *Newsweek,* March 17, 1980, 23.

25. Linda M. Fasulo, *Representing America: Experiences of U.S. Diplomats at the UN* (New York: Praeger, 1984), 230.

26. Ibid.

27. Roeder, "Donald McHenry Irks the Israelis," 9.

28. Charles Stuart Kennedy, "Interview with Ambassador Donald F. McHenry, October 1, 1998," *Frontline Diplomacy: Foreign Affairs Oral History Collection of the Association for Diplomatic Studies and Training, 1986–1998* (Washington, D.C.: Library of Congress).

29. David B. Ottaway, "South Africa Questioning U.N. Fairness in Namibia," *Washington Post,* September 10, 1980, A22.

30. Colum Lynch, "Meet the Key Players in the Iran Sanctions Debate," *Foreign Policy,* February 4 and 10, 2011, http://turtlebay.foreignpolicy.com.

31. "Phlashgordon," in response to Will Inboden, "How to Get Serious on Sudan," *Foreign Policy,* March 18, 2009, http://shadow.foreignpolicy.com/posts/2009/03/18/how_to_get_serious_on_sudan.

32. "Interview: Ken Rudin and Ron Walters Discuss How the Dominant Agenda May Affect the Presidential Race," *Newsweek,* May 17, 2004, 52–59.

33. As quoted in Lynch, "Meet the Key Players," February 4.

34. As cited in ibid.

35. Lorenzo Morris, "Symptoms of Withdrawal: The U.N., the U.S., Racism, and Reparations," *Howard Scroll: The Social Justice Law Review* 6 (2003): 6.

36. See, e.g., http://turtlebay.foreignpolicy.com.

37. Colum Lynch, "So, Where the Heck was Susan Rice?" *Foreign Policy*, June 2, 2010, http://turtlebay.foreignpolicy.com/posts/2010/06/02/so_where_the_heck_was_susan_rice.

38. Susan Rice, "Statement of U.S. Permanent Representative-Designate to the United Nations," U.S. Senate Foreign Relations Committee (January 15, 2009). Cited in "Susan Rice's Confirmation Hearing," Council on Foreign Relations, April 2014, www.cfr.org/international-organizations-and-alliances/susan-rices-confirmation.

39 Lynch, "Meet the Key Players," February 4.

40. Luke Johnson, "Jim Clyburn: Susan Rice Attacks Are Racial Code," *Huffington Post*, November 20, 2012, http://www.huffingtonpost.com/2012/11/20/jim-clyburn-susan-rice-attacks-racial_n_2164195.html.

41. Richard Downie, "Africa at the U.N. General Assembly," Center for Strategic and International Studies, September 18, 2009, http://csis.org/publication/Africa-un-general-assembly.

42. Colum Lynch, "U.S. Uses Veto to Block Anti-Israel Vote at U.N.," *Washington Post*, February 19, 2011, A13.

43. Susan E. Rice, Corrine Graff, and Carlos Pascual, *Confronting Poverty: Weak States and U.S. National Security* (Washington, D.C.: Brookings Institution, 2010), 38.

9

Obama, African Americans, and Africans

The Double Vision

IBRAHIM SUNDIATA

Early in 2012, columnist E. J. Dionne raised the question "Can a Messiah Win Twice?" Looking back wistfully on Obama's first presidential campaign, he commented:

> Four years ago this week, a young and inspirational senator who promised to turn history's page swept the Iowa caucuses and began his irresistible rise to the White House. Barack Obama was unlike any candidate the country had seen before. More than a mere politician, he became a cultural icon, "the biggest celebrity in the world," as a John McCain ad accurately, if mischievously, described him. He was the object of near adoration among the young, launching what often felt like a religious revival. Artists poured out musical compositions devoted to his victory in a rich variety of forms, from reggae and hip-hop to the Celtic folk song. . . . Electoral contests rarely hold out the possibility of making all things new, but Obama's supporters in large numbers fervently believed that 2008 was exactly such a campaign.[1]

It may be easy to forget the euphoria that surrounded Obama during his first presidential campaign. There was euphoria and expectation. In Paris, *Libération* opined that the new leader of the French Socialist Party should be someone with Obama's profile: "The French Left seeks a charismatic leader, age 46, of mixed race, to deliver a message of hope and unity. At a time when American Democrats are discovering their new hero, it would be a good time for the Socialist Party and their friends to find a Barack Obama to end their internal quarrels."[2] In London the *Guardian* noted the changes in America since the death of Martin Luther King and proclaimed, "It is hard to know whether to weep or shout for joy now that it has arrived—probably both—but it is a lesson to the world."[3] An editorial in the *Examiner* was more poetic: "The election of Barack Obama, the son of a Kenyan goatherd, as the 44th President of the United States of America is a moment to savour, proof that the promise of a better day, expressed in prose that rises like poetry, can still carry an electorate. The margin of victory was emphatic and, whatever else follows, today the world changed."[4] The editorial writer mused that "from today, a black child born in America will look on his nation with greater pride because he will feel that the highest office in the land is open to him. . . . In the eyes of the world, the slate will be clean and the pretext, always spurious, for anti-Americanism has been removed."

In spite of these encomia, Obama's victory did not mark the transcendence of race at home or abroad. In the United States, Obama may have been elected despite his race, white opposition being offset by the votes of African Americans and Hispanics.[5] Looking abroad we must examine the impact of Obama's election. Has having an African American commander in chief shifted American foreign relations in any appreciable way? The auguries are mixed. Certainly President Obama's election has meant that even more careers are open to talent in the American foreign policy apparatus. What had begun with a man like Ralph Bunche in the 1940s and continued through diplomats like Colin Powell and Condoleezza Rice came to fruition in the election of an African American commander in chief. It seems certain that the American diplomatic establishment will be integrated as never before.

Obama's rise has a special resonance in postindustrial multiracial societies like those of Western Europe. As *Newsweek* noted in the wake of the 2008 election, "A vast range of people, some oppressed, some powerful, some just opportunistic, have embraced the Obama mystique as they imagine it. In the process, they are revealing a great deal more about their own societies, their frustrations, and especially their problems with racism and ethnic tensions, than they are about the President-elect of the United States."[6] Importantly, color is not the global common denominator. We know that language, culture, and religion are ongoing unifiers and dividers of humanity. There are men in al-Qaeda, for instance, of widely different colors. For them, Obama's American-marketed "blackness" is an irrelevance or semantic trick.

In many parts of the world, the man first elected in 2008 was perceived as an improvement on his predecessor. Africa's African American son Barack Hussein Obama is popular on the African continent. A BBC poll during the 2008 election found that he was the preferred candidate of 71 percent of Nigerians and 87 percent of Kenyans.[7] In 2012 the percentage of respondents in those two countries who preferred the Democratic candidate was 66.[8] In Obama's homeland, the United States, Africa itself continues to be viewed by many as either the primitive home of famine, disease, and civil war or an idyllic mother/fatherland. For President Barack Obama it must be both. Gradually the distance between the ideal and actual Africa has had to be relinquished by the first African American president. Failed states and the fear of international terrorism have prompted a new realism. Also, in his stance against Muammar Gadhafi and Robert Mugabe, Obama has set himself against older notions of Pan-African solidarity. In doing so he has disappointed important elements of his own base. Furthermore, Obama's stance on social issues like women's rights and same-sex relationships has the potential to alienate African governments and peoples still in the midst of an AIDS crisis. An international evangelical crusade may be uniting some Africans around "moral" issues they find more significant than skin color. The bonds of race may have been trumped by the bonds of faith. At the same time, the president cannot alienate the social left of his party at home by failing to champion human rights, including sexual orientation rights, abroad. This is a coming dilemma.

First, let us consider Pan-Africanism. As an overall ideology, Pan-Africanism preaches that black folk, wherever they reside, have certain cultural commonalities and a common struggle against white supremacy. Blacks in the United States and the Caribbean have a duty to work for the uplift and eventual freedom of the mother continent. Once achieved, African liberation would aid blacks in the diaspora to break the chains of racial oppression. For more than twenty years, Obama belonged to a Pan-Africanist organization in Chicago—Trinity United Church of Christ—which has missionary outreach in Liberia, Ghana, and South Africa. Significantly, in light of "birther" preoccupations about his origins, Obama's church proclaimed, "We are an African people, and remain 'true to our native land,' the mother continent, the cradle of civilization."[9]

The civil rights movement had coincided with the rise and triumph of anti-colonialism in Africa. On issues that were clearly black and white—that is, black versus white—the formation of a consensus was fairly easy. The fear that the rhetoric of Pan-Africanism might translate into action was prevalent in certain quarters. In 1962 a number of civil rights leaders formed the American Negro Leadership Conference on Africa (ANCLA). Three years later two members of the National Security Council wrote that the Johnson administration was "quite concerned over the prospect of an imminent Negro leadership conference to set up an organization to influence U.S. policy on Africa."[10] In 1967 Stokely Carmichael (later Kwame Touré) said, "The best protection for Africa today is African-Americans inside the United States because when we start to move against South Africa, if the United States dares to come into this continent, the African-Americans will burn that country down to the ground."[11] In a 1978 National Security Council (NSC) memorandum, policy makers considered the consequences of an alliance between African states opposed to apartheid and African American activists opposed to United States policy on South Africa: "These factors taken together may provide a basis for joint actions of a concrete nature by the African nationalist movement and the U.S. black community." The NSC feared "attempts to establish a permanent black lobby in Congress including activist leftist radical groups and black legislators; the reemergence of pan-African ideals; resumption of protest marches recalling the days of Martin Luther King; renewal of the extremist national idea of establishing an 'African Republic' on American soil." Ominously, the memo suggested that "leftist radical elements of the black community could resume extremist actions in the style of the defunct Black Panther Party."[12] The emergence by the early 1980s of TransAfrica, an antiapartheid black lobbying group was, no doubt, one of the kinds of development feared. Perhaps even more troubling to those wishing to maintain the status quo in South Africa was the passage of the Comprehensive Anti-Apartheid Act of 1986 after intensive lobbying. Congressman Charles Diggs and others had spearheaded an effort that began as a rivulet of protest and then widened into a stream.[13]

Aside from the apartheid struggle, few African issues have dominated the black American consciousness. The African American community in the United States is not, nor has it ever been, monolithic. Political scientist Tony Smith says, "African American leaders are preoccupied most by domestic economic and political concerns, for assimilation is not assured. Funds are short (and often derived from sources outside the community). There is no strong external state or clear foreign enemy to encourage ethnic cohesion with respect to foreign affairs." In addition, "Their membership rolls involve smaller proportions of the community. And their organizations lack interlocking directorships and depend instead on strong (and therefore often competitive) personalities."[14] Michael Clough has noted, "While there is significant black support for increased aid to Africa, there is no consensus on who should receive that aid and for what purposes."[15] Andrew Young and others worked to push commercial links between black America and Africa. The Corporate Council on Africa (CCA) was established in 1993 and works with governments, multilateral groups, and business organizations to improve the African continent's trade and investment climate and to raise the profile of Africa in the American business community. Unity of action and thought, however, is not constant. When an African trade bill went before the U.S. Congress in the summer of 1999, African American opinion stood divided on whether to support or oppose its provisions. Thirteen years later the African American–sponsored Leon Sullivan Economic Summit in Equatorial Guinea highlighted the divergence between African American dreams of an economic El Dorado and the rapacious politics of the continent's autocrats. The Obama administration sent no representative or greeting to longtime dictator Teodoro Obiang Nguema Mbasogo, endeavoring to make the point that political reform must precede any embrace of authoritarian regimes.[16]

The assumption that, once independent, Africa would meld into one giant "black man's land" has proven tragic. Given this situation, how are African Americans to approach a continent three times the size of their own country, one with a multiplicity of ethnicities and polities? Present-day African realities and the growing irrelevance of political Pan-Africanism present Obama with an interesting juggling act. More than twenty years ago he traveled to Kenya, the land of his father's birth, and eight years later he published his remarkable autobiography, *Dreams from My Father*. On the eve of his trip, Obama mused: "Africa had become an idea more than an actual place, a new promised land, full of ancient traditions and sweeping vistas; we engaged struggles and talking drums. With the benefit of distance, we engaged Africa in a selective embrace—what would happen once I relinquished the distance?"[17] Indeed, how does the often poetic Africa of the Pan-African imagination interdigitate with the real one? What of continuing genocide, civil war, and poor governance? In the last decade more than ten million people have died in the internecine wars ravaging the Congo Basin. Darfur was and is a human rights tragedy of epic proportions and one that only fitfully gathers the attention of some of the American public.

Are the authoritarian successors of the European proconsuls to be lauded or condemned? Pan-Africanism had seen a host of worthies: Gamal Abdul Nasser, Kwame Nkrumah, Sekou Touré, Patrice Lumumba. They all ran afoul of U.S. policy. African Americans might be able to unite against white minority rule in South Africa, but it is very difficult to tell friend from foe in intra-African conflicts. The divisive conflicts that marred the continent after the 1960s were hard to disentangle based on the logic of the "color line." Blacks in the policy apparatus, like Ralph Bunche, were criticized for their betrayal of the dreams of Pan-Africanism, as in the case of the Congo. In the mid-1990s minister Louis Farrakhan and Senator Carol Moseley-Braun both visited brutal Nigerian dictator Sani Abacha. Farrakhan and Obama's pastor Jeremiah Wright visited Muammar Gadhafi's Libya in the 1990s. At the end of the decade the Clinton administration sent Jesse Jackson to Liberia as a special peace envoy. Relying on contacts made years before in black America, Jackson lavished praise on Liberian warlord Charles Taylor and his Sierra Leonean colleague Foday Sankoh. Both Taylor and Sankoh were later implicated in the murder and mutilation of thousands, as well as in the impressment of hundreds of child soldiers.

How might we account for these lapses? Some Africans, such as George Ayittey and Alex Kabou, think the African American view of Africa is racially reductionist or worse. Ayittey has declared African American leaders naïve, incapable of seeing beyond the black/white duality of American race politics. In his opinion, because they are desperate for validation, "it is . . . gratifying when black Americans come upon black African presidents—living proof that blacks are capable of running a country."[18] Immigrants from Africa like Ayittey are likely to maintain a growing interest in their home continent, although this interest is likely to be far more focused and even, at times, more parochial than before. It is also more likely to be well-informed.[19] The new black arrivals experience both the reality and contradictions of the American racial dynamic. Like Barack Obama's father, they did not leave their homelands to become pariahs. One authoritative survey of American-born blacks and West Indian and African (Ghanaian and Nigerian) immigrants concluded that while these groups shared appreciation of a common African heritage, "preconceived notions and myths about each other . . . allowed only a surface cordiality."[20] Living within their own historical narrative, locked within their stories of bondage and blame, some African Americans may have difficulty fathoming the stories of others. As Ira Berlin notes, "The nature of slavery outside the bounds of the United States, the world-wide struggles against colonialism, and the origins of independence in the Caribbean or Africa constituted unknown territory."[21] Tensions of adjustment are inevitable.

Obama's greatest run-in with the lingering legacy of Pan-Africanism came in his showdown with Muammar Gadhafi. The Libyan leader was an authoritarian Pan-Africanist who had played host to dozens of African and African American leaders. He had been one of the spearheads of the African Union and had sponsored armed groups in Liberia and Sierra Leone with generous petrodollar assistance. The North African supported the struggle against apartheid in South Africa, and, indeed, Nelson Mandela named one of his grandsons after him. In addition, Gadhafi had invited in thousands of black Africans from neighboring countries. Already in 1998 the flawed and erratic patron of African unity announced, "I had been crying slogans of Arab Unity and brandishing the standard of Arab nationalism for 40 years, but it was not realised. That means that I was talking in the desert. I have no more time to lose talking with Arabs." A turning point had come: "I am returning back to realism. . . . I now talk about Pan-Africanism.[22] Gadhafi claimed the title "King of Kings of Africa" in 2008 in the presence of more than two hundred African traditional rulers and kings. In the following year he staged a coronation ceremony to coincide with the fifty-third African Union Summit in Addis Ababa. In addition, he was elected head of the African Union for the year. True to old-time Pan-Africanism, Gadhafi told the assembled African leaders, "I shall continue to insist that our sovereign countries work to achieve the United States of Africa."[23]

During the Libyan uprising of 2011, minister Louis Farrakhan of the Nation of Islam lambasted Obama as a traitor to his people, saying, "Who the Hell do you think you are!"[24] After the fall of Gadhafi, Representative Jesse Jackson Jr. said he would raise the question in a congressional committee whether the Obama-backed rebels were guilty of "crimes against humanity." Rev. Jesse Jackson Sr. wrote a newspaper article titled "U.S. Can't Stand by While Racism Ravages Libya."[25] An admonition also came from Walter Fauntroy, a veteran civil rights activist and former D.C. congressional representative. He went to Libya during the fighting and concluded, "We believe the true mission of the attacks on Gadhafi is to prevent all efforts by African leaders to stop the recolonization of Africa."[26] Obama had backed a coalition of former colonial powers (Britain, France, and Italy) in attacking Libya. Thus, the Arab ruler most deeply identified with black Africa was overthrown with the aid of a black American president by rebels accused of massacring black Africans.[27]

Stereotypes die hard. Obama as a "son of Africa" has frequently been attacked as the stealth representative of Pan-Africanism and "third worldism" in the White House. Dinesh D'Souza continues to see the president as motivated by anticolonial *revanchisme*:

> So this is what this son of Africa came to offer Africa: virtually nothing. He now has the power, but he doesn't know how to use it effectively. That's because Obama still cannot bring himself to abandon his father's anti-colonial ideology. That ideology calls for transfers of wealth from the colonizers to the colonized. If Obama can't convince Congress to approve more foreign aid for Africa, then he has no idea what else to do. The tragedy is that even if Congress were to approve the aid, it would not provide any lasting benefit. President Obama is still trying to apply his father's discredited formulas from the 1950s even though they have no relevance to the world we live in today.[28]

In spite of such animadversions, the president has been quite critical of the spendthrift strongmen of Africa, some of them remnants of anticolonial struggles. Obama has noted that "ruling elites have not thought about reinvesting what resources these countries have into the development of ordinary people."[29] The son of a father who suffered from the caprices of African politics,

Obama is not enamored of strongmen; "for far too many Africans, conflict is a part of life, as constant as the sun. There are wars over land and wars over resources." Tellingly, he condemned the cult of "Big Men," for "it is still far too easy for those without conscience to manipulate whole communities into fighting among faiths and tribes."[30] Looking at the postcolonial "blame game," the chief executive has observed:

> It is easy to point fingers, and to pin the blame for these problems on others. Yes, a colonial map that made little sense bred conflict, and the West has often approached Africa as a patron, rather than a partner. But the West is not responsible for the destruction of the Zimbabwean economy over the last decade, or wars in which children are enlisted as combatants. In my father's life, it was partly tribalism and patronage in an independent Kenya that for a long stretch derailed his career, and we know that this kind of corruption is a daily fact of life for far too many.[31]

In Accra in 2009 the president addressed the Ghanaian parliament on problems of "democracy, opportunity, health; and the peaceful resolution of conflict." In a complete contradiction of D'Souza's later claims, the president had proclaimed, "Aid is not an end in itself."[32] The case of Kenya, the birthplace of Obama's father, is illustrative of the complexities of the relationship between Africans and African Americans. In 2006 Obama warned that the government of his father's homeland was "rooted in the bankrupt idea that the goal of politics or business is to funnel as much of the pie as possible to one's family, tribe, or circle with little regard for the public good. It stifles innovation and fractures the fabric of the society."[33] Nairobi dismissed his comments as the "very poorly informed" ruminations of a "junior senator." After December 2007 hundreds of Kenyans died in postelection violence that pitted the Luo, the ethnic group of Obama's father, against others. Raila Odinga, a relative of the American candidate, was the losing candidate. Kenya and the rest of Africa are more than just a metonym for "black man's land." They are more than just the background for the history of the black diaspora. Africa has its ethnicities and its ethnic conflicts. Government figures show that a Kenyan born in Luoland today can expect to live several years less than one born in Kikuyuland.[34] An obvious paradox is that Barack Obama has a better chance of being elected in the United States than in his father's homeland. In the seething Kenyan electoral politics of 2013, little assurance emerged that President Obama could helicopter into Nairobi and soothingly impose order.

The demands of U.S. foreign policy necessitate the projection of American power abroad. At present the United States has military assistance agreements with fifty-three African states. In October 2011 more than two thousand Kenyan soldiers entered Somalia with American backing. Part of their aim was to guard against the attacks of the Islamist group al-Shabab. In 2011 Obama's government provided his father's home country with $700 million in mostly military aid.[35] Military aid is not confined to Kenya, however. The United States African Command (AFRICOM) was bequeathed to Obama by the Bush administration. Its goals have been defined as preventing "oil disruption," "terrorism," and "the growing influence" of China.[36] Then secretary of state Hillary Clinton enunciated the policy objectives of "combating al-Qaeda's efforts to seek safe havens in failed states in the Horn of Africa; helping African nations to conserve their natural resources and reap fair benefits from them; stopping war in Congo [and] ending autocracy in Zimbabwe and human devastation in Darfur."[37] The United States has bases in Djibouti, Kenya, and Ethiopia and seeks to strengthen governments in the Sahel against any impending Islamist threat. Advisers have been sent into northern Uganda in an attempt to aid in stabilizing the region. Early in 2013, reacting to instability in Mali and the Maghreb, the administration announced that it was setting up drone bases in Niger.

Domestic considerations impinge on foreign relations in sometimes unforeseen ways. Obama leads a center-left coalition that espouses causes that are increasingly anathema in many parts of Africa. The AIDS pandemic has had a political impact. In 2006 Senator Barack Obama took an HIV test in western Kenya near the place where his father had grown up. His high-profile test was intended to spotlight the need for such action and to lessen the shame surrounding AIDS. No doubt it did good, but, equally, there can be little doubt that shame remains. In the eyes of some leaders, the damage to Africa's image resulting from AIDS is an evil greater than the pandemic itself. It is perhaps not so surprising (but still unfortunate) that former president Thabo Mbeki of South Africa would attack those who, "convinced that we are but natural-born, promiscuous carriers of germs, unique in the world . . . proclaim that our continent is doomed to an inevitable mortal end because of our unconquerable devotion to the sin of lust."[38] Increasingly homophobic official pronouncements seem to be spreading in the wake of the health crisis in countries as diverse as Senegal, Zimbabwe, Uganda, Gambia, Nigeria, Ghana, Namibia, and Kenya. Many African churchmen and women have become part of a global family values coalition that often falls back on nostalgic views of the Western nuclear family. Often corresponding with the American social-values conservatives that oppose Obama at home and fueled by a perfervid rhetoric ("Obama's War on Religion"), it remains to be seen if the allure of America's black president will overcome the African continent's newly homegrown homophobes. Uganda, in particular, gained notoriety in 2010 when a bill was introduced to make homosexuality a capital offense under certain circumstances.

As churches established under colonial empires decline in influence, new groups, many of them white Americans, have entered the fray armed with money and a fundamentalist self-confidence. For example, secretive right-wing religious groups like "The Family" and the "College of Prayer" have long reached out to Uganda. For his part, pastor Rick Warren, who gave the invocation at the first Obama inaugural, visited Uganda in March 2008 and dismissed the idea that gay rights are human rights. Senator Jim Inhofe (R-OK) and Governor Sam Brownback (R-KS) have become close to the Ugandan regime not only religiously but also politically. When Inhofe proclaims, "I'm a Jesus guy, and I have a heart for Africa," thousands on the continent listen. When Reverend Warren declares Uganda and Rwanda "purpose driven" nations, millions listen. As in the nineteenth century, missionaries provide access not only to the Bible and the plow but also to funds and outside contacts.

On the eve of the 2012 primary season, Secretary of State Hillary Clinton declared that the rights of LGBT (lesbian, gay, bisexual, and transgender) individuals were human rights. In addition, the administration seemed to throw down the gauntlet to several African regimes. "President Obama," noted Secretary Clinton, "[has] put into place the first U.S. Government strategy dedicated to combating human rights abuses against LGBT persons abroad. . . . The President has directed all U.S. Government agencies engaged overseas to combat the criminalization of LGBT status and conduct, to enhance efforts to protect vulnerable LGBT refugees and asylum seekers, to ensure that our foreign assistance promotes the protection of LGBT rights, to enlist international organizations in the fight against discrimination, and to respond swiftly to abuses against LGBT persons."[39] This statement may have strengthened the president with his domestic base, but it is bound to raise hackles on the African continent. In his 2013 State of the Union speech, the president spoke approvingly of same-sex marriage. In the same month a political firestorm erupted in Ghana when political opponents accused President John Dramani Mahama of knowing gay activists in the United States.[40] Politicized religious fundamentalism has been able to put down roots where Pan-Africanism has shriveled up and died. This should be of no small concern to a leader like Obama, who boasts of living links with the Dark Continent. Anti-gay activist and Ugandan legislator David Bahati has remarked that "the good thing with the West is that we know that Obama can influence the world only up to 2016."[41]

Barack Obama's ascension to the presidency was a great step forward in United States race relations. African Americans entered into all levels of the foreign policy apparatus. However, the contradictions between the bonds of ethnic solidarity and the demands of American foreign policy will persist. Barack Obama presents a grand paradox—the accession of a "son of Africa" to the American presidency may well sound the death knell of traditional Pan-Africanism.

Notes

1. E. J. Dionne, "Can a Messiah Win Twice?" *Washington Post,* January 3, 2012, www.washingtonpost.com/opinions/obama-can-a-messiah-win-twice/2012/12/30/giqahwwyup-story.html.

2. As quoted in Soeren Kern, "Obamania: What Europeans Are Saying about American Democracy," *Brussels Journal,* January 30, 2008, www.brusselsjournal.com/node/2920.

3. "President Obama," editorial, *Guardian,* November 4, 2008, www.theguardian.com/commentisfree/2008/nov/06/barackobama-uselections2008.

4. "Opinion Round Up of Historic Obama Win," *Examiner,* November 5, 2008, www.examiner.com/article/opinion-round-up-of-historic-obama-win.

5. Michael S. Lewis-Beck, Charles Tien, Richard Nadeau, "Obama's Missed Landslide: A Racial Cost?" *P.S.: Political Science & Politics* 42 (2009): 69–76.

6. "Reflecting on Race Barriers," *Newsweek,* November 14, 2008, http://www.newsweek.com/obama-and-global-race-barriers-84743.

7. BBC, "Obama Win Preferred in World Poll," September 10, 2008, http://news.bbc.co.uk/2/hi/7606100.stm.

8. BBC World Service, "Global Poll: Obama Overwhelmingly Preferred to Romney," October 22, 2012, http://www.worldpublicopinion.org/pipa/pdf/oct12/BBCElection_Oct12_rpt.pdf.

9. Trinity United Church of Christ, "About us," www.trinitychicago.org/index.php?option-content&task=view&id=12&itemsd=27.

10. Michael Clough, *Free at Last? U.S. Policy toward Africa and the End of the Cold War* (New York: Council on Foreign Relations Press, 1992), 32, citing memo to McGeorge Bundy from R. W. Komer and Rick Haynes, March 30, 1964, National Security Council files, Lyndon Baines Johnson Presidential Library, University of Texas at Austin.

11. Locksley Edmundson, *Africa and the African Diaspora: The Years Ahead* (New York: Third Press, 1973), 11, citing Stokely Carmichael (Kwame Touré) interview with the *Sunday News* (Dar es Salaam), November 5, 1967.

12. National Security Council, Interdepartmental Group for Africa, "Study in Response to Presidential Security Review Memorandum NSC-46, Black Africa and the U.S. Black Movement," March 17, 1978, Supplied by Wallace Short, Howard University. Available at http://www.finalcall.com/memorandum-46.htm.

13. At the beginning of the civil rights era, only 1 percent of African Americans, in contrast to 6 percent of whites, could name as many as five African territories; 70 percent of blacks, compared with 55 percent of whites, could not name any at all. Yossi Shain, *Marketing the American Creed Abroad: Diasporas in the U.S. and Their Homelands* (New

York: Cambridge University Press, 1999), 136, citing Alfred O. Hero Jr., "American Negroes and U.S. Foreign Policy: 1937–1967," *Journal of Conflict Resolution* 13, no. 2 (1969); Clough, *Free at Last?*, 32, citing Joint Center for Political Studies, "Africa in the Minds and Deeds of African American Leaders," draft report to the Rockefeller Foundation, May 14, 1990.

14. Tony Smith, *Foreign Attachments: The Power of Ethnic Groups in the Making of American Foreign Policy* (Cambridge, Mass.: Harvard University Press, 2000), 116.

15. Clough, *Free at Last?*, 34.

16. Elizabeth Flock, "Politicians Bow Out of High-Profile Summit Hosted by Africa's Longest Serving Dictator," *U.S. News and World Report*, August 6, 2012, http://www .usnews.com/news/blogs/washington-whispers/2012/08/06/politicians-bow-out-of-summit-hosted-by-africas-longest-serving-dictator.

17. Barack Obama, *Dreams from My Father: A Story of Race and Inheritance* (New York: Three Rivers Press, 2004), 302.

18. George Ayittey, *Africa in Chaos* (New York: St. Martin's, 1998). Also see George Ayittey, *Defeating Dictators, Fighting Tyranny in Africa and Around the World* (New York: Palgrave McMillan, 2011). See Howard French, "An Ignorance of Africa as Vast as the Continent," *New York Times,* November 20, 1994, citing Axelle Kabous, *Et si L'Afrique refusait le développement* [What If Africa Refused Development?] (Paris: L'Harmattan, 1991).

19. African immigrants have the highest levels of education among newcomers. See Ira Berlin, *African America: The Four Great Migrations* (New York: Viking, 2010).

20. Ibid., 228, quoting Jennifer V. Jackson and Mary E. Cothran, "Black versus Black: The Relationship among African, African American, and African Caribbean Persons," *Journal of Black Studies* 33 (2003): 576–604.

21. Berlin, *African America,* 219.

22. Abdelaziz Barrouhi, "Libya's Gaddafi Turns Attention to Black Africa," *Reuters,* September 16, 1998.

23. "Gaddafi Vows to Push Africa Unity," BBC News, February 2, 2009, http://news .bbc.co.uk/2/hi/africa/7864604.stm.

24. "Farrakhan Blasts Obama," WVON, Chicago, March 19, 2011, http://www.youtube .com/watch%3Fv%3Du27XF9QVkSE.

25. Jesse Jackson Sr., "U.S. Can't Stand by While Racism Ravages Libya," *Chicago Sun-Times,* November 8, 2011, www.suntimes.com/news/jackson/86674940–452/us-cant-stand-by-while-racism-ravages-libya.html#.U1LMEvldVpc.

26. Valencia Mohommed, "Walter Fauntroy, Feared Dead in Libya, Returns Home— Guess Who He Saw Doing the Killing," *Afro,* September 7, 2011, http://www.afro.com/ sections/news/national/story.htm?storyid=72369.

27. "Amnesty: Libya's Rebels Must End Abuse of Blacks," Associated Press, August 31, 2011. The statement was made by David Nichols, senior executive officer, Amnesty International.

28. Dinesh D'Souza, *The Roots of Obama's Rage* (Washington, D.C.: Regnery, 2011), 215.

29. Transcript from "President Obama's African Journey," *Anderson Cooper 360,* aired July 19, 2009, http://transcripts.cnn.com/transcripts/0907/19/acd.01.html.

30. Remarks by President Obama to the Ghanaian Parliament, Accra, Ghana, July 11, 2009. Transcript available at http://www.whitehouse.gov/the-press-office/remarks -president-ghanaian-parliament.

31. Peter Firtsbrook, *The Obamas: The Untold Story of an African Family* (New York: Crown, 2010), 244.

32. Ibid.

33. Speech by Senator Barack Obama, "An Honest Government, A Hopeful Future," University of Nairobi, Kenya, August 28, 2006. See also Jeffrey Gettleman, "East Africa: The Most Corrupt Country," *New York Review of Books,* January 14, 2010, www.nybooks .com/articles/archives/2010/jan/14/east-africa-the-most-corrupt/?in src=toc.

34. Murithi Mutiga, "Why Kenya's Pride in Obama Victory Is Tempered," *Independent,* November 5, 2008, www.independent.co.uk/news/world/africa/why-kenyas-pride-in-obama-victory-is-tempered-994355.html.

35. W. T. Whitney Jr., "Annals of U.S. Imperialism: Africa Update," H-Net List for African History and Culture, January 5, 2012, http://h-net.msu.edu/cgi-bin/logbrowse .pl?trx=vx&list=H-Africa&month=1201&week=a&msg=tkcN%2BVKVAua09096ChP xAA.

36. Daniel Volman and William Minter, "Making Peace or Fueling War in Africa," *Foreign Policy in Focus,* March 13, 2009, http://www.africafocus.org/editor/africom0903 .pdf.

37. Charles W. Corey, "Hillary Clinton Outlines Obama's Africa Policy," *allAfrica.com,* January 24, 2009, http://allafrica.com/stories/200901240009.html.

38. Theodore Sheckels, "The Rhetoric of Thabo Mbeki on HIV/AIDS: Strategic Scapegoating?" *Howard Journal of Communications* 15, no. 5 (2004): 69–82.

39. Secretary of State Hillary Rodham Clinton, "Remarks in Recognition of International Human Rights Day," Geneva, Switzerland, Palais des Nations, December 6, 2011. Transcript available at http://iipdigital.usembassy.gov/st/english/texttrans/2011/12/2011 1206180616su0.4842885.html#axzz2yVGRIAkH.

40. Andrew Solomon, "In Bed with the President of Ghana," *New York Times,* February 9, 2013, http://www.nytimes.com/2013/02/10/opinion/sunday/in-bed-with-the-president -of-ghana.html.

41. Josh Kron, "Resentment toward the West Bolsters Uganda's New Anti-Gay Bill," *New York Times,* February 28, 2012, http://www.nytimes.com/2012/02/29/world/africa/ ugandan-lawmakers-push-anti-homosexuality-bill-again.html.

Epilogue

The Impact of
African Americans
on U.S. Foreign Policy

CHARLES R. STITH

I have spent a good part of my adult life helping to affect public policy. For most of those years it was as a civic leader from the outside. During the Clinton administration, however, I worked inside the formal structures of government, first as an informal adviser to the president and as a member of policy working groups dealing with domestic matters and foreign affairs, and later as U.S. ambassador to the United Republic of Tanzania. As someone who has been intimately involved in policy formulation and action, I know that the end game in development of public policy is not *input,* but *impact.*

How is impact made and measured in the process of policy formulation? In terms of foreign policy there are tactical and strategic sides to this question. From a tactical perspective, one can make an impact on foreign policy formulation in three ways: (1) being elected president or appointed by the president to one of any number of posts in the executive branch that are involved in policy formulation in the foreign policy sphere; (2) being a member of Congress, which has legislative and budgetary powers to affect policy formulation; or (3) being an advocate (or activist), outside the formal structures of power, but able to affect the strategic choices about specific matters of policy. Obviously the opportunity to push for a particular position can be taken from more than one of these positions. Furthermore, the more positions from which one can operate, the more power one has. The more power one has, the more potential impact one has.

The other part of the question of how impact is affected is strategic: is there a particularly substantive perspective one provides that is reflected in the eventual policy? This is a book about African Americans and U.S. foreign policy. From my perspective it is impossible to conclude a book like this without asking whether blacks have had an impact on United States foreign policy. For blacks to have had a historic impact on foreign policy presupposes they have had the power and perspective to do so.

Throughout the history of the United States, African Americans have had an interest in affecting the critical foreign policy issues of the day and a varying ability to do so. In surveying the story of that impact—whether historical or personal—several factors stand out. First, I see the foreign policy concerns of African Americans as major and mainstream from era to era, whether the issue was the slave trade or the war against terrorism, African colonization or the struggle against South African apartheid.

Second, the unique quality that African Americans have brought to the foreign policy mix is to see America's geopolitical interests through the lens of human rights. In the early days of the new republic, the issue was slavery and it was the humanity of African Americans that was at stake. Post-slavery, in the era of Reconstruction, whether the issue was Native Americans or immigration policy, the affinity for human rights remained the same. During the civil rights era, with a newfound ability to influence foreign policy as policy makers in the executive branch of government, as leaders in the legislative branch, and as advocates in the press or grassroots organizations, I contend that in general African Americans have pushed American policy in the direction of human rights and, in particular, advanced a more progressive agenda for U.S. foreign relations with non-Western countries.

During the current era, in which the country is being led by its first African American president, who by law is the nation's foreign policy officer in chief, the expectations are consistent with the historic role that African Americans have played in the foreign policy sphere. During Obama's first campaign for the presidency one question relative to foreign affairs was whether he was seasoned enough and tough enough to use America's considerable power to protect and project America's interests abroad. Every signal—domestic and foreign—is that his domestic base and the world expect something more in terms of foreign policy than simply military power, soft power, or smart power. The expectation in Obama's case seems to be: can he find the common thread to weave a web of global community based on hope over fear, a sense of our common humanity rather than conflict and confrontation?

The third point that is suggested in any survey on the bearing African Americans have on U.S. foreign policy is that the breadth of foreign policy interests by African Americans has reflected their position and power within the American body politic. The more power, the broader the spectrum of interests and impact by African Americans. In the early days of the republic, the power of African Americans was limited by law, but, like a laser, the limited power they had was focused on the one issue they needed to change. As America has developed and the status and standing of African Americans has evolved, the areas of influence in the foreign policy sphere have grown. Era to era this point proves true, with the capstone being the election of America's first African American president.

There are four *eras of impact* that reflect an African American imprint on U.S. foreign policy. Those are the slavery era, the Reconstruction era, the civil rights era, and the post–civil rights era. Each era is noteworthy for its changes in status and power of African Americans and thus has implications relative to the question of impact. Each era also had its distinct foreign policy issues and challenges. As many of the historical matters within each era are covered in great detail throughout this volume, I will just briefly outline several elements of each era. Where relevant, I also reflect on the practice of American foreign policy as informed by my own career and highlight African American efforts to help shape and promote American foreign policy abroad.

The Slavery Era: 1776–1865

The first foreign policy issue of importance to African Americans was the slave trade and slavery.[1] While generally thought of as a domestic issue, the slave trade can also be understood as a matter of foreign policy. Moreover, it was about commerce, the rights of the seas, and bilateral relations with European nations. These are clearly matters that affect the relations between nation-states. It was the formulation of African American opposition to the slave trade that is noteworthy in this discussion of foreign policy. The opposition that African Americans mounted was not framed in terms of "equal rights" (which are domestic), but rather in terms of "human rights" (which are universal). As a human rights issue slavery ceased to be merely national; it became international and thus an issue of foreign policy. Grasping this point is important because not only does it provide a historical context for answering the question about impact, but it also brings into focus a lens through which African Americans engaged the debate about this policy and the legal framework that supported it. During the slavery era, the tactical options of African Americans to affect U.S. foreign policy were unquestionably limited. Without access to formal levers of political power, blacks were limited to being activists in order to forward a particular policy perspective.

The most notable examples of activists to make the case against the slave trade and slavery were Frederick Douglass and Harriet Tubman. There were also lesser-known figures like Henry Highland Garnett, who opposed war and slavery as flip sides of the same coin of America's moneyed class, and Josiah Henson, who was believed to have been the person after whom Harriet Beecher Stowe modeled the seminal character in *Uncle Tom's Cabin*. There were black women other than Harriet Tubman who carried their share of the burden in the fight against slavery. Sarah Parker Redmond, who led the charge in carrying the fight against the slave trade abroad, and Maria Stewart, who wrote for the *Liberator,* were such stalwarts. Prince Hall, the founder of the African American Masonic Movement, was a staunch abolitionist. The African Methodist Episcopal Church, founded by African American clergymen Richard Allen and Absalom Jones and born in response to the indignities suffered by black Christians at the hands of their white compatriots, was an equally prominent force in the fight against slavery. The black press, to the extent that it existed, was a force in the fight. Such newspapers as the *North Star* and *Freedom's Journal* fought the fight against slavery with a focus and ferocity matched by few.

On this critical U.S. foreign policy issue African Americans had an impact without holding elective or appointive office. A change in the law about trafficking African slaves—the Webster Ashburton Treaty of 1842—was but one example. Blacks used the considerable power they had as advocates to shift American policy on slavery. Understanding this success despite limited access to formal mechanisms of power also brings into focus an important dynamic going forward in the effort to assess African American impact on U.S. foreign policy. That is, the arch of influence of African Americans on U.S. foreign policy has reflected the trajectory of political power of the African American community. Given the extent to which U.S. domestic politics have preoccupied black political concerns and have been the barometer by which black political power is measured, the relationship between power and foreign policy can be missed.

The Reconstruction Era: 1866–1896

In 1866, with a newly legislated status as free persons, a rather dramatic turn was made in the ability of African Americans to have their views aired and acted upon.[2] From 1866 to 1901 twenty African Americans were elected to the House of Representatives and there were two blacks in the U.S. Senate. Blacks could influence policy through the ballot box and through public officials having seats at the table where decisions were made, which in terms of foreign policy meant there was an opportunity to have an influence that was not previously possible. By definition, it meant that in addition to advocacy, with the option of elective office there was another available potential lever of power at the disposal of African Americans to affect U.S. foreign policy. There were a number of foreign policy issues and interests on which African Americans weighed in from their leadership positions in Congress. One unique issue falling into this category was the treatment of Native Americans. Ironically, blacks moved from the margins to the mainstream during the Reconstruction era; Native Americans were considered foreigners in their own land and were dealt with by the U.S. government as it would any foreign power. During this era there were a number of major treaties signed with Native American nations, such as the Treaty with Kiowa, Comanche, and Apache (1867) and the Fort Laramie Treaty (1868). Most blacks in Congress included the treatment and status of Native Americans as a part of their congressional portfolios. Consistent with the point of view and values incubated during the debates about the slave trade and slavery, most people insisted on fair and humane treatment for Native Americans.

Another foreign policy issue that generated attention among African Americans was the issue of emigration, principally to Liberia. Most African Americans were against emigration to Liberia (or any destination outside the United States). However Congressman Richard Cain, who represented South Carolina from 1873 to 1875 and again from 1877 to 1879, eventually became an advocate for emigration because of the erosion of black rights in the South during his second term. In 1878 he offered a bill that would have established routes for seagoing traffic to Liberia. The bill never made it out of the Commerce Committee.

The long and short of the meaning of the Reconstruction era as far as the impact of African Americans on foreign policy was twofold. On the one hand, because of the legislative power African Americans possessed, they were able to place their imprimatur on foreign policy. On the other, the impact of African Americans on U.S. foreign policy during this era had less to do with the issues than with the institutional role they were able to play because of the political possibilities that defined this period. My emphasis on the legislative role African Americans played in this era in terms of foreign policy is not meant to diminish their civic involvement in this area; rather it is to underscore their power, and thus their impact, in these new roles.

The Civil Rights Era: 1954–1980

As a result of the civil rights movement there was a reemergence of African Americans in Congress as a political force to be reckoned with. This era also marked the appointment of blacks to positions in the executive branch that in an unprecedented way positioned them to enter the foreign policy fray. As barriers fell, opportunities in other areas of influence also opened up, including the mainstream media and the corporate sector.

Harlem's Adam Clayton Powell (D-NY) was elected to Congress in 1948 on the cusp of the civil rights movement and the early days of the postcolonial era. Powell personified the geopolitical changes that defined this era. A decade later Charles Diggs (D-MI) was elected to Congress and took legislative interventions on U.S foreign policy by an African American to a new level, proudly wearing the moniker "Mr. Africa." Coinciding with the independence of Ghana in 1957, Diggs accompanied then vice president Richard Nixon on a tour of Africa, following that up with his attendance at the All-African Peoples Conference in Ghana in 1958 and leading a 1969 fact-finding mission to Nigeria against the backdrop of the Nigeria-Biafra War. Other African American influencers on foreign policy in the Congress during this era included Charles Rangel (D-NY), Andrew Young (D-GA), Barbara Jordan (D-TX), Mickey Leland (D-TX), Bill Gray (D-PA), and Ron Dellums (D-CA). Their efforts, spanning a twenty-year period, represented a new plateau in terms of African American influence on U.S. foreign policy in the legislative arena.

These interventions were both dramatic and effective. During this era there was a shift in U.S. policy that brought an end to minority rule in Rhodesia and laid the foundation for a revolutionary turn in U.S. policy vis-à-vis Africa in the years to come. Beyond legislative efforts on the House side, the modern era has seen three African Americans serve in the U.S. Senate. In addition to the Senate's "advise and consent" role on matters of foreign policy and its role in the ratification of treaties, Edward Brooke (R-MA), Carol Moseley-Braun (D-IL), and Barack Obama (D-IL) each made a difference in U.S. foreign policy in specific ways. This era also marked a time of unprecedented access and impact in the executive branch of government. Jimmy Carter's 1976 election was due in no small part to the support of Coretta Scott King, Andrew Young, Jesse Hill, Joseph Lowery, John Lewis, Maynard Jackson, and others in the civil rights establishment. Carter made human rights the linchpin principle for American foreign policy. He tapped then congressman Andrew Young to join his administration as his United Nations ambassador and to be the public face of this new approach to U.S. foreign policy. Ambassador Young's appointment (and that of his successor Donald McHenry) meant African Americans were an integral part of cabinet deliberations regarding U.S. strategic interests and concerns globally.[3]

Also during this era African Americans were appointed in unprecedented numbers to positions in the foreign policy establishment. The list of distinguished African Americans in such capacities has a long history.[4] Yet it is in the civil rights era that African American impact in this area not only set a new standard reflecting the exceptional skills of those appointed but, as important, also reflects the critical mass selected to such positions. Starting from the likes of Clifton Wharton, Patricia Harris, Carl Rowan,[5] Terrance Todman, Edward Perkins, and Edith Sampson to a bevy of contemporary stalwarts like Ruth Davis, Shirley Barnes, Mattie Sharpless, Johnnie Carson, Wanda Nesbitt, Michael Battle, and USAID administrator Alonzo Fulgham, African Americans have played prominent parts on the stage of foreign policy formulation and action. Close to 150 African Americans have served as diplomats over the years, with most being appointed during this and the succeeding era.

The impact of African Americans on U.S. foreign policy, however, cannot (and should not) be solely defined by the formal roles they played in the process. These formal roles were complemented by the advocacy work of groups like TransAfrica, Opportunities Industrial Centers (OIC), the Phelps Stokes Fund, the Coalition of Black Trade Unionists, and Africare, to name a few. The black church and black press were also effective advocates and collaborators in affecting U.S. policy. This impact was visible from Martin Luther King's call to conscience about Vietnam to the clarion call to oppose apartheid involving churches like Union United Methodist Church in Boston, which I pastored. Black journalistic standard bearers like *Ebony, Jet,* and the *Amsterdam News* played a prominent role in the fight to end apartheid. The role that journalists played was not limited to the historically owned black press. African American reporters and columnists in the mainstream media, such as former *Newsweek* stalwart and Pulitzer Prize winner Les Payne, former *Washington Post* reporter Leon Dash, ABC News reporter Kenneth Walker, PBS and civil rights icon Charlayne Hunter Gault, CBS News reporter Randy Daniels, the *New York Times'* Sam Fulwood, and *USA Today's* DeWayne Wickham, played critical roles in shaping public debate through the coverage and commentary they offered.

At the beginning of this chapter I noted that there are three ways in which an impact can be made on foreign policy—namely, through the executive and legislative branches of government as well as advocates and activists. During the civil rights era, for the first time in history, African Americans were firing on all cylinders and their impact on U.S. foreign policy reflected it.

The Post-Civil Rights Era: 1980 to the Present

The final chapter in terms of the impact of African Americans on U.S. foreign policy is what I call the post–civil rights era. I draw the line of demarcation for this period at the beginning of the Reagan administration. Most certainly in terms of domestic policy Reagan saw his policy aims as representing a post–civil rights agenda (some would argue that it was an anti–civil rights agenda). With respect to foreign policy, this era is worth noting as such because the presence and impact of African Americans on matters of foreign policy have taken a quantum leap forward.

Given Reagan's conservative views and anti–affirmative action policies, it is ironic that the influence of African Americans on U.S. foreign policy increased exponentially from the previous administration. By naming General Colin Powell as his national security adviser, Reagan ensured that African Americans would move even higher in the foreign policy establishment. This was borne out in Powell's being named chairman of the Joint Chiefs of Staff during the administration of George H. W. Bush. It also resulted in a young Stanford scholar by the name of Condoleezza Rice being appointed as special director of Soviet and Eastern European Affairs at the National Security Council. With these appointments, the presence and power of African Americans in terms of U.S. foreign policy reached a new plateau. With regard to Africa, while Reagan's policy of "constructive engagement" with the apartheid regime in South Africa was appalling and his view that African nation-states were legitimate battlegrounds to prosecute the Cold War with Russia was fraught with problems, the presence of Powell in the positions that he held marked an unprecedented opportunity for African Americans to impact U.S. foreign policy.

With the election of Bill Clinton, the impact and presence of blacks in the foreign policy sphere continued to grow. During the Clinton administration there was a monumental shift not only in U.S. foreign policy on Africa but also in terms of commercial policy more generally. That shift was personified in Ronald H. Brown, the first African American secretary of commerce. With the Brown doctrine on Africa, the emphasis on Africa policy shifted from "aid to trade," and in a broader sense, as commerce secretary Brown was the face of commercial interests abroad. Specific to Africa policy, other African Americans were on the fulcrum of policy formulation. These included people like George Moose and Susan Rice, both of whom served as assistant secretaries of state for African Affairs, and Rosa Whitaker, who served as assistant U.S. trade representative. I had the pleasure and honor of working with all three of them. Under Ambassador Moose's watch, in 1994 I was a part of President Clinton's official delegation to monitor the first democratic multiracial elections in South Africa. As U.S. ambassador to Tanzania, I served under Dr. Rice. I am aware of the extent to which she had the president's ear and helped shape policies on everything from terrorism to trade, which diplomats like me were called to represent.

One of the major foreign policy initiatives of the Clinton administration, and its signature policy initiative regarding Africa, was the Africa Growth and Opportunity Act (AGOA). The act reflected the philosophical sensibilities of Secretary Brown, and its passage reflected the strategic and tactical savvy of people like Rosa Whitaker. Setting this policy in place required more than crafting the policy; beyond formulation it required action to get it passed. There were key actors in the business community to be convinced of the act's merit and the need to support it on Capitol Hill. There were key members of the African diplomatic corps who needed to be organized to lobby for the act's passage. There was a need for a coordinated strategy within the Clinton administration to bring together all of the elements. At every level, from inside players to outside agitators to opinion leaders, African Americans were involved in the effort to get the act passed. Foreign policy professionals like Ambassador Johnnie Carson, as deputy assistant secretary of state for African Affairs, and USAID's Alonzo Fulgham played critical parts in fashioning AGOA as well as helping to craft the tactical approach to ensure its passage and implementation. On Capitol Hill, congressmen Charles Rangel and the late Donald Payne galvanized congressional support. In the private sector one of the most formidable forces on U.S. foreign policy on Africa is the Corporate Council on Africa. Its founding chairman, Percy C. Wilson, a longtime friend and colleague of mine, was a key advocate for the act. African American journalists like DeWayne Wickham, a columnist for *USA Today*, did much to clarify the stakes and challenges of getting the act passed.

In terms of the paradigm I outlined earlier for having and measuring impact on foreign policy, AGOA was a textbook case of African American enterprise and execution. As an ambassador at the time, I was involved in the deliberations to get the act passed and was called upon to give input on the importance of AGOA to further America's strategic relationship with Africa and recalibrate that relationship to one defined by trade as well as aid.

With the 2000 election of George W. Bush, African Americans reached a new benchmark (at the time) in terms of U.S. foreign policy. With the appointment of Colin Powell as secretary of state and Condoleezza Rice as national security adviser (and later secretary of state), the bar was raised to what some thought was an unimaginable level. The roles Powell and Rice played and the weight they carried in crafting and carrying out U.S. foreign policy during the eight years of the Bush presidency were significant. On every foreign policy question or issue of the day they were seen by the world as the face of the administration and symbols of American power.

When Secretary Powell assumed his position as head of the State Department, the first bureau he visited was the Africa Bureau. The most cynical suggested that this choice simply reflected the fact that Africa was first alphabetically (a view that I reject). Whatever the motive, with that visit the die was cast. Africa would receive higher priority, and it would be an African American at the helm of the State Department who would be guiding this change. That Africa would get higher priority was borne out by the progressive policies of the Bush White House on that continent. With Powell as secretary of state (and followed by Rice), an unprecedented and comprehensive policy agenda for Africa took shape. As was the case with the passage of the AGOA during the Clinton administration, there were others, like assistant secretaries of state for African Affairs Dr. Constance Newman and Dr. Jendayi Frazier (and Dr. Cindy Courville at the National Security Council), who were not only involved in policy formulation but were also involved in the mechanics of moving the Bush agenda forward. PEPFAR—Bush's HIV/AIDS, tuberculosis, and malaria initiative—represented a new benchmark in terms of humanitarian aid to Africa. The first strategic military command, AFRICOM, was a new beachhead in terms of military and security partnership with Africa. Though technically AFRICOM is not a policy-making body, it is worth noting that its first commander, General William E. Ward, is African American. The Millennium Challenge Initiative, which enabled democratic regimes in Africa to build roads, bridges, and ports, literally charted new waters in terms of development on the continent. One of the least heralded, but no less effective, initiatives was USAID's Africa Education Initiative, headed by USAID veteran Dr. Sarah Moten. This effort provided $600 million to support African education programs in teacher training, textbooks, and scholarships for girls in twenty-one African countries.

African American impact on U.S. foreign policy was obviously capped with the election of Barack Obama as president and commander in chief. Beyond his role as president, with his appointment of blacks to key positions African Americans have been involved in the foreign policy process in meaningful ways. At the cabinet level, among those who have been involved on matters of foreign policy are National Security Adviser (and former U.N. Ambassador) Susan Rice, Attorney General Eric Holder, and U.S. Trade Representative Ronald Kirk. At the sub-cabinet level those who have been involved are people like Cheryl Mills, chief of staff to the secretary of state, (immediate past) Assistant Secretary of State for African Affairs Johnnie Carson, current Assistant Secretary of State for African Affairs Linda Thomas-Greenfield, and Assistant Secretary of State for International Organization Affairs Esther Brimmer. At the time of this writing, while Obama's foreign policy agenda remains a work in progress, he is certain to leave an indelible imprint on U.S. foreign policy. What that imprint will be is another question. Having said that, the expectations about the foreign policy framework that should define his presidency are clear.

A telling example of those expectations is reflected in an experience I had the morning after the 2008 election. On election night I had boarded a flight for Berlin. It was well before the election results were in. On the way to the airport, I stopped by the Obama campaign headquarters and picked up a bag of campaign buttons. I figured that whatever the outcome, the buttons would be a hot commodity in Berlin and for the second leg of my trip, which was to be the African continent. I've taken this transcontinental flight more times than I can remember. I am usually asleep within minutes after "wheels up," but this night was different. No doubt anxious about the election, I didn't sleep a wink. When the plane landed, before the pilot announced that we had safely arrived at our destination (as is customary), he announced the election results. With all the drama of a presenter at the Academy Awards, he started cryptically: "Ladies and gentlemen, the election for the United States presidency has been decided." He then paused for dramatic effect. "And the forty-fourth president of the United States is Barack Obama." Cheers erupted from every corner of the aircraft.

After we deplaned, passenger after passenger came up to congratulate me. It was the extra-large Obama/Biden button on my jacket, I think. Two comments struck me profoundly. One person said, "This is a great day for your people." Given the extent to which race has been a crucible around the neck of America, threatening to strangle the promise the United States represented, how right that stranger was. It was an important day for blacks all over the world. Others offered a response that was more general but no less poignant, which was "This is a great day for the world." In terms of expectations, what that comment betrayed was a sense that U.S. foreign policy under Obama would be less heavy-handed and more high-minded, which would put this presidency clearly within the tradition of justice and human rights that has defined the impact of African Americans on U.S. foreign policy over the years.

Whether Obama's impact is monumental or incremental in terms of a shift in policy remains to be seen. With Obama's election, and looking backward to the first forays into foreign policy by blacks in the eighteenth century, it is clear that African Americans have made significant strides in U.S. foreign policy and will continue to do so.

Notes

1. Regarding the dates here, American slavery obviously predated the establishment of the United States as a nation-state. Because this is a book about the impact of African Americans on "U.S. foreign policy," I start the slavery era coterminous with the founding of the Republic.

2. I use 1896 as the end of the Reconstruction Era because it coincides with the *Plessy v. Ferguson* Supreme Court decision, which codified the doctrine of "separate but equal." This case was the legal predicate for segregation, the result of which was the wholesale disenfranchisement of African Americans, particularly in the South.

3. See chapter 8 of this volume.

4. See chapter 1 of this volume.

5. See chapter 3 of this volume.

Contributors

LINDA HEYWOOD is Professor of African and African American History at Boston University. Professor Heywood is the author of *Contested Power in Angola* (University of Rochester Press, 2000), editor of and contributor to *Central Africans: Cultural Transformations in the American Diaspora* (Cambridge University Press, 2002) and co-author with John Thornton of *Central Africans, Atlantic Creoles, and the Foundation of America* (Cambridge University Press, 2007), which won the Melville J. Herskovits Award for the best scholarly work on Africa published in English in 2007. Her articles on Angola and the African diaspora have appeared in the *Journal of African History, Journal of Modern African Studies, Slavery and Abolition,* and the *Journal of Southern African Studies.* She has served as a consultant for numerous museum exhibitions, including *African Voices* at the Smithsonian Institution; *Against Human Dignity,* sponsored by the Maritime Museum; and exhibits at Jamestown, Virginia. She was also one of the history consultants for and appeared in the PBS series *African American Lives* (2006) and *Finding Oprah's Roots* (2007). She has just completed a biography of Queen Njinga of Angola. Dr. Heywood holds a BA in history from Brooklyn College, a masters in international affairs, and a PhD in history from Columbia University.

ALLISON BLAKELY is Professor of History Emeritus at Boston University, where he arrived in 2001 after teaching for thirty years at Howard University. He is the author of *Blacks in the Dutch World: The Evolution of Racial Imagery in a Modern Society* (Indiana University Press, 1994); *Russia and the Negro: Blacks in Russian History and Thought* (Howard University Press, 1986; winner of an American Book Award in 1988); several articles on Russian populism; and others on various European aspects of the black diaspora. His interest in comparative history has centered on comparative populism and on the historical evolution of color prejudice. Among the awards he has received are Woodrow Wilson, Mellon, Fulbright-Hays, and Ford Foundation Fellowships. He served as national president of the Phi Beta Kappa Society from 2006 to 2009 and is on the editorial board of its journal, the *American Scholar*. In 2011 President Obama appointed him to a six-year term on the National Council for the Humanities. Dr. Blakely holds a BA in history from the University of Oregon and an MA and PhD in history from the University of California, Berkeley.

CHARLES R. STITH is the founding director of the African Presidential Archives and Research Center and adjunct professor of international relations at Boston University. Before assuming his present position, Stith served as ambassador extraordinary and plenipotentiary of the United States to the United Republic of Tanzania in the traumatic period after the August 1998 bombing of the U.S. embassy in Dar es Salaam. Stith is the author of *Political Religion* (Abingdon Press, 1995) as well as numerous articles that have appeared in such publications as the *Wall Street Journal, Denver Post, Atlanta Journal-Constitution, Boston Globe, Boston Herald, USA Today, Los Angeles Times, New York Times,* and the *Chicago Sun-Times*. He holds a BA from Baker University, an MDiv from the Interdenominational Theological Center's Gammon Theological Seminary in Atlanta, and a ThM from the Harvard University Divinity School.

JOSHUA C. YESNOWITZ has been a lecturer in American politics and research methods at Boston University, Suffolk University, and Simmons College. He writes about American political and intellectual development with a focus on higher education, social movements, minority politics, and youth political socialization. His writing has appeared in the *Journal of Political Science Education, Le Monde diplomatique, New Political Science, Polity,* and *Social Movement Studies*. Joshua holds a PhD in political science from Boston University, an MA in political science from Boston College, and a BA in American Studies and Government from Skidmore College. He is co-editor and multiple chapter author for *Agitation with a Smile: Howard Zinn's Legacies and the Future of Activism* (Paradigm Publishers, 2013).

WALTER C. CARRINGTON is a former U.S. ambassador to Senegal (1980–1981) and Nigeria (1993–1997). He previously served as director of the Department of International Affairs of Howard University; executive vice president of the African-American Institute (1971–1980); and in various capacities in the U.S. Peace Corps (1961–1971), including that of regional director for Africa. From

2004 to 2007, Ambassador Carrington was the Warburg Professor of International Relations at Simmons College in Boston. He is a graduate of Harvard Law School.

LISA DAVENPORT completed her MA in American history at Howard University, focusing on African American history and culture, and her PhD in twentieth-century American history at Georgetown University with a focus on U.S. diplomacy. She has published articles on jazz and diplomacy and also worked as a research consultant for a nonprofit foundation in New York. Dr. Davenport is the author of *Jazz Diplomacy: Promoting America in the Cold War Era* (University Press of Mississippi, 2009). She is now an independent scholar and also works as a freelance writer.

VERA INGRID GRANT is director of the newly founded Ethelbert Cooper Gallery of African and African American Art at the W.E.B. Du Bois Institute at Harvard University. She has curated several installations at Harvard University's Rudenstine Gallery and Stanford University's Women's Center and the Reading Room at the Center for Comparative Studies in Race and Ethnicity. She was previously the executive director of the Du Bois Institute and associate director of the African and African American Studies program at Stanford University. She completed an MA at Stanford in Modern European History and is currently completing a PhD project titled: "'Fused Encounters': Transnational Race in the U.S. Occupation Zone in Germany, 1918–1923." She is author of "Black Shame: Popular Imagery in 1920s Germany" in *The Image of the Black in Western Art,* vol. 5, *The Twentieth Century* (Harvard University Press, 2014).

BRANDI HUGHES is an assistant professor of American Culture and History at the University of Michigan, Ann Arbor. Her research and teaching examine the role of religion in the reconstruction of the post-emancipation United States and the significance of Christianity in the cultural and political development of the African diaspora in the nineteenth and early twentieth centuries. Hughes is currently completing a manuscript titled "At the Cross: Redeeming Emancipation in the Mission Fields of African America," which studies the entanglements of evangelical nationalism and diaspora in African American missions to colonial Africa.

MICHAEL L. KRENN is a professor of history at Appalachian State University. He received his BA in history from Weber State College (now University), his MA from the University of Utah, and his PhD from Rutgers University. Professor Krenn has written five books; edited seven volumes; and written numerous articles, chapters, research notes, and book reviews on the history of U.S. foreign relations. His two most recent books are *Fall-Out Shelters for the Human Spirit: American Art and the Cold War* (University of North Carolina Press, 2005) and *The Color of Empire: Race and American Foreign Relations* (Potomac Books, 2006). He is currently at work on several projects, including a study of the early nineteenth-century natural scientist Samuel George Morton.

LORENZO MORRIS is professor and chair of political science at Howard University. Professor Morris has published five scholarly books, including the co-authored *One-Third of a Nation* (Howard University Press, 2001) and *Elusive Equality: The Status of Black Americans in Higher Education* (Howard University Press, 1979), as well as more than one hundred articles on a variety of political concerns. He is currently researching African Americans in national elections and ethnic issues in French political parties. Professor Morris has served as a consultant on several development assistance projects, including projects for political party organizing in Haiti and improvement of electoral structures in Senegal and Benin. He also has been invited by the State Department to advise and lecture on electoral organizing and voting rights in Benin, Cameroon, Guinea-Conakry, Madagascar, and Sierra Leone.

IBRAHIM SUNDIATA formerly held the Samuel and Augusta Spector Professorship in History and African and Afro-American Studies at Brandeis University (now professor emeritus). In 2002 he was awarded a Du Bois fellowship at Harvard and continues to be a nonresident fellow there. In addition, Dr. Sundiata is a member of the Council on Foreign Relations and has served on the board of the Association for the Study of the Worldwide African Diaspora (ASWAD). He has taught at Rutgers, Northwestern, Universidade Federal da Bahia, and the University of Illinois at Chicago. Professor Sundiata completed his undergraduate work at Ohio Wesleyan University and received his PhD from Northwestern University. He is the author of *Black Scandal: The United States and the Liberian Labor Crisis* (Institute for the Study of Human Issues, 1980); *Equatorial Guinea, Colonialism, State Terror, and the Search for Stability* (Westview Press, 1990); *From Slaving to Neoslavery* (University of Wisconsin Press, 1996); and *Brothers and Strangers, Black Zion, Black Slavery, 1914–1940* (Duke University Press, 2003). Sundiata's current project, *Not Out of Dixie: Obama and the American Identity Crisis,* focuses on the interplay between ethnic identity, politics, and public policy.

JEFFREY C. STEWART is professor and chair of the Department of Black Studies at the University of California, Santa Barbara. He received his PhD in American Studies from Yale University in 1979 and has taught at Yale, Tufts University, UCLA, Scripps College, Howard University, Harvard University, and George Mason University. Professor Stewart's research focuses on issues of race and culture in art, history, literature, and music, and he has made strong contributions to studies in the Harlem Renaissance, black criticality and social movements from slavery till the 1960s, and on the work of Howard University philosopher and thinker Alain Locke. He has been a guest curator at the Smithsonian Institution's National Portrait Gallery, where he curated the exhibition *To Color America: Portraits by Winold Reiss* (1989). Stewart also organized the national traveling exhibition *Paul Robeson: Artist and Citizen (1998–2000)*; helped curate the permanent exhibition at the Reginald Lewis Museum in Baltimore, Maryland; and assisted in the research and conception of numerous other applied history projects. He has authored several books, including *1001 Things Everyone Should Know about African American History* (Three Rivers Press, 1998).

DAMION THOMAS is an assistant professor of Physical Cultural Studies in the Department of Kinesiology and affiliate faculty in the African American Studies Department at the University of Maryland. He received his BA, MA, and PhD in history from the University of California, Los Angeles. Dr. Thomas's research interests include sport and United States race relations, black internationalism, African American popular culture, U.S. foreign relations, and black masculinity. His book *Globetrotting: African American Athletes and Cold War Politics* (University of Illinois Press, 2012) provides a transnational perspective to the study of domestic American racial affairs by examining U.S. government attempts to manipulate international perceptions of U.S. race relations during the early days of the Cold War. Recent publications include articles in the *International Journal of the History of Sport, Sport and Society*, and the *Journal of Sport and Social Issues* as well as book chapters in *Out of the Shadows: A Biographical History of African American Athletes* (University of Arkansas Press, 2006) and *East Plays West: Sport and Cold War* (Routledge Press, 2006).

Index

The University of Illinois Press
is a founding member of the
Association of American University Presses.

Composed in 10.25/13 Minion
with DIN 1451 display
by Jim Proefrock
at the University of Illinois Press
Manufactured by Cushing-Malloy, Inc.

University of Illinois Press
1325 South Oak Street
Champaign, IL 61820-6903
www.press.uillinois.edu